Perth born Renato Bonasera is the son of Sicilian migrants. He was baptised Catholic in infancy but became serious about his faith after a conversion experience just before his 16th birthday. His desire to fathom the mysteries of faith and life has led him into the *Cloud of Knowing*, that place in which one meets, albeit in veiled form, God in our midst.

Reflecting on personal experiences and those of others whose stories have been the catalyst for deeper insight into life, suffering, death and the supernatural, Renato provides a heartfelt reflection on God's presence in lives spanning nearly a century, in three continents.

Renato is married and is a father of five children.

Reviews of *Into the Cloud of Knowing (First Edition)*

"In 1974 a book by James Wm. McClendon Jr. entitled *Biography as theology: How life stories can remake today's theology* helped to reinvigorate the art of doing theology via story telling. In this most recent publication by Renato Bonasera this tradition is being kept alive still. Renato's book gives voice to people whose lives have crossed his and he reflects on the way their stories can and do shape one's theology. This book illustrates Alasdair MacIntyre's contention that a 'man is essentially a storytelling animal…personal identity is just that identity presupposed by the unity of the character which the unity of the narrative requires.'"

– *Dr Philip Matthews, School of Philosophy & Theology, The University of Notre Dame Australia, Fremantle*

"We live in a society selling the message that God is dead. Renato Bonasera's book reminds us that this could not be further from the truth! He takes us through both his personal journey as well as events happening in the wider world and demonstrates time after time how all things work out for good for those who love God and who are called according to his purpose (Romans 8:28). Through worldly eyes we can't always see the bigger picture – whether it's our road to conversion or whether it's a major tragedy such as death. Renato demonstrates that by looking through the eyes of faith, each experience reveals a God who is truly active in our lives and in the lives of others. Life is really a journey towards knowing."

– *Jane Borg, Principal of Acts 2 College of Mission and Evangelisation, Disciples of Jesus Covenant Community, Perth*

"Bonasera's *Into the Cloud of Knowing* is an intriguing collection of anecdotes and testimonies of people's encounter with the Divine and supernatural. These stories serve as an assuring reminder that God is present and is in our midst. As a non-Catholic you will learn more about Catholic devotions and spirituality and why, for example, Catholics hold a special place in their hearts for the Blessed Virgin Mary. *Into the Cloud of Knowing* will inspire you and touch your heart."

– *Stephen Spiteri, Teacher, Apologist and Speaker, Perth*

Reviews of *Into the Cloud of Knowing (Second Edition)*

"Bonasera's fine piece of writing is a valuable gift for discouraged dads, overburdened mums, weary spiritual intercessors or anyone who is just plain jaded by the suffering that they see about them everywhere.

The author himself has easily fitted into one or more of the abovementioned categories at varying stages in his life journey. From these rich experiences, he has shared his hard- earned insights, using raw and skillful imagery. Bonasera creates an inviting prose that is honest, transparent and candid, with all the warmth of traditional Sicilian hospitality. The result is a true 'word feast'.

It is easy to find titles full of victories and astounding miracles, in which goodness makes an obvious triumph over evil. 'Into the Cloud of Knowing', however, dares to examine the dark mists as much as the silver lining. Bonasera courageously dissects the mystery that is suffering, generously sharing the wisdom that he has taken time to reach.

His collage of stories will treat the reader to tales which range from the intense, to the tragic, to the downright frightening; to that which is thoroughly entertaining. The reader of this book will find themselves overtaken by drama very much akin to a daytime Soap Opera, but with much more style and purpose."

– *Amy Harry, Perth*

Into the Cloud of Knowing

(2nd Edition)

RENATO BONASERA

Copyright © 2020 (Renato Bonasera)
All rights reserved worldwide.

No part of this book can be stored, changed, sold, copied or transmitted in any form or by whatever means other than what is outlined in this book without the prior permission in writing of the person holding the copyright, except for the use of brief quotations and certain other non-commercial uses permitted by copyright law.

Publisher: Inspiring Publishers,
P.O. Box 159, Calwell, ACT Australia 2905
Email: publishaspg@gmail.com
http://www.inspiringpublishers.com

A catalogue record for this book is available from the National Library of Australia

National Library of Australia The Prepublication Data Service

Author: Renato Bonasera
Title: Into the Cloud of Knowing
ISBN: 978-1-922327-58-1
ISBN: 978-1-944244-34-7 (First Edition)

www.renatoantonio.com

Extracts taken from various texts in this book with permission include the following titles.

RACHEL'S TEARS by Beth Nimmo and Darrell Scott. Copyright © 2000 by Beth Nimmo and Darrell Scott. Used by permission of Thomas Nelson. www.thomasnelson.com.
LEFT TO TELL by Immaculee Ilibagiza. Copyright © 2014 Hay House, Inc., Carlsbad, CA
OUR LADY OF KIBEHO by Immaculee Ilibagiza. Copyright © 2014 Hay House, Inc., Carlsbad, CA
"*Step Into the Wild*", by Joe Yogerst, Qantas The Australian Way, September 2014.
JESUS CALLED HER MOTHER by Dee Jepsen. Copyright © 1992 by Bethany House Publishers. Used under permission for fair use, Baker Publishing Group.

Unless otherwise indicated, Scripture quotations are from The Holy Bible Catholic Public Domain Version Original Edition. Copyright © 2010 by Ronald L. Conte Jr.

The author and the publisher have made every effort to contact copyright holders for quotations used in this book. Any person or organisation that may have been overlooked should contact the publisher.

Cover design by Renato Bonasera. Photographs from pixabay.com released free of copyrights under Creative Commons CCO.

Some names have been changed to protect the privacy of those interviewed. Some dialogue has been dramatised for literary effect without altering the meaning and truth of the events described.

≈ ≈ ≈ ≈ ≈ ≈ ≈ ≈

To the Most Holy Trinity who continually reaches out to us in both ordinary and extraordinary ways on our earthly pilgrimage.

To the "Cloud of Witnesses" interceding for us from Heaven, especially the Queen of Angels and Saints.

To my Mother and Father, who chose to accept another life into the world and thus give me the opportunity of becoming a child of God.

To my wife, whose love and support is balm to me, I look forward to sharing many more God moments with you till death do us part.

To my beloved children, you are my most treasured gifts, now and forever.

To those whose stories appear in this book and have inspired me on my journey of faith, I am indebted to you for your witness.

To those who have walked with me in life, you know who you are. Your friendship is a treasure to me.

To my brother and sister, extended family, friends, and students, may this book say what I have not been able to in person.

To those who have proof-read my work, provided feedback and kindly written a review, I will be forever grateful.

And to those who feel that God is far away I pray that this book may provide reason for renewed hope.

≈ ≈ ≈ ≈ ≈ ≈ ≈ ≈

CONTENTS

Forewords by Dominic de Souza xiii
Forewords by Edward Russell.. xv
Preface xvii

Part 1 – "Do not be overcome by evil, but overcome
evil with good" (Romans 12:21) 1
   Introduction to Part One.. 2

LET THE CHILDREN COME TO ME 5
   Innocence 6
   Remembering Petey.. 8
   The Laminar Flow... 13
   The Mask and The Lady... 16
   In Her Arms... 20
   Letting go.. 24
   I Can Run... 26
   The Slaughter of Children 31
   Sofia... 35
   Martyr of Columbine.. 40
   His Grace is Enough... 45

DELIVERANCE... 49
   Serpents... 50
   "Mummy, I'm Scared".. 52
   The Phone Call 56
   Spiritual Armour... 59

PARADISE LOST.. 65
   Descent 66
   Vultures 70
   Entombment.. 72

THE REBEL AND THE CHILD SOLDIER..................................... 77
   The Call.. 78
   Meheba.. 81
   Suspicion... 85
   Gunshot 88

IS LOVE ENOUGH?	93
Viktor Frankl's Beloved	94
Turning the Tide	96

Interlude: "Sir, I don't believe in God anymore!" ... 102

Part 2 – "I will do Wonders" (Exodus 34:10) ... 105
    Introduction to Part Two ... 106

THE UNLIKELY CONVERT	109
The Upper Gallery	110
Invitation	114
The Healing Touch	117
Slain	119

AND THEY SHALL BE HEALED	121
Cup and Spill	122
Tumour	124

TOUCHED BY GRACE	127
The Calling	128
The Rosary Priest Down Under	131
Sacred	133

ENTERTAINING ANGELS	137
An Angelic Ministry	138
Angel at the Foot of the Bed	141
The Vaal River	144
Angel on the Roof Top	147
The Brush of an Angel's Wing	149

SICILY: ISLAND OF SAINTS AND WONDERS	151
Ancient Roots	152
The Cloud of Witnesses	157
Conon and the Barbarian	158
St. Anthony & St. Calogero	160
St. Rita and the Police Officer	164
St. Rita and the Necklace	167

ALL SHALL CALL HER BLESSED 169
    The Madonna 170
    Roma 176
    The Scandal of Mary 180

Interlude: Blog – Conversation with an Agnostic 183

Part 3 - "I will establish My covenant between Me and you
and your descendants after you" (Genesis 17:7) 187
    Introduction to Part Three 188

THE PROMISE 191
    Mystery Unveiling 192
    Final Sojourn 195
    Gutted 199
    Dreams and Visions 201
    Weeping 205
    The Promise of Jeremiah 208
    The Italian Lady 210
    17th Day of the 7th Month 215

COVENANT 219
    Out of the Mouths of Babes 220
    Jonah's Song 224

THE MUSTARD SEED FAITH 229
    Dodo Bird on the Roof 230
    Moving Mountains 232
    The Christmas Interrogation 235

ALL IN THE HANDS OF GOD 237
    Lost Innocence 238
    A Not-So Blind Faith 240
    Beyond the River Nile 242
    The London Blitz and Doodlebugs 244
    Abandoned 248
    Currant Buns 251
    The Getting of Wisdom 253

DARING TO BE A JOSEPH 257
    Fatherhood 258
    Joseph's Legacy 259

THE HOUND OF HEAVEN 263
    The Pope and the Pilgrim 264
    My Father and I 267
    Apocalyptic 269

Epilogue 272

FOREWORD

Any attempt to chart the human soul, much less the designs of God on the human heart often ends in confusion, or abstraction. Not with Renato Bonasera's new book 'Into the Cloud of Knowing'.

In the spirit of the Incarnation, Renato draws us quickly into an incarnated view of God's hints and hunts for the elusive love of a human heart. Starting with the dark episode of his mother's sudden death, Renato seems to be staggering around looking for answers, and finds them not necessarily in Scripture, or candlelit churches, or in letters of fire swept across the heavens.

He finds the answers meant for him in the moments of his life, in his cultural upbringing, in the moments of joy and tragedy that punctuate his past. With a welcoming and compelling narration, he draws us into his search for the face of God, glimpsed through the glances of dying children and laughing infants, troubled family and prayerful parents.

In the Eastern tradition of iconography, it is understood that painters 'write' the icons from dark shades to lighter, a theological discipline echoing God's creative act of bringing things to light.

In the same vein, Renato shares how he has been forced to grapple with the darkest of questions, the presence of evil alongside an almighty, good God, the pain and suffering of children, the persecution and sorrow of the innocent, war, loss, martyrdom and grace. He finds answers and the truth, but like Christ, the Truth incarnated as man, each answer is found in a person, in a situation wrapped in the humanity and experiences of individual lives and breathing people.

Set against the ruddy backdrop of Western Australia, and deeply birthed in the banks of the Swan River, the colleges and cliffs of Fremantle and Yangebup, join Renato in a sketch of life as a Catholic searching for truth. Himself the child of Sicilian immigrants, he turns to his heritage and delves into the blustery, faith-soaked culture of Sicily to rediscover the greatest influences of his childhood. It's one of my favourite chapters, written in an engaging and sense-driven style that keeps alive the excitement of discovering traditional foods and ancient shrines.

But as a child must mature into a man, so must the book turn its focus onto the harder questions, and Renato doesn't shy away from them, partly because he can't. The beauty and tragedy of being connected to the human family means that we share in each other's joys, and also each other's pain. As Renato realises, often in hindsight, these moments of black, bleak suffering and anger are the brightest chances we have to be divine conduits of grace for each other.

'Into the Cloud of Knowing' is not only a sketch of his life, but also a series of character sketches. From a young boy dying of complications, a young girl martyred for her faith, and a deeply devoted panel of mothers and fathers, Renato leads you into the uniquely Sicilian gallery of his Australian mind, formed by the Christian yearning for the face of God looking at us from each other.

His swift pen traces the stories of missionaries and martyrs in Africa, whisking you into dusty refugee camps fraught by gunfire to the shivering patience of children watching British bombers during the Second World War. It is in these dark moments of war and death that the face of evil emerges, visible as a gnawing, personal presence.

Renato peels back the layers of the human experience to include the impact that angels and demons have on us. Join him in a chapter devoted to stories of haunting and oppression, to a chapter rippling with the teasing tension of angelic guidance.

He comes full circle with his own children, and the transformation they bring to him as a father. This book, his love gift for them and for posterity, is a single, sweeping ride through history and hagiography, replete with stories of saints living and canonised, a journey through what it means to be Catholic grounded in the immediate sun and sand of a person's life.

It is assumed that the mystical life is a dark reality, reserved for the greatest, most meditative saints. 'Into the Cloud of Knowing' shows every Catholic that each of our lives is filled with a million moments to help us slip through a rift, a *Narnian* wardrobe that we will recognise as personally familiar and forever new.

We live in a cloud of angels and witnesses, and if we pray for the eyes to see, we will find that God is present in everything.

Dominic de Souza
Catholic Author
Front Royal, Virginia, USA

FOREWORD

In this beautifully honest book about his life, and the story of those who have touched his own from around the globe, Renato takes us on a journey that is not only personally historical but also spiritual. In fact, the two are not separated.

Renato's love for family and God are so intertwined that for Renato it is as the same thing; one without the other does not seem possible no matter what joys or tragedies come his way. And it is in these, along with his love for family history from Sicily to Australia, that his unshakable love for his Catholic faith shines through every word and becomes a lived testimony that I found inspiring.

This book is a great testimonial of God's miracles and love for a soul in its mystical journey into the Cloud of Knowing. In this way, it is truly inspired.

Edward Russell FMI, SD.
Catholic Evangelist/Preacher/Author
Perth, Australia

(Edward – known affectionately as Eddie – passed away in 2019. May he rest in peace).

PREFACE

My home had just become a battlefield. Jacob, my second son, only six years of age at the time, had rushed towards me like the Flash, ramming into me. As he returned for another bout, I remembered how to make the chaos stop as their mother had taught me. *Just start reading. If they don't listen and won't come, just start and they will stop what they are doing.*

"I'm reading now," I called out, pulling a cushion under me, my torso propped up by my elbows, with the book laid out in front. Within thirty seconds of commencing the Disney classic, *The Rescuers Down Under,* the tactic had worked like a dream. One, two and then three children sat around me, mouths shut and bodies still. I read from cover to cover, my daughter asking me a few questions to which I responded with a few predictive replies. They were enthralled. I was relieved. The calm had been restored.

There is something about story telling that captivates the mind. But it does much more. Story telling is the place where memory and longing meet, and where only that which is describable in the soul can be expressed, albeit without full understanding.

Death was the first impetus for this book. My mother's passing in 2003 left me with a longing to remember what could easily be lost – my mother's own memory and the imprint that her life had made on my soul.

Then came the desire to share the story of others. Soon my heart's longing to grab hold of all the treasures of the past, and to see my life in its context, quickened all the more. And as I got older, married and became a father to five children, with many cherished memories of what God had done for me, these treasures became more brilliant and more coveted. Indeed, the sufferings that inevitably came only intensified this longing.

I do not want these treasured memories to be lost to the sands of time. I want to continue to be a father to my children beyond my sojourn here and lead them to see the footprints of God in their midst. Accepted as pure gift, spiritual experiences draw us ever deeper into the 'cloud of knowing', wherein lies both the mystery and the assurance provided by our Christian faith, and where we hear God speaking with that still and small voice.

With St. John Fisher I testify that all the great kindnesses of God that form the pool of grace-filled memories should be recorded so that "all Christian people who come after us may bear them continuously in mind."

This task has become ever more pressing as the threat of evil in the world, as always, appears omni-present. It is as if the world is the new Middle Earth, to paraphrase Tolkien's cosmology, where the battle for the survival of good is being fought. Humanity appears to be continually under threat, if not through the corruption of the human heart, then, through natural disaster, famine and, more recently, through a microscopic enemy known as COVID-19. As I write these words, the pandemic, inflicting fear on a global scale, disrupting cultural life and economies, and literally killing tens of thousands, is reminding all of us that longed for utopias will never be realised this side of Heaven. The temptation to lose hope is very real. But for those who hold on to hope, so is the invitation to remember that there is so much more to this life, than an end to it.

It is my desire that my children, and all who read this book, will remember and rejoice in what our *inscrutable* and yet personal God continues to do for those journeying towards him in faith. He desires not one to be lost and calls us each by name.

PART ONE

"Do not be overcome by evil,
but overcome evil with good"

(Romans 12:21)

INTRODUCTION TO PART ONE

The day the blond-haired middle-aged woman walked into my Year 8 classroom and was introduced as our guest speaker for the day, was the day my walk with God really began. The conversion itself would take another few years to blossom fully. But, as Roma Martino spoke of her journey from atheism to Christianity and told stories of healings and other wonders wrought through prayer and prophecy, I breathed new life. In hindsight, I think I understood better what the disciples of Jesus must have felt that day at Emmaus when they proclaimed, after meeting the Resurrected Christ, "Did not our hearts burn within us while he talked to us on the road, while he opened to us the Scriptures?" I knew that day, at the age of 12, and would never come to doubt again, that God was as real as you or I. He loved me – the fat little boy - all 84 kilograms of me.

During the many visits to Roma's home and through the correspondence between us that followed our *chance* meeting, Roma came to call me her *third son*. She shared stories of inspiration and hope, miracles and wonders, with an adolescent boy struggling to find meaning in a world becoming increasingly secular. And increasingly evil.

I realised that the evil I was hearing about in the world, was not just occurring on the physical plain, in war, famine or crime. This evil that I had read about in horror stories even at a young age, such as in *The Omen*, *The Amityville Horror* and Stephen King's *Salem's Lot*, suddenly took on more significance in the spiritual awakening I was experiencing. Saints I read about had experienced evil too, in ways that were claimed to be historical and not just legendary. I was intrigued by the diabolical battles fought between one of my favourite saints, the stigmatist priest Padre Pio, and demons who ravaged his monastery cell. Or the demonic apparition in the form of a wild dog that chased another mystic saint, polish nun St. Faustina, in the corridor of her convent. And I was in awe when I learned that exorcists (priests involved in expelling demons) actually still existed, even before I came to meet the exorcist in my own diocese many years later.

But matters went deeper for me. Soon, the fascination was replaced by the cloud, at times tempestuous, of temptation. Where was God in all this? How could God allow for evil, demonic or otherwise, to even "hang around" on earth and do what it did, whether in "fascinating" ways or just through the act of tempting the human race to run amok? Why was being good so hard? Why did we have to suffer? I had known of little children dying from cancer. How could one even begin to accept that? For a while, I turned away from God as adolescence and the "demands" of Catholicism became enemies and seemingly irreconcilable. And though I would return to God again, just before turning 16, through my second and permanent conversion, the problem of evil remained, especially the evil of the suffering of the innocent - and addressing it was a necessity - or my faith would be meaningless.

LET THE LITTLE CHILDREN COME TO ME

⌘

*Allow the little children to come to me, and do not choose to prohibit them.
For the kingdom of heaven is among such as these.
- Matthew 19:14*

⌘

1
Innocence

It is just after 6 a.m. and there is an excited knock at the door. I awake with a jolt as my six-year-old son Joshua marches in triumphantly. Despite my reminder, for the thousandth time, that he should never wake people up regardless of the hour, Joshua's childish wilfulness reigns supreme. "But Dad, it is past 6 o'clock," he protests, continuing with the inevitable apology for waking me from my all too short yet blissful slumber. The portal has been opened. Soon three little bodies will be using my body as their morning gymnastic session. My four-year-old son, Jacob, enters, donning his Santa hat as if oblivious that Christmas Day had come and gone. But, as time and place are flexible in the world of the child, soon the Santa hat is on my head and I am invited to check it out in the mirror!

Anything can happen in the delightful wonderland of children's imagination. A room will become an *Octopod* in which everyday household items are transformed into anything from a steering wheel to hatch openings, bringing the *Octonaut* family to life replete with a customised Gup. (If this is gobbledygook to you just watch one episode of the children's series *Octonauts* that was sending my children into a spin in 2012).

The siege soon continues unabated. The living area, bedrooms and playroom will become the scene of a major battle as a different children's classic comes to life. Daddy has become the villainous Gargamel, through no choice of his own, and his Smurf children have decided to defend themselves against their nemesis. Basketballs are thrown at my head as I duck and determine to play it their way. Entering their make-believe world, I begin to name and then chase *Grumpy* Smurf, *Smelly* Smurf and *Pretty* Smurf (Marie Grace, the youngest of my children at the time). With squeals of excitement and foreboding danger the three Smurfs disperse as *Gargamel-Daddy* chases. They look a little worried but the smile on their faces reveals that this is just way too cool!

Scenes like the one above, have been repeated countless times. Children can delight us with their cuteness, their *joie de vivre*, their unexpected whit and unabashed affection. They bring out the best in us and even the most "adult" kind of parent, who has forgotten that the world of a child was once theirs, finds it easy to rediscover their own long-lost innocence in a child's loving arms. It is indeed easy to bathe in the joy of family life when all is going to plan. And with enough love even the regular winters that visit every home become surmountable. But, when winter becomes a deluge that snatches away the life of a precious child, how can the ark of human strength alone be capable of keeping the besieged family afloat? During those tragic moments the anchor of grace is the difference between despair and hope, the lifeline that keeps us in touch with a deeper reality. Those affected, plunged into a dark cavern, cry out to the only one who can possibly provide any meaning.

2
Remembering Petey

Melina Crea was still in a dark pit when, just a few weeks after the senseless death of her four-year-old son, she courageously returned to the funeral home where Peter's vigil had been held; this time to comfort a friend in mourning. She had to be there. She had felt sick all day just thinking about it which only abated when, just before the start of the Rosary, Melina felt an indubitable warmth and energy surge through her body. Total peace, albeit brief, flooded her soul. *Petey's* presence was so tangible that Melina fought the temptation to turn and look, afraid that if she did, the experience would end.

"He brought Frank and I so much love and joy," Melina told me tenderly, fighting back tears, when we met over coffee in January 2012. "But in his suffering and death I learnt more than I could have learnt in a lifetime."

It was in early May when Peter, at only two and a half years old, began to complain of leg pains. "Mummy, I have a sore," he said. Melina and Frank thought nothing of it, at first. at first. After all, it's not unusual for children to experience random growing pains. However, when her tender mummy kiss would do nothing to make Peter's sores go away, Melina knew there was something very wrong. *There's nothing wrong with his legs* she was told each time she took him to the doctor's. The same verdict was passed down each time. He's just seeking attention, they said.

"Do you honestly think my two-year-old would be pretending Doctor?" With a persistent, righteous anger, Melina kept asking the doctors to look further, continuing to advocate for her little boy despite setbacks, until one day they met Dr Jacqueline Scurlock.

When this doctor walked into their lives it was both a blessing and a curse. Promising to remain with them until she knew what was wrong with Peter, Dr Scurlock pondered at first the possibility of juvenile rheumatoid arthritis.

"Mrs. Crea, I am not going to argue with a mother's intuition so we will continue searching till we find the answer," she had told Melina. "What do you think he has, Mrs. Crea?" Unable to keep in her intuition any longer, Melina, her expression fallen, finally spoke the words her ears did not want to hear. "I think it's bone cancer Doctor."

With Peter not having a distended liver, Dr Scurlock had been convinced it could not be cancer. A lumber puncture and bone marrow aspirate were advised, and with the results in, Melina made her way back to Dr Scurlock's office, on May 27, 1990, accompanied by her sister-in-law Carmel.

Melina wondered why Dr Michael Willoughby, Head of Oncology, greeted her when they arrived. *Oncology Department? Why is an oncologist here?* Time stopped briefly. But Melina remembers, albeit as if in a dreamy haze, the words that came from the oncologist's mouth, rebounding like a canon firing a number of shots in succession. "I am sorry... the tests show that Peter has acute myeloblastic leukaemia." Melina looked at Carmel whose pale complexion spoke volumes. "Unfortunately, it is an aggressive type of Leukaemia. It is a rare form of cancer normally found in men over twenty-five years of age," continued Dr Willoughby. Peter's body is already 80% covered with the cancer."

Melina was speechless as the shockwaves assaulted her, as did her racing heart and something about her husband being called. Regaining her composure briefly, Melina asked, "What are you telling me? Is there treatment?"

"Yes, but the recovery rate in children is 30-40% and so we need to start treatment right away. Peter will need to stay with us, Mrs. Crea."

Carmel watched as Melina set into action, the fire of a mother's love lighting the way forward to the obvious yet potentially illogical solution. "Okay then. We need to sell everything up and go to America". The bargaining stage of the grief cycle had already begun.

"You don't need to uproot. We use the same protocols as America and the same treatment," Dr Willoughby replied gently, reassuring Melina there would be no need to add further strain to the family.

Frank arrived, the fear in his eyes mirroring that of his wife's as they embraced, distraught, yet still seeking the comfort they knew would not be coming any time soon. In an instant, their family's life had changed forever.

Practicalities distracted the couple briefly as arrangements were made for the long road ahead. As Peter could not return home, and with her mother having arrived to stay with Peter, Melina and Frank went home. What about their seven-year-old Jessica? They made their decision. For as long as Peter's treatment lasted, and with the help of parents and siblings, Melina would stay at the hospital during the week and Frank would remain with his daughter at night, after visiting his son after work each day. Walking out of that office with the full weight of the knowledge on her shoulders, Melina was plagued by visions of what her precious toddler would have to go through.

While pleading to understand what had just happened to their family as they arrived home to collect their belongings, Melina punched and kicked doors as the haunting quiet of her home gave its permission for her anger to burst like a dam, unable to contain its load. *Why our family?* And, just as soon as that thought appeared again, a new resolve punched through as well. *We have to remain strong for Petey's sake.*

Peter could not have known why his mummy had hugged him so hard the day of the diagnosis. And in the weeks that followed he would see a loving smile on her face that tried to mask her broken heart. "It is just my allergies Petey," Melina would tell her observant son. Fortunately, as Melina suffered from hay fever and often had watery eyes, she could use her allergies as an excuse to hide the tears that Peter could see in her eyes from time to time. Her smile and warm embrace became Peter's sanctuary as his little body was wracked by months of intensive chemotherapy at Princess Margaret Hospital for Children.

The day of Petey's first treatment soon came. "Petey, you need to stay in hospital for a while longer. You have a bug that doctors have to get rid of in the body. You will need a lot of medicines but don't be scared. I will be with you all the time."

"Okay mummy," replied Peter, looking at her trustingly with his dark brown eyes. Melina could not believe how accepting he was of it, but encouraged, she continued.

"I want you to imagine all these soldiers in your body coming in to attack the bug to get rid of it," Melina proposed, sparking her son's imagination and turning as much as possible into a game. The days when Peter had to be taken into theatre, however, were especially difficult. Melina would accompany him in theatre each time until the anaesthesia had done its work. Leaving him asleep, Melina would go outside quickly and, each time, break down privately.

The time Peter spent in an isolated room in the hospital ward was never spent alone. With a steady flow of visitors, the family came to practically live in the waiting room as the number of people at any given time exceeded the permitted numbers in his room.

"C'mon Petey. Pretend you are the doctor," his father or cousins would say as everyone would have a go at allowing him to "insert" an IV drip in their arm so that he didn't feel that he was the only one who had to go through the treatment. The company, gifts and laughter all made his more difficult moments a little more bearable. One small consolation. One small relief in a sea of confusion, pain and trauma.

Most of Peter's chemotherapy was inserted via his small veins. At times, doctors had to use a long-term vascular access device that was inserted through Peter's narrow neck and chest vein, which distressed the toddler greatly. On one occasion, the unsuspecting child had just completed a course of chemo at around 7 in the evening while he was still asleep. Melina had gone to the bathroom and soon heard her son's screams. He had woken up and stood up just as the chemo had finished, causing the central lines to become detached. As I listened to Melina tell her son's story and as she shared photos of his journey, I had a glimpse of the horror that they had to endure. I couldn't imagine the panic as the surgeon had to urgently reinsert the tubing in the middle of the night. I think of my own children and don't ever wish to know whether I could go through the same inhuman spectacle. What amazed me the most was the smile on Peter's handsome and mischievous little face. In so many photos I saw Peter giving his thumbs up, even in surreal images that betrayed his intense pain.

Peter had to readjust to not being able to enjoy life's simple pleasures. "Mummy, I wish I could run down that hill," Peter blurted out one day as he glanced longingly outside his hospital window to the children running up and down the green hill. "Eventually you will, Petey," she reassured him. Melina knew that 'eventually' may be further away than she would like to reveal to her beautiful little boy. The side effects of the chemotherapy he was receiving soon became the latest major concern.

Like leaves detaching themselves from autumn trees, Peter's gorgeous curls began to shed. Upon awakening each morning, Peter would cast a glance at his pillow and ask, "Mum, could you ask dad to bring the dust buster?" The naivety of his innocent question did not diminish the sadness of the situation for Melina who abhorred the poison that was being administered through her son's small body, pledging to help save his life, but not before it depleted her boy's fledgling immune system.

The weeks passed, marked continuously by the administration and effects of chemotherapy that had extended its claws through every part of the Crea family's life. Peter, his immune system thoroughly compromised, had to now enter the "room" that would be his home for the next fourteen months. The *Laminar Flow*, a room made famous in *"The Boy in the Plastic Bubble"* starring John Travolta, was Peter's custom made 'bubble', replete with the necessary arsenal of medicinal weapons, ready to do battle against any airborne disease or infectious bacteria or virus that might pick a fight with the little boy.

3

The Laminar Flow

The Laminar Flow Room is upsetting enough for an adult, but for a child of two years of age, it brings with it an extra challenge and risk.

"Mrs. Crea, the Laminar Flow is a room for those people whose immune system is so low that even the slightest cold could become fatal. Petey will have to be in there 24/7 until his body's immune system is back within tolerance limits."

"Does that mean we can't be with him at all? We can't comfort him?"

"You can, Mrs. Crea, but only under certain strict conditions."

Since the air in the room was purified air being continually pumped out from a side wall, anyone entering the room from outside had to be completely covered with a head cover, gown, mask, latex surgical gloves and sanitised booties. The day Peter first entered, he had to be bathed, wrapped up in a sterile sheet and placed directly on the bed. No contact could be made with anything that had not been sterilised. If a toy dropped to the ground it had to be kicked away and sterilised. A week later it would return in special packaging. Even gifts for his birthday had to undergo the procedure a week before his birthday, after which it would be wrapped in a special type of blue paper.

Just touching his mother's face was enough to initiate another sterilisation procedure for Peter. At times it was hard to prevent him from seeking to touch his mother's face and from wanting to get out of bed. When he accidentally did get out, during particularly stressful moments, Peter faced an immediate scrubbing. The only light in the abyss that was the Flow, was Peter's adorable sanguine personality. Maintaining his larrikin attitude, he would sometimes threaten his mum mischievously. "Look mum, I am going to touch you," or "Look mum, I am going to touch the floor." Melina, having taken the bait, would say, "You wouldn't dare!" These were the moments that made it all just a little more bearable. Peter, now barely 3 years old, was Melina and Frank's strength.

No matter what was done to him, Peter was always hugging, kidding and demonstrating optimism surprising for a young child. It was not that rare to see Peter wearing underpants on his head for a laugh or not wearing underwear at all just because he could or felt like it!

Peter hardly ever lost his smile or facetiousness. With a slight grin, Melina recalls how they compensated for his need to get off his bed and walk around his room. They made shoes out of two sterile dishes, "the ones shaped like kidneys", and Peter would march around his bed triumphantly. Fortunately, one could visit him by remaining on the open side of the plastic sheeting that served as the room's outer wall. Peter could also communicate with friends in adjoining rooms, facing each other and holding up their various toys.

The hours, days and months blended into each other as Peter made the Laminar Flow his home. While tubes, IV pumps, sterile hospital gowns, vomiting, general illness, drips, horrible mouth care treatments, frustration and loss of free movement became commonplace for Peter, he was never left alone. The staff did whatever they could to make his stay a little more pleasant. When his mother asked, "How are you feeling, honey?" up would come Peter's thumbs again to indicate he was doing okay.

The Flow was decorated with all of Peter's favourite icons, including posters of the *Wildcats* and *Eagles* sports teams. There were puppet shows, craft activities and a constant flow of visitors from cousins to uncles and friends to grandparents. The joy on his face was infectious when some famous characters including the Ninja Turtles, Fat Cat and his beloved Humphrey Bear visited him. His excitement about the Wildcats was intensified the day he got a visit from Ricky Grace, who played for the *Cats* at the time.

Stories with Peter's Aunt Nadia were precious, and he was very protective of her. For a time, he cottoned on to the infatuation the Radio Lollipop gentleman was developing for his beautiful Aunt and made sure to caution him. "She is *my* aunt," he warned. But above all, Peter was comforted by his second "mum", his older sister Jessica, who at five years his senior, continued to be protective of Peter just as she had been before his diagnosis. Jessica and Peter were close. And Jessica was feeling it all too!

Each day, Peter would eagerly await Jessica's visit, whether after school or on weekends, and watched tenderly as he saw her walking past the plastic sheeting that led to the entrance of his room. Jessica responded just as eagerly, visibly upset on those days she wasn't allowed to visit. She loved her baby brother dearly and looked forward to reading to him, playing with him and above all consoling him, which in some small way also helped her not to feel so useless. On a number of occasions, when Peter had high fever, Jessica was a pillar of strength, not leaving Peter's side.

"Mum, Peter will be okay, won't he?" Jessica would ask her mother often, praying with her that he would make a full recovery.

"We take one day at a time Jess and thank God for each day that he is with us." Melina hoped that her words of entrustment to the Divine Will would comfort her daughter, who, in her own way, was a victim of this mad illness that had struck her beautiful little boy. "At the tender age of 8," Melina explained to me, "Jessica had to deal with such a grown-up situation, but she listened and tried the best that she could."

Whether it was due to the visitors, his favourite story book entitled *You beaut Juicy Fruit*, or the immense love with which he was showered each day, Peter was a bastion of courage, coping with whatever was dished out to him; even the bone marrow transplant that he needed, using his own bone marrow which had been extracted, stored, chemically purified and then reinserted into his fragile body after a relapse, was not enough to quell his hope and brave demeanour. Peter had matured rapidly and not just emotionally, developing a faith that would see him through the darkness. Each day, Melina taught her son to pray with a spirit of gratitude for what they did have. Touching Melina deeply were the times Peter would call a blessing upon his mother.

"This is the day he came out of the laminar flow in time for Christmas," Melina shared proudly, showing me the photo of Peter with a Santa's hat and a smile of a Cheshire cat, on one of the rare times Peter could exit the flow for a break, when his immune system had improved. Another photo clearly showed the tears of joy in his Aunt Pamela's eyes when she embraced him, and they made face-to-face contact. I can only imagine what it must have been like for Melina and Frank when they were able to kiss him after such a long time.

And then came the news. The all-clear was pronounced. After 14 months of near solitary confinement, Peter could leave the hospital. The nurses could almost see the Crea dust fall to the ground as they left like a tornado ripping through an old town leaving nothing in its wake. Jessica was beaming! For a while, it seemed that her prayers for his complete physical recovery had been answered. Peter could now return to the completed new family home on the five-acre block in Herne Hill, in the luscious Swan Valley region of Perth.

4

The Mask and The Lady

The sand dunes which Peter had enjoyed running up when the home was being built, had now been replaced by a quaint colonial style home nestled safely in the foothills of the Darling Ranges and surrounded by open fields and fresh air.

Peter beamed as he rode on the tractor with Jessica and other visitors, or as he ran with the wind at his back past the rainwater tank and the barn that was the humble abode of his horse named Bonny. It seemed that the time Peter had spent away from Bonny had done little to quash the friendship they shared. It was to Bonny's gate that Peter ran with expectant enthusiasm, as soon as he was able to.

At almost twice the height of Peter, the stunning chestnut Gelderland was a real beauty. With her long and flat majestic head just in front of that muscular neck and her prominent whither, Bonny made her way to her young friend, even though Peter was told not to stay too close to Bonny, to avoid contamination for Peter's still not perfectly healthy body.

Peter didn't care. The extent to which he disregarded his mother's warning was evident each time Melina saw Peter hanging off his beloved horse, or walking under her, all of which Bonny seemed to enjoy immensely. "Bonny wouldn't take to anyone else but Peter," Melina recounted, "and what I found amazing was that she wouldn't be afraid of Peter at all but would be frightened of sheep."

Time passed again. Some months. The relapse, sudden, plunged the family again into the abyss. The toxic chemotherapy would be replaced by a new toxin. It was decided that Peter would be dosed with daily radiation at Sir Charles Gairdner Hospital over a six-week period. Peter was now a wise four-year-old whose faith, while strong, would undergo further development.

As the treatment required having to wear a special mask and suit, it was not something Peter was particularly fond of.

"To ensure that the treatment will work properly, Mrs. Crea, we will need to take a mould of Peter's face and chest," Dr Willoughby said. *Don't you understand he's just a child?* Melina listened incredulously as Dr Willoughby continued. "We need to make an appropriate mask to be placed over his face and chest. Then we need to bolt this down onto the bed so as to restrain Peter while the ten minutes of radiation treatment pass. In other words, Mrs. Crea, Peter has to lay down perfectly still," he continued, almost matter-of-factly yet not without compassion. Perhaps he saw the exasperation on Melina's face which she consciously switched off when she spoke with her boy.

"Petey, it is there to help you. It is only for two minutes and they just want to make sure they get all the bugs they need to." To Melina's surprise and with a confidence beyond his years Peter's initial distress was replaced with a candid and astonishing promise. "Mummy, pray to Our Lady, and I promise you I will keep still without the mask."

The fascination that Peter had with the woman he knew as *Jesus' mum*, was a long standing one. During his stay in hospital, it was a framed image of the Blessed Virgin Mary that sat on his bedside table. With the same instinct that made Melina believe her son was not fabricating stories about his sore legs, Melina trusted her son would keep his word now.

"Mrs. Crea, that is impossible. We would have to sedate him every day for six weeks." Dr Fiona Cameron, head of Radiation at Sir Charles Gairdner at the time, did not share Melina's faith in her four-year-old son.

"He is telling me he won't move, and he won't," Melina responded frankly.

"Mrs. Crea, you know your son better than anybody else. So, if you tell me he will keep still I will talk to Fiona and see what we can do," pledged Dr Willoughby. He did indeed keep still and managed to convince Dr Cameron to give it a go.

The night before the first radiation treatment, mother and child prayed together. For the following six weeks Peter lay as still as a statue without any aid in the radiation unit, much to the disbelief of the medical staff. "No way," gasped one nurse, in awe, when she walked in routinely during the session. Her presumption that Peter had been sedated was soon corrected. By the end of the treatment, Peter had been donated the "mask" as a trophy and testimony to his brazen accomplishment. He also took in his stride, jokes about him being as red as a beetroot!

For a second time, it seemed that Peter had seen the end of the disease that lay dormant in his body. But then, one morning, things changed drastically once more.

"Petey, good morning sweetie." Melina knew something was horribly wrong when she saw his distorted face. It looked like he had Bell's Palsy on the left side. A lumbar puncture revealed that Peter's spinal fluid was 80% covered with cancer. Just one cancer cell had escaped and made its way into the brain where it had hibernated and then spread. Paralysis of the face was one of the symptoms.

Weak at the knees and fighting back tears threatening to burst that dam again, Melina asked how long her son had. Hesitating at first, the doctor exclaimed, "I am so sorry. Peter has only a few weeks to live…. We can look after him here or he can go home and be with his family."

It was Peter who made the decision.

"Mummy, I want to go home and see everyone," Peter requested. He knew he was dying. As the sun began to set on Peter's young life, forcing a maturity that was well beyond his years to shine before the eyes of all, Peter desired nothing else other than being with those he loved, at home, and in time to celebrate an early Christmas.

At Peter's request they all decorated the Christmas tree. Melina spent her days calling up random people to come over for a visit, especially aunts and uncles, again at Peter's request. All of them dropped whatever they were doing and visited their cherished nephew. It was not rare to see a host of cars parked outside the family home.

For a while, Frank and Melina kept him active and happy. His uncle took the family on his boat. He spent time with his dad in the office, sitting on his lap while Frank completed work that could not be put off. He was able to enjoy playing with a pet dog and begged of his mum, "Can I touch him mummy?" When he was reassured that he could, he grabbed the pet for dear life and hugged him tightly, enjoying one of the few earthly joys remaining to him. Peter had been so used to having to stay away from "germs" for most of his young life. Hygiene mattered little now.

With the cancer spreading it was not long before Peter lost the ability to speak and swallow. A nasal gastric tube had to be reinserted. Soon he could only keep eye contact. With one of those cruel twists of irony taking hold, Peter's beautiful hair was growing back. Frank continued to take him on tractor rides while Peter's family smiled in front of Peter, hiding their anguish, the façade ceasing only when Peter began drifting in and out of a coma.

But something more was happening in Peter than just a failing battle with a disease that was viciously ravaging his tiny body. It seemed as if Peter's soul was being prepared for a transition, and soon, this reality became tangible and even visible.

5

In Her Arms

Before he had lost his ability to speak in the two weeks leading up to his death, Peter came up to his mother one day and reassured her. "Mum don't worry. I'll be alright." He revealed dreams that featured friends who had died. Peter said to Melina one day, "Mum, I am going to be seeing Missy soon," a dear friend of Peter's who had passed away some months before. Melina looked down at her beautiful son's eyes and, brushing his prophecy aside simply said, "Oh, sweetie. It will be a long time before you will be seeing Missy." But Peter was insistent. "No mum, but it will be okay, really." Perhaps he sensed that this was a conversation his shattered mother was not ready to hear.

Where had Peter obtained that assurance of his impending reunion with Missy? Perhaps it was a natural intuition? Perhaps Peter, although a small child, understood more than the adults around him thought? While nobody in the family can be sure, the answer may lie dormant in two experiences that Peter and his Aunt Nadia had in the last two weeks of his life. Through Nadia, it would seem that a message was being conveyed from a not so distant place.

The special love that Peter had for Mary, *Jesus' mum,* was a devotion that had been nurtured in his family and which united his loved ones in prayer for Peter. The Rosary, a well-known Catholic prayer, brought relatives and friends to the Crea home, who joined Melina and Frank in praying for their son, hoping that they could somehow contribute to ending Peter's suffering and help him find peace. The prayer meeting was led by Gabby, the same lady who had spread the news of his cancer around various prayer circles in Australia when Peter had first been diagnosed. At this stage, the prayer sessions were daily, and Nadia faithfully attended, demonstrating the compassion that Melina has always loved in her sister. Always ready to chat, to help, and always smiling, Nadia would fight spiritually for Peter who had touched her to the depths of her soul. Then, one night, she shared an experience with Peter she never forgot.

The family had just finished the prayer session and Peter was resting on the mattress on the floor as usual. Nadia had remained seated near him while Melina and most of the family went into the kitchen for some refreshments. Nadia is not what you would call a charismatic Christian, accustomed to visions or other wonders associated with the charismatic gifts of the Holy Spirit. In fact, when I asked her if she were, she wasn't sure what I meant. And yet, on two separate occasions Nadia was gifted with two visions that could only be explained as *otherworldly*, confirming that the veil that separates this world from the next is only hidden from our view just for a time.

As she sat to Peter's right, wanting to be near him, Nadia reached down and rested her hand on his shoulder as she normally did. She gently closed her eyes. Before too long, Nadia was *transported* to another place with her nephew. Twenty years later, Nadia still remembers the details clearly. "I remember it to be white and lovingly warm," she explained. She saw thousands of children in this place. They were unmistakably happy as they ran and laughed joyfully. Nadia was standing behind Peter, her hand still resting on his shoulder, and together they watched as the children played. The sight itself filled Nadia with happiness.

Soon, a beautiful "woman" walked gracefully through the crowd of happy children. Nadia wondered if this woman was actually an angel. Lovingly, the angel bent down in front of Peter, directed her gaze at him and asked, "Peter, are you ready to join us now?" Nadia bent down behind Peter and whispered, "Peter, are you ready to go?" Instantly, he yelled out, "No!" It was then that Nadia found they had both been 'transported' back to the lounge room. Nadia bent down again and said, "Peter, it is okay. You don't have to go if you are not ready. Everything will be okay."

As Nadia discovered, Peter's *no* had been heard by Melina. "Nadia, what happened?" she asked, obviously perplexed and worried as she returned hastily to the lounge room. Nadia recounted the experience.

By the time Melina's family and friends had gathered once again for the Rosary only a week before Peter's death, it wasn't through words that Peter communicated.

"Mel, how is he?" asked Carmel who was one of those relatives who had shared deeply in the journey of the Crea family for the past two years. "He can't speak anymore, Carmel. His saliva has dried up and he can't swallow," replied Melina. Together these two women had shed many tears, Carmel still unable to accept that her beautiful little nephew would soon die. Jessica was struggling terribly, battling her fears and utter sadness, upset with the doctors for not curing her baby brother, and wounded deeply by God's apparent silence. *Why have you not heard my prayers, God?* Even now, Melina kept trying to make Jessica understand. "Sweetie, I know how difficult this is. We can't think like that. We need to remember just how blessed we have been to have Petey with us. He has been such a caring and loving brother, hasn't he?" Jessica nodded while she held back more tears. "We are going to continue praying that Peter will not be in pain and that we have the strength to deal with what has to be."

Together with her aunts, Jessica once again sat around Peter that night. They continued to entrust Peter to the Lord, praying together through the intercession of the Blessed Virgin. As the prayers of the Rosary continued, Peter seemed to be at peace and in some degree even comfortable.

It says in Scripture that where two or three are gathered in Christ's name he is there in their midst. That night someone else would also be in their midst. The subdued voices of those present rose up to Heaven in unison. Melina was sitting beside her sister and suddenly noticed that Nadia had stopped praying. Instead, she had her eyes transfixed on Peter.

Melina turned her gaze towards Peter at this point and noticed that her little son appeared to be attempting to prop himself up, an action he repeated a number of times. Melina wondered what he was doing as she saw Peter's shoulders return to the mattress each time. Before the final prayer was uttered Melina felt Nadia tighten her grip on her hand.

"Nadia what is it?" asked Melina.

"Did you see that, Mel?" she asked, looking like she had seen a ghost. The realization that only she had seen this vision suddenly hit Nadia. Even though she felt as if she were watching everything with her eyes wide open, her sister had not seen anything at all.

"Mother Mary was here, Mel!"

Melina's head spun as she listened to Nadia describe the sight that filled her with an overwhelming peace.

Before her eyes, Nadia saw Peter enveloped by a warm, soothing white light emanating from a woman Nadia could only describe as beautiful, her eyes gazing lovingly upon Peter, full of compassion, like any caring mother gazing at her child in need. The woman's brown hair was partly covered by a veil. This woman was not the woman that had greeted both her and Peter in her previous vision. To Nadia it was clear that this woman was the one that Peter knew as "Jesus' mum!" Nadia felt like she knew exactly what was happening.

As Nadia continued to watch, enthralled, she saw Mary reach down ever so gently in order to scoop Peter up in her arms; just like a mother carefully picking up her child while sleeping peacefully in the cot, supporting the back of his neck and shoulders. A number of times Mary tried to lift Peter up but Nadia could sense a tension in Peter. She could feel his resistance, not in an angry way but in a way that said, "I want to go - but I am not ready yet!" Nadia saw Mary try a couple more times and then just put him down gently, released her embrace and faded away, the white light accompanying her, now gone. Yet, the loving warmth that had enveloped Peter, remained. Peace fell upon Peter who rested, perhaps more than he had rested in months.

Nadia knew at the time that the visions she had been gifted with had not been about her. Even though Peter and his Aunt Nadia had always had an extra special connection, Nadia has come to realise that Melina was the reason for her gift. If it happened to anyone other than her cherished sister, Melina may not have accepted it. She may not have accepted the meaning of the experience. As tears welled up in her eyes, tears of both joy and pain, Melina came to finally accept that the doubts that had plagued her about her son's recovery would be confirmed. The miracle she had been hoping for would not occur; Peter would not be healed in this life. But there was at least the consolation of knowing that he would be taken home, to a place filled with the love that this beautiful little soul deserved.

6
Letting go

Melina had prayed that he would be at peace and that she and Frank would have the strength to cope with his loss. From the night of the vision onwards, Melina noticed that Peter no longer struggled with sleep.

As painful as they are, certain moments that define our lives should never be forgotten. They are a mirror of our hearts and teach us to learn the unmistakable story of love that unites all humanity into one family and one destiny. Embarking on that final walk with Peter on the day he was called home, Melina could never have been more certain of this truth.

The night of Peter's death, when he finally said *yes* to the angel of Nadia's first vision, began like many that had preceded it. Melina and Frank were keeping watch over Peter in what had become his makeshift bedroom in the lounge room. It was not big enough to accommodate all the visitors that would be constantly streaming through. It was also a room that enabled Peter to make a new friend, the most unlikely of creatures.

As his mattress had been pushed up against the main window of the room, Peter had a good view outside. Every morning, a Willy Wag tail would greet Peter. This enchanting little bird, native to Australia, New Guinea and the Solomon Islands, is so named for its movement. As it forages on the ground it has a habit of wagging its tail horizontally.

It was 2 a.m. and dawn was still a long way off. The darkness outside had cast its shadow over the Crea home like a blanket. As Melina cautiously fixated on her son's laboured breathing and on his frail body, she knew that he was facing his final struggle. Unlike her husband, Melina had come to some degree of acceptance before this final night. A prayer made long ago had been answered. "Lord, if it is not for me to keep our son, please help me to let him go." Each passing minute was a death knell that penetrated the room. The time had come to give permission for her precious little boy to go.

Choking back tears, feeling as if her heart was being torn from her body, Melina turned gently to her husband, and pleaded. "Frank… you have to tell him that it's okay for him to go. You have to let him go.

Petey is waiting for us to tell him it's okay." She knew that Peter was bravely holding on just for the sake of his parents. "I can't do it…" Frank cried desperately, his words only a glim reflection of what his shattered father's heart could not utter.

Time passed agonisingly. It was now around 3.45 a.m. Summoning his remaining strength, fuelled only by the desire for his son's peace, Frank accepted the inevitable. He gave his son one last gift. He bent over, Melina by his side, and whispered in his son's ear quietly. "Son, you go… It will be okay… We love you… Go to Jesus." Melina's hands, which were resting cautiously on Peter's chest, unexpectedly received his prompt reply. Just moments after Frank uttered his words of permission Melina felt her son's heartbeat fade until it stopped completely. Peter had heard the voice of his father.

Peter Crea, 4

7

I Can Run

Parents are simply not meant to bury their own children. Gazing down at her son in his white suit, the day before his funeral, Melina reflected on the appropriateness of the red bow tie that Peter was wearing. Peter had loved the one worn by a doctor at the hospital. It was fitting that he should be buried wearing one, in his favourite colour. With Rosary beads clasped in his tiny hands, Peter finally looked at peace. "He was perfect," Melina exclaimed proudly. "Just as God gave him to me, he took him. Perfect!"

Relatively joyful too would be Peter's funeral, more a celebration of his life, his unconditional love and mischievousness, his vivaciousness and kindness. Melina asked everyone attending the funeral to refrain from wearing black but instead to dress in bright coloured clothing. At the cemetery, with Peter's favourite music in the background, and surrounded by a crowd of mourners that reflected the colours of a rainbow, red balloons were released and began to soar towards the heavens.

As the small coffin descended into the ground, the reality of Peter's physical absence would not snuff out completely the hope and knowledge that he was truly now at home, bathed in that warm and compassionate light once again, just as he had been blessed with briefly before his death.

While hope remains, the pain, of course, never departs, and memories, while they can be a blessing, can also make the grief ever present. The absence of the child they hugged and held closely, is a vacuum that nothing can ever fill. What Melina and Frank were going through was no different for Jessica.

Right up to the funeral, Jessica begged for Peter to remain on the farm. "Why do we have to take Petey to the funeral parlour mum? Why can't he stay in his room or be buried on the farm that he loved so much?" Jessica simply could not understand a lesson that most people only learn as they get older. She wanted Peter to remain close by, not ready to let go. And her parents, completely exhausted, still tried to explain to their beautiful, anguished daughter, that Peter's spirit would be with them even though his body had to be taken. "Peter will always be with you, Jess."

As time dissolved, the chaos remained. It can at times be surprising how the mere mention of one's deceased loved one can stir up a well spring of tears. The raw emotion is always just under the surface, especially when family traditions and rituals in memory of Peter are enacted. Peter's birthday is celebrated still today. A birthday cake is made, a birthday candle blown out and the family remembers. So too, are used, the Christmas tree decorations Peter requested on that last early Christmas celebration.

The bitter sweetness of these iconic family rituals can be seen each time his birthday approaches. Melina is reminded that his death was the day of Petey's liberation and freedom. Peter had not lost the battle. He had won it in a way that this world cannot understand. The birth of the Christ child at Christmas is a gentle reminder too that life in Christ is always transformed.

Yet, even those who have a faith, regardless of their conviction, are left with the stark reality of the existence of evil and death in this frail world. Melina and Frank, like other parents whose children have died of cancer, would experience all the stages of grief that time would guide them through: the profound numbness, yearning and anger, emotional despair and withdrawal which at various times and periods were eventually replaced by a reorganization of their lives and a letting go. For Frank the experience of withdrawal would mean the need to leave Herne Hill. The place that had been their home held too many dark memories.

Peter's continuing presence was a gentle stream that became a flowing river after his death. Signs and consolations were immediate. The very morning of his death signs of Peter were experienced by various people simultaneously. Just ten minutes before Peter's Aunt Carmel got the phone call, and while in a dream-like state, she lifted her head off the bed and saw this little boy with curly blond hair illuminated by a glorious light emanating from his body. And she just knew.

Her son Angelo, who was only three years of age and who was very close to Peter, also saw Peter sitting on his chest of drawers in his bedroom. Peter's other friend named Greg stunned his parents when he woke and said, "Mum, I had a dream about Petey. He came to me and said goodbye."

Then, the night before Peter's burial, while Melina and Frank were in in the lounge sitting quietly with their extended family, numb and silent, and Jessica had already been in bed for an hour, Jessica cried out.

"What is it, Jess?"

"Mum, can't you see it? There is a gold light standing in front of me, reaching out to me," continued Jessica. Melina saw nothing. To this day Jessica is convinced that Peter was letting her know that he was with her.

Another friend was witness to the bonds of friendship that death cannot sever. During his time at Princess Margaret Hospital Peter had struck a chord with a little girl named Nikki even though she was twice his age. She had the same rare cancer as Peter but was not told that Peter had died. When Nikki's mother phoned, Peter had passed away but a few days. "I don't know what to tell Nikki, but I don't want to tell her that Petey has passed. She wants to see him and see you too." It took a while but Melina courageously obliged and went to see Nikki.

My son has just died, and Nikki has the same cancer. This thought accompanied Melina on her walk to Nikki's front door. As expected, Nikki asked, "Aunty Mel, where's Peter?" Thinking she would burst into tears, Melina put on a brave smile.

"Petey is asleep Darling and is not able to come. But I'm here."

"Aunty Mel, I have to tell you my dream," shared Nikki. "We all went for a picnic by the river."

"Did you really?"

"Yeah, we were having a picnic and we were having so much fun." Melina couldn't believe what she was hearing. A few weeks earlier Melina had organised a picnic for both families by the Swan River but as Nikki had been unwell her mother hadn't even told her about it. Peter had been without his friend that day. Now, in Nikki's dream, the two of them were together once more!

A few other things enabled Melina to find encouragement after Peter's death. Melina doesn't normally dream of Peter but on one occasion she did. It was a dream that fused a past pain and a present joy. It reminded Melina of that time some years before when Peter had first been diagnosed and had been placed in a room that overlooked a beautiful green hill. Peter would look out the window and watch the happy children playing. "Mummy, I wish I could be there too. I wish I could run but my legs are too sore." With her reassuring voice, Melina had told Peter not to worry. "You will do it one day, Petey". In Melina's dream she saw Peter walking towards her wearing the same hospital pyjamas. He awoke her to show her something. "Mum look out the window," he shouted with joy. "I can run." And he *was* running. He was running up and down the sloping hill.

While Melina says that she has never asked why God has allowed Peter to die so young, she has wondered how innocent children can suffer in the way her son did. I believe it is this question of suffering which is the hardest for any Christian to be challenged with. The suffering of innocent children is the hardest to bear and can shake even the firmest foundations of one who has the metaphoric faith than can move the largest mountain.

My time with Melina, hearing the shattering story of her son, seeing the tears in her eyes and thinking about the honour Melina had bestowed on me, is something I hold dear to this day. It was my turn to bestow a small gift on Melina. A story of another child who had passed away just a few years before Peter had, and whose funeral I had attended. I no longer knew the 8-year old's name, but I had written about the experience in my journal. I read it directly to Melina.

"My friends gave an account of what happened. I am inspired each time I hear it and it gives me much hope. I pray it will do the same for all those with loved ones who are dying. The little girl was in her mother's arms and the mother could hear her saying, "Keep going, keep going." The mother asked her why she was saying that and the girl said that she could see a tunnel with a big light at the end of it and could hear joyful people saying the words. The girl died in her mother's arms ... and my friends say that the mother knew she had reached the 'joyful people' when she closed her eyes and died with a smile on her face." (May 30, 1989).

I am comforted by the thought that Peter was welcomed by the "joyful people" as his heart stopped beating. Surely it is for such a place of light that little children in particular belong? Melina turned her eyes to Heaven as soon as Peter had died, and she knew that Peter's death was not the end of his life. As Melina said to me, with a rock-like faith that has kept her going until this day, "I know I will see Petey again. I know that Peter is in perfect peace and with the Creator." I share her hope that all who die in Christ, whether knowingly or unknowingly, and in a way known only to God, will also know the meaning of the great apostle Paul who was given a glimpse of Heaven before his death, declaring that this phenomenal reality we call Heaven can only be described as what "no eye has seen, nor ear heard, nor the heart imagined." It is the dimension which God has *prepared for those who love him* (1 Corinthians 2:9); a place in which Peter Crea is still running up and down that beautiful green hill of life, his legs no longer in pain, his soul free.

Notwithstanding the presence of Heaven in Peter's story, one question remains for the times we simply cannot see beyond the impenetrable stone of death's expressionless gaze. Can there be meaning found in the awful death of a child, even if the consolation of Heaven is obvious? And can that meaning be expressed in such a way that it is not just interpreted as a platitude to get God off the hook?

8

The Slaughter of Children

I walk through the staff room on my way to the coffee machine. A smile splashes across my face.

Coffee! My one beloved addiction!

I go straight to the machine with the "Strong Coffee Beans" label and hit the "Espresso" button. No need for the mild stuff this morning. *Now* I can get to work, as the slogan on my mug reminds me—*No coffee, no workee*. With my secular mantra now enacted, I proceed to my classroom.

Exiting the staff room, I notice the daily newspaper on one of the tables and consider stopping to check the headlines. It isn't long before I regret the decision. I know that what I will see will dampen my spirit, *and* my coffee experience. But I know I need to look. I have already stopped watching the television news and just tolerate news on the web, which I need as a portal into this world, ablaze as it is with turmoil. Still, I take a look.

What I see is evidence of what could arguably be called the vilest age in history, if the prevalence, quality, and quantity of evil are considered. Not just bad news but energy-sapping news. Demoralising news. A dead baby found in a teenager's bag as she is shopping in a top New York store. The bag's contents, mistaken for booty, instead betray this teen's crime: murder of her own child! She had given birth the day before. The umbilical cord is still attached to the child. This baby didn't fare any better than the ones that of late have been thrown into the garbage.

What else do I see? I see corrupt governments inflicting violence on their people, imposing unjust laws, or ignoring terrorist acts that are so barbaric that pure evil is the only explanation. I see fundamental rights being denied, and genocide, an old eugenics programme made famous under Hitler and now back in vogue but in a different guise. Multiple wars, and the consequent destruction, poverty and famine, prevail. Ideologies that deny human rights and the inherent goodness of new life abound and are protected by law. I read stories of children as young as 12 arrested for rape and sexual offenses, or thrown into the world of prostitution, victims of pimps—all while governments, via neglect or direct strategy, permit these situations to continue.

We are continuing to fight the wars on drugs, homelessness, and crime. The destabilisation and redefinition of the family knows no limits. Our senior citizens are mugged and euthanized. Euthanasia has even become law in my home state of Western Australia. Young children are molested and then murdered to cover the perpetrators' tracks.

The older I get, and the longer I walk with the Lord, the more do events that epitomise the intensity of the evil "in my time" trigger questions and doubts, tempting me to retreat into denial. Such doubts then become broken records that keep playing the same tune, challenging the boundaries of my faith and my ability to see light in the midst of darkness.

The aftershock of one event that shook me, began its journey from half a world away just before Christmas, in 2012. Ironically, the evil of the event mirrored the real events that serve as the backdrop to the authentic Christmas, more than the fairy-tale "Jingle Bells" version ever could.

Of the two dozen or so children who perished at the Sandy Hook School in Monroe, Connecticut, the vast majority were elementary-school-age children. They were massacred at gunpoint. The slaughter at Bethlehem was repeated. It was Christmas in the shadow of the cross—the biblical Rachel weeping for her children once again, because they are no more.

The children who were spared could thank their brave teachers who protected them with their ingenuity and acute intuition. One of those teachers, 27-year-old Victoria Soto, hid her young pupils and saved their lives before the gunman, Adam Lanza, killed her. She was a light in the darkness, but not enough light to prevent Sandy Hook from becoming the tragedy it did.

Bloodbaths like the one at Sandy Hook simply should not happen. Children slaughtered? Really?

Haven't we gotten past that madness after so many centuries of supposed civilization? Photos and video footage brought the carnage into the homes of millions across the world. Frantic relatives were shown waiting for word or screaming desperately upon receiving the news. Pervasive among the parents heroic enough to be interviewed, was the need to cling to memories of their children as heralds of goodness. They needed to recall their smiles or their *joie de vivre*, as if at least one thing would continue on, even though the physical nearness of their children was a vapour dissipating with each passing hour. Whatever the tragic event might lead an outsider to dwell on—gun ownership, personality disorders, broken families, acts of heroism, or the fact that God has been 'taken out' of U.S. schools—the mourning of those affected, and the horror they witnessed, have confined the parents to a prison from which there seems no escape. Their cherished children will not return home. Their absence will remain a gaping wound that will not heal.

It is a sobering thought to accept that perhaps what the psalmist wrote in Psalm 9:16 might in fact be true. The current state of any nation on the globe could well be a direct result of its own fidelity, resonating with a pattern that God identified for Israel of old:

"The Gentiles have become trapped in the ruin that they made. Their foot has been caught in the same snare that they themselves had hidden."

Should we be surprised, on a spiritual level, if evil fills in the void that is created when God is thrown out? What is hardest to accept is when the child appears to be the special target of evil. It is the child whose nature ironically witnesses to the glory of God, and to the mystery of the wonder of the human being. While a delight to the Lord, the child can be a constant sign of contradiction to the enemies of life.

The temptation during these times is somehow to explain the evil away: "God's ways are not our ways," we might reason. "There is a purpose for everything, even though we don't understand it." Or "we live in a fallen world where bad things happen." Citing Original Sin, Satan, a fallen world, and free will are good as initial responses to the mystery of evil, but they will not provide all the missing pieces of the puzzle. I am certain that if someone had tried citing Original Sin or free will to a Sandy Hook parent, it would not have touched the real question their hearts were screaming: How could you allow such an evil to occur, God? The quest for an answer to this question, often asked in anguish, is what theologians call *theodicy*. For the layman, this simply means attempting to reconcile the stench of evil with the goodness and love of God.

Have you, like the Sandy Hook parents, or like Peter's parents Melina and Frank, ever been in that dark place of doubt and confusion and asked the real question? I think God is big enough to take it. I know *I* have asked the question, as I did in 2006, when my parish community experienced the devastating loss of one of its smallest members.

9

Sofia

I felt at home in Mater Christi parish in the Perth suburb of Yangebup. I was involved in its beautiful liturgy, embellished by gifted musicians, serving as one of the cantors, particularly when I led the congregation in the Exultet for the Easter Vigil, arguably the most elaborate liturgy in the Catholic Church's calendar. Its readings from Holy Scripture, most of them sung, trace the entire narrative of salvation history. It all makes for a long Mass, but it was a deeply spiritual experience for me.

The church's beautiful stained-glass windows and the local stories behind some of the images found in them (including the parish priest's cat) only added to the sense of family and community we experienced while we were there.

Nine-year-old Sofia Rodriguez-Urrutia-Shu was buried by the parish priest, Fr. Bryan Rosling, a few days after her brutal murder. Throughout the heart-wrenching funeral, and in the days and months that followed, through the challenge of media interviews, legal proceedings, and court trials, the Rodriguez family responded with a tranquillity I have not seen paralleled by anyone else I have known under such duress. They smiled and were always gracious, never losing their composure despite the darkness that enveloped them. Sofia's parents, Gabriel and Josephine, organised social get-togethers for families after Sunday Mass, in order to celebrate family life. While we remained in the parish, my family joined in these gatherings and was enriched by their friendship.

When I once walked past the toilet block at the Livingstone Shopping Centre into which the 21-year-old killer had lured Sofia, I found it all surreal, especially given the violence with which the man had taken Sofia's life. The circumstances of her death meant that things were never the same in the parish. A chapel—the Chapel of the Innocents—was erected in Sofia's honour. It stands as a lasting reminder that, with Sofia's death, Mater Christi parish lost some of its innocence. It is a permanent memorial not only to Sofia but also to the dignity of the child, which triumphs even when man's moral sickness has had its way.

Ironically, just before the news of Sofia's death had struck the airwaves, a Year 8 student raised his hand and asked the question that so many choose to keep in the silence of their heart: "Sir, why does God allow evil to occur?" When he asked it, you could have heard a pin drop.

As a teacher, I love that silence like an awe held in suspended animation. It means that the proverbial chord has been struck. In the depths of their being, people long to discover God, even if the culture that surrounds them denies God's existence. There is really only one reason for finally giving up one's search for God — the notion that God's goodness is false, proven by the meaningless suffering of the innocent.

To an adolescent trying to decide, perhaps for the first time, whether or not the Christian faith of his parents is worthy of acceptance, or just a fairy tale like the rest of the world says, the question of God's goodness is *the* question. And I have always felt called to tackle it if I am to be serious about my teaching. It may not be too difficult to believe in God if all that is required is to accept that he exists. But it is more difficult if you cannot trust that he will protect you from a suffering that makes absolutely no sense.

This was a moment when the students were craving truth. Their eyes revealed an eagerness to find some reason to hope in a loving God. I knew I needed to seize the opportunity.

Looking back at the student briefly, before answering his question, I began walking to the rear of the classroom. Standing beside a poster of Psalm 23 that was hanging on the back wall, I said, "You may have heard about Psalm 23, which speaks of the Lord as our Shepherd. Well, there is an important verse in the psalm which says, 'Even though I walk through the valley of the shadow of death, I will fear no evil, for you are with me.'" I continued. "You see, God has never promised that we will avoid suffering. In fact, he himself did not avoid it on the cross. But he has promised to be by our side in our darkest moments."

It hadn't been that long since I had really come to understand this truth myself, so I was teaching it to them with the excitement that comes with fresh discovery. It is an insight that I cherish to this day. God has never promised an easy life. Instead, he has said more challenging things, like "take up your cross" and "in this world you will have trouble." He has even prepared us for battle with Satan, who seeks to sift us like wheat, or with our own brother, father, sister, mother – even our own child - with whom we may experience division because of our faith in Christ. Yet these sobering words have been given to us along with his promise to be with us always. He has assured us that his yoke is easy and his burden is light, and that he has "overcome the world." Of course, these assurances presume that we will allow him to pull us towards him and not pull ourselves away from him.

By the time I was standing before another class, this time comprised of Year 9 students, I had learned that some friends of Sofia's brother were among them. We agreed that we should try to bring some comfort to the family. "What do you think, guys?" I asked. It was unanimous. We would make gift hampers and produce some sympathy cards that we would then deliver to the family through Fr. Rosling. The school's principal approved our plan.

The hamper items began streaming in by the following lesson. Could one, two, or ten hampers do anything at all to ease the family's pain? Probably not. Certainly, they would not provide anything more than a momentary distraction. But they were better than nothing.

When my students entered the classroom, with its white walls and bluish-green carpet, it was a set of coloured cards, paper, crayons, and texters strewn all over the front desks, that accosted them.

I called them to come up and collect what they needed for the decoration of the cards. "Try to write something that will bring comfort to the family," I encouraged them. They began the process, some with head down, busily colouring, others walking to and fro, gathering their wares. Feeling they might need a little help, I decided to look to the Scriptures for some inspiration.

A grey cupboard on the left side of the room housed a copy of the Bible. *I will collect it*, I thought, *return to my desk, and begin ploughing through it.* Does that *"open the Bible and see what your eyes fall on"* trick really work? I had tried it before with uncanny success. So now, I would try it again.

For some reason I didn't wait until I had returned to my desk. Instead, I opened it thoughtlessly, as soon as I had picked it up from the shelf. Reading the first words my eyes fell upon - the first few verses of the third chapter of the Book of Wisdom – I was stunned.

Immediately, I called out to the busy students, forgetting the decorum and professionalism expected between student and teacher.

"Hey, guys. Stop! I can't believe this. Listen!" They all turned toward me. With my face lit up, I explained what I had just done, then read out loud the following:

"But the souls of the just are in the hand of God, and no torment of death will touch them. In the eyes of the foolish they seemed to die, and their departure was considered an affliction, and their going away from us, a banishment. Yet they are in peace."

"That's amazing!" gasped a boy known for his gentle nature. I couldn't wipe the smile off my face, and my students were visibly touched. Was God indeed speaking to us? Had he just answered my question about how to reconcile evil with his loving kindness? But more importantly, was he expecting us to share this wisdom with Sofia's family?

In time I did write to them and tell them what happened that day in my classroom. That day in June 2006 when I opened the Bible to the Book of Wisdom, the Lord convinced me that our perception of human realities is not the same as God's. The Lord seemed to be confirming what I myself had been pondering in my thoughts and prayers since I had heard about Sofia's passing.

But I wasn't able to tell them one other interesting 'coincidence' of that day which I only realised in 2019, as I began work on the second edition of this book. The word, *wisdom*, is the English translation of the Greek word, *Sofia*!

Regardless of how difficult it is to stomach the suffering of the innocent, our Christian faith, and this experience, shows me that God does indeed walk through that valley of death with us. I choose to believe not only that Sofia is with the Lord today but also that he was with her in a tangible way in her final moments in this life, giving her the knowledge and strength of his presence, perhaps even taking away her fear.

How could God not *have been with her if anything we believe about God is true?* What the world sees as utter destruction, God sees with the eyes of eternity. Sofia, his "just one," is now in peace.

Sofia, 9

10

Martyr of Columbine

What *does* the Christian tradition say about the suffering of the innocent? Is there, in the lives of the saints, in scripture and in the witness of today's believers, anything that gives us reason to hope that the invisible realities present during acts of evil are just as real as, if not more so, than the physical realities we see with our eyes and feel with our hearts? The evidence, I have come to see, is overwhelming.

The same story has been repeated again and again in the lives of martyrs, both ancient and new, testifying to the same truth that Christ himself once uttered to the Apostle Paul when he begged to be delivered from his mysterious *thorn in the flesh* - "My grace is sufficient" (2 Corinthians 12:9). With spiritual insight, he came to see meaning and purpose in his suffering. Christ did not promise to heal him, but he did promise to walk by his side with his grace. Something more meaningful was going on for Paul that he would come to understand only in time. *All of his suffering was part of Christ's own work of redemption, which we too are caught up in somehow.* And he came to rejoice in his sufferings, as he told the Church at Colossae:

"For now, I rejoice in my passion on your behalf, and I complete in my flesh the things that are lacking in the Passion of Christ, for the sake of his body, which is the Church" (Col. 1:24).

Through Paul's words, Christians can be filled with hope that the fire that causes all things to *"work together unto good, for those who love God"* (Romans 8:28), is a transforming one. God knows that his power and presence can compensate for the harm done to finite things by helping us to see with eyes of faith, the treasures we are storing up in heaven, where "neither moth nor rust consumes and where thieves do not break in and steal" (Matthew 6:20).

At times, God prepares us for our death through a still small voice, an intuition, or a mystical transport of some sort. In those who have experienced this very thing, I have found a deeper understanding of the "see-through vision" that makes all the difference when considering the question of suffering. In particular, I have observed God working this way in the life of another school-shooting victim, who died 13 years before the tragedy of Sandy Hook; the witness of Columbine. Martyr, Rachel Scott.

Seventeen-year-old Rachel Scott was killed in Littleton, Colorado, on April 20, 1999, in what has come to be known as the Columbine massacre. Much has been said about the fact that she courageously witnessed to her faith in Christ before one of the gunmen, Eric Harris, shot her in the head shortly after he and fellow gunman Dylan Klebold, fellow students, ambushed the school. Rachel had spoken with Eric during the preceding school year and he had known that she was a Christian. Her name was later found on his list of targets.

It was from Darrell Scott, Rachel's father, that I first heard the phrase "see-through vision." He had courageously spoken of a transcendent vision that had enabled him to see beyond the stone that was his daughter's "meaningless" death to the diamond that was her legacy.

The witness of Rachel and others that day has been described as a defining moment for a generation of teens. But how could Scott be sure it wasn't just a mere coincidence? The answer lay in Rachel's backpack, which had been pierced by the bullet that had cut through her body. Hidden inside it was the treasure of Rachel's diary, her final will and testament.

When Rachel's mother and father opened their daughter's bloodstained backpack when it was discovered, and read her diary entries, it must have been like hearing their daughter's voice again, as if from a distant place. Rachel had poured out her thoughts and her prayers to God in that diary. For Rachel's mother, Beth, these prayers reveal an intimacy with God that cannot be denied. They reveal much more too: a desire to make an impact on the world for God, and to submit to his will—in fact, to be nothing short of a warrior for Christ.

For someone so young, Rachel had a deep understanding of spiritual warfare. Recorded in *Rachel's Tears*, written by Rachel's parents, is her diary entry from March 7, 1998. Rachel had been experiencing a mysterious pain in her stomach that was never explained. It led her to write:

"God . . . I have this terrible sharp, dull pain in my stomach. I don't know if it's a spiritual feeling, if the enemy is attacking, or if it's just sickness . . . If it's a spiritual feeling, I ask you to bless it. If it's the enemy, I ask you to bind it. If it's just sickness, I ask you to heal it. Thank you."

Then, in the hours before Rachel and the other twelve victims were shot, she drew a picture that was unnervingly prophetic. In it she depicted two eyes from which thirteen teardrops fell to water a rose. Thirteen tears. There would be thirteen victims at Columbine High School. Scott later discovered another drawing of a rose dated a year earlier. This time it was just a rose with bloodlike drops growing from a columbine plant, the state flower, after which her school was named. Rachel had included a scripture verse in her image: "Greater love hath no man than this, that a man would lay down his life for his friends." These words make the significance of Rachel's pictures even starker. They tell us what Rachel herself somehow seemed to know. On May 2, 1998, she prophesied the following:

"This will be my last year Lord, I have gotten what I can. Thank you."

Rachel knew she would die soon. She had drawn eyes weeping over Columbine. The number of tears matched the number of victims. She would be one of them. Their blood would bring rebirth to Columbine.

Rachel had accepted Jesus into her heart at the age of twelve, asking to be filled with the Holy Spirit. Five years later, Jesus accepted her sacrifice for a purpose that Eric Harris and Dylan Klebold could not have foreseen—the rebuilding of God's Kingdom in the hearts of youth across the world. Rachel had asked God, in one of her prayers, to "deliver me from my ways." She just wanted to do God's will, as unfathomable as it was. She thus allowed what was in our sight merely an evil, to be transformed, in Scott's words, into something triumphant by God's grace.

What God was showing me in the days following Sofia's death, just as he had told Rachel through her inspired diary entries, was that there is meaning in the death of his faithful ones. He was answering the question about evil and suffering in a way he knew I would understand—through his Word, directly from an Old Testament passage that just happened to have a message for someone contemplating the frightful death of an innocent little one and trying to find some hope and meaning in it.

I believe God was saying still more. We need to look at everything in this world through spiritual eyes, even situations that lead only to despair in the flesh because to our physical eyes they reveal only the reality of decay.

Perhaps, even more surprisingly, God was saying that children, whom Christ declared to be the very essence of the Kingdom of

God, are the most powerful co-sharers in Christ's own suffering—what Catholic mystical theology calls *redemptive* suffering. Who else but those who are most innocent and pure, who most closely resemble Christ, would be permitted to participate in Christ's own suffering for the salvation of souls? We may not like it. We wish that it never happened. Yet, Catholics know that at least one precedent for this has already been set, in the well-known story of the little children of Fatima, Portugal.

When the Blessed Virgin Mary appeared to them in 1917 with her peace plan from heaven, before all hell broke loose on Earth through communism, war, and militant atheism, she also came to ask them something: "Are you willing to suffer for God so that the souls of many might be saved?" The three seers aged only seven, nine, and ten, courageously said *yes*.

The Lady from heaven promised to be with them and that God's grace would be given accordingly. It seems that the suffering of the innocent, offered or accepted lovingly and patiently, becomes the greatest act of love and therefore the most powerful weapon against moral evil. Seen with heaven's eyes, this type of suffering, far from being useless and meaningless, can indeed have great power.

It is only with Heaven and the eternal salvation of souls in mind that any Christian can move from questions filled with pain and anguish, which are only to be expected, to statements of faith-filled trust in God's mysterious plan. *Lord, thank you for the good you have brought out of this evil. Jesus, I entrust my child to you as Abraham did Isaac, knowing that you love him more than I ever can. In ways known only to you, not only was my child's suffering not meaningless, but it was also redemptive and has helped me to experience love in a way I would not have thought possible.*

Perhaps you are thinking, "Well, that's all fine and good. Some people have consolation in their suffering. But what about those millions of others who have no faith and suffer innocently? What about them? Does their suffering have no worth? Is God not with them?" I agree. This is an important question. It has often plagued me. And though it still does plague me to some extent, I have found inspiration in the least likely place.

Arguably one of the lesser-known Chronicles of Narnia, *The Horse and His Boy*, by C. S. Lewis, is actually one of my favourites. It is the story of a long-suffering boy named Shasta who was treated like a slave by his foster father. He discovers, instead, that he is the long-lost son of a king and heir to the throne of Archenland, not far from Narnia.

Aslan, the Christ-Lion, reveals himself to Shasta and helps him understand that Aslan has known his suffering all along and has been with him in various ways. But it is what Aslan tells Shasta, when Shasta seeks to understand the suffering of his companion Aravis, whom Aslan has disciplined, that speaks volumes to me. Aslan confesses that he was the lion who wounded Aravis! Yet, the reason for this wounding was not for Shasta to know because he only ever tells one his or her own story, and not that of others! Aslan makes it very clear, that we can never truly understand the story of others.

11

His Grace is Enough

It has not been my own suffering that has scandalised me. Somehow, I have always been given the strength I have needed to survive it, in whichever form it has come to me. In my mother's death, in operations, gut-wrenching betrayals, and intense loneliness, I have seen some reason, something good that has come of it. One night comes immediately to mind. I found myself writhing in pain. Hunched over, but with eyes open, I glanced at the objects in my room—furniture, bed, whatever was in front of me. And for a very brief moment, which nonetheless left a lasting impression, I realised just how empty all of it was. I understood that all of it would pass away, including my body, which was being battered at the time. It all seemed like a counterfeit of reality. Death had suddenly taken on new meaning. It is not a loss but a birth into a deeper, more glorious reality—an attachment to the One who is fullness of reality.

No, it has not been my own suffering that has scandalised me but the suffering of others, the *stories* of countless others. These have plagued me: The Jewish Holocaust. 9/11 and countless victims of terror worldwide. The Rwanda Massacre. Columbine. Sandy Hook. Sofia. The list goes on. And Lewis's brilliance has enabled me to see why.

I had presumed that the story between God and others is written in the same way as my own; that I could somehow judge others' stories in the same way as I do my own. I didn't realise that I will never understand the unique story that the Lord writes on a soul other than my own. I certainly am not privy to the light and graces that God grants to each soul in order for his will to be accomplished in their life, for their salvation to be obtained, and for their role in the salvation of others to be lived out. Perhaps this is why I was left incredulous at the strength of Melina Crea when she was facing her son's suffering, or of Gabriel and Josephine when they were faced with the horror of Sofia's death. I was not given the graces they were given. And the more I reflect on the suffering of close friends, the more I see a pattern emerge.

A dear friend has suffered multiple operations from cancer and its complications and has been at death's door. I hear her tell me how much more she has come to understand the love of Jesus. Her suffering has been excruciating, yet her strength, courage, and hope are a monolithic inspiration. Instead of losing her faith, it has been refined. Her intimacy with Christ astounds me. I know I could not go through what she has. And God knows that too.

Another friend, a father of four, found himself tested through the suffering of his children for at least two years with very little respite. Operations, accidents, epileptic fits, and inexplicable viruses have been his household's regular visitors. None of his children have been spared. "He allows so much," my friend told me, speaking of God's permissive will. He is numb at times from the struggle, but he perseveres, and his faith is unshaken.

Feasibly, the commonly held idea that "God never gives us more than we can handle" does speak a real truth after all. Jesus did indeed mean what he said, especially when we feel like the flame of faith has been extinguished: "My grace is sufficient."

This faith is tailor-made for each individual.

I think about the parents of Sofia, about the parish community of Mater Christi. I ponder the suffering of Peter Crea, of Rachel Scott, of the children at Sandy Hook, and of their parents, who will continue grieving in timeless silence.

The images that haunt the parents of children who suffer violence, illness, and premature death, can never tell us the full story of God's gaze and of what God was working out in the children's hearts and souls as he transformed the evil they experienced, into a good that has eternal rewards.

The answer won't be found in being plagued by the image of their children suffering or being violated. But it may be found in the gentle silence of their prayers and tears, and in the strength of their faith, fine-tuned by the graces that God has offered to nurture its growth. It is found in the sufferer's willingness to see the love of God in the darkness of doubt and fear. Trust does indeed seem to be the only possible response that the Christian can ultimately give to the scandal of suffering, especially the suffering of a child. It is the response of Job, who, despite having everything taken away, still says,

"Naked I departed from my mother's womb, and naked I shall return; the Lord gave, and the Lord has taken away… Blessed by the name of the Lord" (Job 1:21).

Over the years since my conversion, I have come to see that evil comes in many forms, some more mystical than others, not borne just from disordered immorality or from natural evil such as disasters. Some forms of evil have a more radical root and origin that predate human existence.

These more supernatural forms may not have scandalised me as much as the more 'human' ones, but they have certainly left their mark. And, so it was, around the age of 30 years of age, that God placed me in the direct path of this more mystical more primal evil – a bit *too* direct for my liking.

DELIVERANCE

⌘

*Moreover, if it is by the finger of God that I cast out demons,
then certainly the kingdom of God has overtaken you.
- Luke 11:20*

⌘

12

Serpents

The scream pierced the cold air as the young mother's heart skipped a beat. Maria jumped out of bed and reached out to comfort her young son. It was midnight and the scream, right on schedule, was preceded by the loud banging on the roof. As usual, by the time she reached him, he was sitting up, still screaming, his eyes shut. Grabbing her one-year-old son's tiny hand she helped him make the sign of the cross. "In the name of the Father, and of the Son and of the Holy Spirit," she intoned, knowing this was the only thing that would work. And as the ritual was completed, the little boy named Salvatore (after his grandfather), settled and immediately fell asleep.

The one-bedroom stone house was still standing, when I saw it for myself in 1998 on our family trip to Sicily. It was eerily abandoned, untouched, while homes were built around it.

"This is the house," my mother said as we drove past. She had told me the story of the haunted house that my cousins Salv and Carla had lived in for a while in the Sixties. I could easily imagine the snakes that my aunt had seen regularly outside the home, in which she never wished to remain alone, right up until they migrated to Australia. I was grateful for the expansive frontage that provided a comfortable distance from the house as we drove off. I didn't know then what I came to know some years later. Whatever it was that terrified the little boy with the curly black hair didn't just remain in that house. It would seem that it followed the family across the seas, developing a particular fascination with Salv's younger sister, Carla.

There are a number of myths associated with the practice of exorcism and the deliverance ministry. One is that the ritual and practices associated with it are remnants of a backward medieval past. The reality is that exorcisms are still practiced and are increasing.

The first time I gave the practice any real notice was while watching an episode of *60 Minutes*. The voices that issued out of the 16-year-old girl featured in the piece were chilling. I had tried watching *The Exorcist* after that, but the first five minutes were enough to convince me it was not for me. And when I read about the deliverance ministry in various texts I did so as an intellectual activity. I was intrigued by the work of exorcists who distinguished between the various levels of diabolical activity that can occur. Various levels of oppression or infestation and, of course, the rarer possession. I discovered what these experts warn us to avoid – so called doorways that lead to such activity, such as participation in the occult, curses, satanic rites, and even the seemingly harmless 'evil eye' curse which is commonly understood in some European cultures.

Reports of demonic influence and infestation had increased by the turn of the century and, before long, interest in the ministry began blossoming with papal approval even before the somewhat surprising emphasis on Satan that Pope Francis made an unlikely hallmark of his pontificate.

Pope Francis spoke on the devil twice in the first two days of his pontificate. And he didn't stop there. It was Francis who in 2014 formally recognised the International Association of Exorcists that has had a conference every year since 1994. The Church, it would seem, is meeting the demand with a task force of priests ready to do battle.

Without expecting or asking for it, my personal interest in the deliverance ministry swiftly took on new meaning at the dawn of the new millennium. What I had read about and understood intellectually suddenly became part of my own story, crossing paths with the story of the little boy with curly hair, his beautiful sister, and the spirit that seems to have followed them from their home in Sicily to Australia.

13

"Mummy, I'm scared"

When Carla first recalled what had been happening in her home in the Perth suburb of Beechboro, I didn't know it had been going on for seven years. We were at my Aunt Caterina's house in 2000, chatting about spiritual realities. Carla may not have been deeply religious, but she was spiritual and was one of the few relatives with whom I could speak so openly about all things mystical. She had the gift of prophetic dreams, meant for others more than herself.

One such dream had occurred a week before our grandfather died in the Eighties. She dreamt she was walking in a funeral procession. The following day she asked our *Nonno* what it meant. He just shook his head, but his eyes betrayed a concern. A week later, Carla found herself at our grandfather's house again just after watching a movie containing a funeral scene. Without any specific reason he hugged and clung to Carla as if afraid he would never see her again. "Call your father," he asked her. "Tell him I want to see him." Nonno died that night.

Dreams are one thing. But I was a little taken aback when Carla began to explain what she had been experiencing in her home, while she was still awake!

"Things began happening pretty much as soon as we moved into the house in 1993," she said. "We would hear footsteps out in front of the house. My daughter, Domenica, would hear strange noises too." Domenica was nine by the time the activity in the home had increased. Sweet and loving by nature, Domenica was perhaps an easy target. It was when Carla was pregnant with her that an inexplicable bang as loud as an explosion erupted inside the home, heard by Carla's mother, Maria, who was there at the time.

"What other strange noises?"

"Toys would go off in the middle of the night – sounds you couldn't put down to one's imagination. Dom shared a room with Jessica who would hear someone running up and down the side of the house. She would cry hysterically every night and refused to stay in her room. I would ask what was wrong and she would say, 'I don't know, mummy! I just don't want to be in there. I'm scared.' So, one night I decided I would check it out myself, and I slept in her bed. I realised she wasn't making it up – it wasn't just a normal running noise. It was terrifying!"

My eyes were fixed on Carla's serious gaze that nonetheless did not detract from her youthful Sicilian beauty. "It wasn't just the sounds either. Things would move - and we saw things. In the morning we would find Daniel's toys all over the place in the room that used to be a playroom when his sister Jess was only two. Back then I remember her saying 'Mummy, there was a man outside the window.' I would tell her there *was* no man. But she would insist."

It seemed that the children were under special attack. Daniel, a mature little boy with big brown eyes, also experienced things an eight-year-old shouldn't. One day he was home from school and he and his mother were facing the window as they chatted. Suddenly Daniel was distracted.

"Oh," he exclaimed.

"What is it darling?"

"No, nothing Mummy. You wouldn't believe me even if I told you," he replied maturely.

"No, baby, tell me," Carla insisted, concerned a good deal more than her face was indicating.

"A naked man just ran by the window," he said matter of fact.

"Where, darling?"

"He just ran by that way running from the back of the house to the front." Carla started praying and asked them to get out of the room. There was only so much she could take, and as things became crazier, with more than one thing occurring each day, fear for her children increased. And her husband? He refused to speak of anything he had seen or heard.

"Renato, I used to have dreams about Domenica – her head spinning and a terrible voice coming out of her mouth. I would wake up in a fret and go to her room, bless all the kids each night and sit on their bedroom floor praying for them. By then, Daniel had stopped going to sleep on his own. I had to stay with him, especially after his dream. He said he saw his floor open up. He saw fire. What scared me the most was when he said, 'Mum, the pig was there trying to get me, trying to come out!'

As Carla continued, I became transfixed by what I was hearing. "I didn't disbelieve him. I had experienced things too. I remembered when I was pregnant with Jessica and living somewhere else. One night I felt like someone was sitting on my chest, crushing me. I tried screaming but nothing came out – and then, just as quickly as it came, it stopped!"

I realised that whatever it was that was causing all this in her home, the children had not been the only targets. Carla revealed that she had experienced things as early as she could remember. Her nightmares consisted of monstrous dark shadows that came into the room and approached her brother Salv. But Carla wasn't actually asleep. In her mind she could hear these shadows saying that they would harm him. When she tried to scream, she couldn't – just like that time with Jessica.

"I could do nothing then," she said. "I didn't know about prayer yet!"

I hadn't bargained for any of this. But what she told me sounded more and more like what I had read in the books of exorcist Fr. Amorth. Of spirits that somehow attach themselves to certain people, sometimes the eldest child or eldest female child – spirits that move with their desired *companion*.

"Carla, do you think this has something to do with the house where you were born?"

"Maybe. I know that the whole town believed that the house in Naso was haunted. Maybe the spirit followed me. Because even when we moved to Tuart Hill I would wake up screaming in the night and

mum would comfort me. And then, when I married Remo and we stayed with Mum and Dad for three years, things didn't change. Near the window we both heard a demonic growl that would be followed by a huge bang into the garage door. But there was nothing outside. We would sleep with the window shut from that point on – that didn't stop the sound of the tennis ball that bounced through the corridor at night, though!"

Marvelling at how calm Carla was as we spoke, and not knowing what else to say, I said the one thing I knew would make sense. "Carla, I really think you should call a priest."

14

The Phone Call

For some time after that night, we didn't discuss the matter again. I could sense that Carla was not too keen for a priest. "Calling a priest" is something my extended family usually see as a practice initiated when close to death!

Months passed. But in that time, and not without a tinge of irony, I crossed paths with a priest, recently arrived in the archdiocese of Perth, who unlike most priests, not only spoke of the devil but claimed he had done battle with the diabolic. I heard his testimony – a powerful witness to the reality being experienced all over the world even though I didn't know it at the time. The coincidence was uncanny – my cousin's revelation – meeting Fr. David (not his real name) - and it didn't stop there. My involvement with this priest became such that I was asked to join him as part of a prayer team when he exercised the deliverance ministry.

Discerning religious life at the time, I accepted the offer and began to accompany him on home visitations. With his stole around his neck, and armed with the Eucharist, he would pray as he walked through various rooms, elevating the Host, which Catholics believe is transformed into the true Body and Blood of Christ during Mass. A room in a particular home we visited was quite cold. As soon as we approached that room with the Host, the dog outside began barking hysterically. That was the room where the owners said most of the *activity* had been occurring.

It was a deliverance in Fr. David's own chapel, however, that spooked me out completely. There I was, kneeling in prayer at the back of the chapel while Fr. David continued his work with a woman whom I will call *Rita*. Father never told me the finer details of her situation but I knew she regularly attended his healing masses. I saw her there the first time too – vomiting during one of the sessions. This wasn't the first session he had ministered to her. I watched as Father began his prayer, wearing once again his stole as a sign of his priestly authority, prayer book in hand, both he and Rita positioned near the altar.

At times, Rita obeyed the priest's commands. Other times she played him. "In the name of Jesus, go to the foot of the cross and submit to the power of Christ," commanded Fr. David. Ignoring him completely, Rita stood erect in mock obedience and walked right past the cross with defiant, robotic-like strides. The change to Rita's voice, convinced me there was much more here than just a woman needing healing.

"Why are you with Rita?" Father asked

"She is beautiful," came the reply. "I have been with her a long time. I love her!" A demon speaking of *love*?

The session having ended, I left with the distinct impression that Rita's deliverance would not be an easy one.

Some time passed when I received a call from Carla. I had had enough time to dwell on her situation by then, couched as it was in my mind by my recent involvement in the deliverance ministry. And when the phone rang and I answered, hearing her voice, I didn't give her a chance to speak.

"Carla, I have been waiting for your call. You need to see a priest," I said, this time much more convicted. A brief silence followed. Slightly shaken, Carla responded. "That's why I phoned.... As you said that the hairs on my arm stood on end."

"Carla, I think what is happening in your home is demonic."

"I know. And things have gotten worse."

Things had indeed progressed, the activity more frightful. Domenica had begun hearing voices – so much so that teachers phoned home concerned about it.

One night, as Carla went to the bathroom, its door suddenly rattled, as if someone was holding it on both sides, shaking it for dear life.

Another night, Carla went to the toilet and left the door slightly ajar. She heard Dom calling fearfully, "Mummy, Mummy!"

"Come here, sweetie," Carla soothed, only becoming confused when Dom didn't come to her for comfort as she normally would. That was strange! When the voice became a mocking chant, however, the confusion was replaced with terror. This was *not* her daughter. Cautiously returning to her bedroom, Carla's gaze was drawn towards the kitchen. Standing there, still and threatening, was an outline of a dark shadow. Carla jumped into her bed, petrified; all her children were by this stage accustomed to sleeping in *Mummy's room*, their mattresses strewn all over the floor.

In bed, heart racing, praying for her children's protection, Carla then noticed the door to her room shift inwardly. Moments later, Carla felt as if whatever had entered had made the foot of her bed its resting place.

"Renato, it was then that I knew I needed to call and ask for a priest," she confessed. "Things have been worse still since I called a medium into the house."

"Who was it, Carla?"

"It was a friend of a friend. She came in, sat down and said there was the spirit of a half-cast aboriginal who thought my home was her land. When I asked her if I should get a priest she said emphatically, 'No, that will only make things worse'."

"Carla, that's exactly what you *have* to do. I will call one, okay?" Carla accepted.

What followed leading up to the day of the visit was somewhat unnerving. When Fr. David tried to call Carla, the phone would go dead. Eventually, the persistent priest got through.

"I think it is best if I come sooner, rather than later," he said. A time was booked. And the process arranged. I would chauffeur and accompany Fr. David to my cousin's home.

15

Spiritual Armour

It was the morning of July 16th, 2000, the Feast of Our Lady of Mt Carmel, when Fr. David was scheduled to arrive. I was home alone. Being mindful that I had not been praying for protection regarding my involvement in a deliverance, a situation that would make me extremely vulnerable – where my fear would play against me and I needed to be clothed with spiritual armour - I walked to my bedroom to pick up my Bible, the diary of St. Faustina (a mystic saint who had dealings with the demonic), and my Rosary beads.

As I began making my way out of the bedroom, I was almost swept up by the garish explosion of repetitive banging that resounded behind me. What sounded like my cupboard getting a wild beating gradually lessened in intensity the further away from my room I ran, shooting off to the kitchen at the other end of the house with my heart about to puncture my rib cage.

With Rosary beads in hand I quickly began praying the Divine Mercy chaplet. My finger traced the beads as I prayed the prayer taught by Our Lord to St Faustina. "For the sake of his sorrowful passion, have mercy on us and on the whole world." More hammering, but it began to subside and then stopped completely. For whatever reason, the *intrusion* was kept at bay in my bedroom.

I sat down at the kitchen table, my back to the window, so I could keep an eye on anything that might pop out in front of me, not leaving anything to chance. Opening up the scriptures to where I had left off the previous time, my eyes fell on the following, unexpected passage.

And he called the twelve. And he began to send them out in twos, and he gave them authority over unclean spirits (Mark 6:7).

Not sure whether to laugh or cry, I took a deep breath. I knew then that what I had heard in my room was indeed not of human origin. I also knew that God was in the midst of it all. Fr. David and I would not be alone.

A fresh knock, this time one of the more natural kind on the front door, startled me again. I made it out of the kitchen, slightly reticent as the journey to the front door would bring me closer to my bedroom. I was relieved when Fr. David confirmed his presence. "Are you okay," he asked. The pale expression on my face told him what he needed to know. His first stop was my bedroom. And then, making our way to my car, we began our trek into the lion's den!

It was late afternoon when we arrived at Carla's home. Both literally and metaphorically the grey storm clouds that hung above us aptly matched the dark atmosphere that we were entering. Carla's younger brother was still over, and he discreetly left before Father blessed the children who were escorted out of the house.

"Carla, if you take all the religious objects down off the wall, I will bless them for you," suggested Father. It began to rain, the wind howling periodically as the priest progressed with the deliverance. He invited Carla to confession in Daniel's room where most of the activity had occurred.

I had read Fr. Amorth's comments about Confession being the most powerful form of exorcism. Even in cases of possession, Satan has no real hold on a person except through our compliance in sin. Fr. David knew this well. His armour consisted of the Sacrament of Confession and the Eucharist more than any other sacramental like holy water or blessed objects.

As I waited outside the makeshift confessional, Father asked Carla to sit on the bed while he knelt.

"Just repeat this prayer," he directed. The tormented scraping and clawing sounds on the venetian blinds which this prayer triggered became progressively angrier. Afraid, she kept her gaze on Fr. David who must have been sensing something too as his voice grew more authoritative. Carla's focus on the prayer intensified and suddenly she felt an empowerment fuelled by the prayer that countered the furious din that offered its protest, as the tingling sensation in her stomach suddenly stopped. Fr. David, at the same time, knew that *an unwanted guest* had left her.

"It's gone," said Fr. David as they finished their prayer. Concerned for her neighbours, Carla asked, "Where has it gone?" Father replied simply. "Where it belongs."

I watched as both priest and penitent came out of the room as Father prepared for Mass in the makeshift chapel set up in the lounge area. He exposed the Host on the golden Paten placed on the kitchen table as candles flickered nervously. Carla managed a smile but the theatrics of it all were hard to dismiss.

As the healing Mass commenced, the wind grew louder. Lights flickered. Carla's expression fell. She glanced at Remo and then back at me. It was as if she was asking, "Can you hear that?" She then looked towards Fr. David who acknowledged, as if by telepathy, what was going on and proffered an encouraging smile. Behind her, emanating from the kitchen, Carla heard growling accompanied by the sound of claws scraping, this time, from her daughter's room. It then stopped – a brief reprieve.

Father began to pray a prayer against curses. "While Father was praying that prayer, I remember feeling as if I was being pushed from the inside of my core," Carla recalled. That explained the raw fear and confusion on her face as her arm and leg jerked uncontrollably.

And then that also stopped. The ordeal was over.

Liberated, and reborn, Carla's life changed from that day. Domenica said to her one day, "Mummy, your eyes look different." Her appearance had obtained a peace that Carla had probably never experienced, and her faith had taken on deeper meaning. Fr. David explained that he felt there had indeed been a demonic infestation in the home and that Carla had experienced diabolical oppression.

Carla's new life was soon blessed with another child whom she named Christian. The bond between them is one that has been formed by the newfound grace post-deliverance. The struggles that have come in rearing all her children since then have been taken on with a newfound strength. It is like the experience she had when Christian was ill as a child. With her child lying down, and her hands placed on him in prayer, Carla would find her hands palpitating and Christian would begin to jerk.

Carla's gift of discerning dreams has also continued as her conversion to Christ blossomed.

In a terrifying dream in the early months of 2010, Carla saw a plane flying really low over land with a distinctive shade of blue visible from beneath the plane, just before it crash-landed. She remembers seeing many people walking away desperately from the wreckage, indicating many survivors. She also saw very clearly that the plane had broken up into *three distinct pieces*. Believing that this dream might be prophetic she curiously tried to work out which airline the plane represented because she was certain it was not an Australian airline.

By the end of the year, the following information was discovered on the Net. On August 17, 2010, an *Aires* Columbian jetliner with blue stripes and distinct bright blue engine casings crash-landed on a Columbian Island in the Caribbean, breaking up into three pieces. The vast majority walked away alive apart from one man who lost his life. The resemblance was uncanny. When her husband Remo saw the news, he was silent. The resemblance was *too* uncanny. (Her father would agree, but with regards to another dream in which Carla found herself in a Piazza in wartime Sicily, together with our deceased Aunt Maria. When her father Giuseppe heard Carla's description of the Piazza, he identified it as the main Piazza in Messina, one that Carla had never seen).

Since my experience with Carla I have crossed paths with others who have had an experience with the diabolic. The story of one in particular is perhaps a clear case of possession right here in Perth.

"Paul" had been exposed to the Ouija board and occult from the age of ten, most likely due to the links his family had with Freemasonry. His testimony to me by phone was incredible and like watching pages turning in an exorcist's book. Witchcraft. Séances. Visible manifestation of a demon. Feelings of torture during his exorcism which took three priests and repeat sessions. He would squirm as the Eucharist was held up close and could feel the demon moving and clawing inside him as he prayed the Rosary. The moment he was finally delivered, the back door of the chapel flung open violently. It had taken nine weeks for a full deliverance.

Some may ask how I can believe "Paul" just from a phone conversation. Well, I could understand that if I hadn't actually met him and come to know him as a practicing Catholic family man who looks like a heavily tattooed ex-bikie member!

For Carla, what may have started in a house in Sicily certainly ended in a house in Perth thanks to the ministry of the Catholic priesthood. Many Catholics might like to ignore the deliverance ministry, but, at the end of the day, doing so would be to deny the teachings and practice of the Church, as well as the experiences of many souls. In an age where there are many in our consumerist and neo-pagan culture willing to introduce our children to the occult, now is perhaps not the time to ignore spiritual realities. The representation of Satan as a comic figure with a 'red dress' who helps sell cars in commercials is an example of a society that sees Satan as a laughable concept at worst, and a useful aid to fame and fortune at best.

Jesus said, "… if it is by the finger of God that I cast out demons, then certainly the kingdom of God has overtaken you" (Luke 11:20). Carla's deliverance brought her closer to this Kingdom. For a while, the problem I had with evil had abated. My teaching and reading, as well as my own ponderings, however, soon brought me into contact with the scandal of another form of evil in which an entire so-called Christian nation was not only oppressed, but apparently *possessed*, with a hatred that was inconceivable. And when I finally met someone who had experienced the effects of this hatred first-hand, I knew the next stage of my search for answers had been engaged.

"The thief comes only to steal and kill and destroy.
I came that they may have life and have it abundantly.
(John 10:10 - English Standard Version)

PARADISE LOST

⌘

If the evil that was unleashed here could be conquered with love, where could evil not be conquered?
- Immaculee Ilibagiza

⌘

16

Descent

The South African Airlines jet began its descent to Kigali airport after departing Zambia nearly two hours before. A year earlier this airspace was the stage for the assassination of Rwandan President Habyarimana, his plane brought down by a surface-to-air missile. It was the final catalyst for the Rwandan genocide that killed up to one million people, hardly raising an eyebrow outside the country's borders. The ineptitude of the United Nations to intervene, and France's alleged complicity in aiding the Hutu murderers, would go down in history as a betrayal of massive proportions.

Francis Leong gazed through the aircraft window, his eyes drawn to haunting black specks hovering above the city centre, the likes of which he had never seen before. Hundreds of preying vultures circled the celestial heights as they monitored the terrain below.

Disembarking the aircraft a few minutes later, Francis made his way into the terminal where staff from the Christus Centre awaited him and the five other delegates from the Meheba Refugee Settlement Camp in Zambia.

"Welcome to Rwanda," said the Jesuit Fathers assembled before him. These were the lucky ones who had been away at the commencement of the genocide that lasted 100 days. Francis noted the smile on their faces, wondering what stories lay behind the happy gaze.

Francis had already met many Rwandese, mostly Hutu, back at the settlement camp where he worked as Director. Over a million fled the Tutsi dominated Royal Patriotic Front (RPF) that liberated Rwanda, seeking refuge from the revenge they were told would come.

Believing this lie was easy. Decades of propaganda about the Tutsi guaranteed it. The *Interahamwe* militia, who had worked alongside the Rwandan police and Presidential Guard as fellow *genocidaires*, also did their best to convince the Hutu, using them as human shields, or as their bargaining chip for their eventual return into Rwanda. The genocide had not been completed! And so, into Zaire, Tanzania, Uganda and the Congo they spread. Reaching as far as Meheba.

Francis recalled the issues with leadership in the Meheba camp. Accusations made between the refugees had to be dealt with and Francis knew that some of the refugees may well have been the perpetrators of the massacres. He was potentially staring into the eyes of assassins. While his job at the camp did not include interrogation about the refugees' complicity, but rather their own need, Francis remained curious. Why had the genocide occurred which had turned neighbour against neighbour and perpetrated the vilest acts of mutilation, rape and terror imaginable?

How the Hutu in his camp could tell who was Tutsi, always intrigued Francis. "We can tell," they explained to him. "But *you* can't." Were Tutsi and Hutu really that different? He did not understand what decades of dehumanization and polarization had accomplished. By the time the 1994 genocide had occurred, Tutsi had become synonymous with cockroaches, needing fumigation, whether in or out of the womb.

Collecting his luggage from the antiquated carousel, Francis followed his hosts outside. The unadulterated natural beauty of Rwanda assaulted his senses with its acute irony as he made his way to his accommodation not too far from the airport. How could such a tragedy have been conducted in what could only be described as a paradise, this land known stereotypically as the land of a thousand hills and as the Switzerland of Africa? In Rwanda, it is said, is where God rested after creating the rest of the world.

Rwanda had indeed become a recess of hell. A year after the genocide had ended was the time chosen for directors of the Jesuit Refugee Service to meet in solidarity in the very place in which the demonic legions had been released. Francis and his team were headed to the *Christus Centre*, one of the first massacre sites of the genocide, which had also prepared the soil for other systematic killings in Kigali and beyond.

"Francis, did you know that the Christus Centre was the same retreat centre that Immaculee Ilibagiza visited after the genocide?" I asked him during one of our interviews together. There would not be too many interested in Rwanda who would not have heard of Immaculee Ilibagiza's dramatic survival. The kindness of a Hutu protestant pastor, who hid her and seven other women in his bathroom, is a tale that has been heard or read by many around the world. The Pastor, though, was only *one* of the instruments God used to spare her life. When I read Immaculee's first book - *Left to Tell* - I was enthralled by the string of divine interventions that peppered the three months she endured in that tiny bathroom. Prophetic dreams, words and answered prayers, and above all the grace to forgive those who slaughtered her family, were just some of the marvels that made the entire story of Rwanda more bearable. And I became the more eager to plumb its depths.

"I do know that now," Francis replied speaking of the importance that the centre played for Immaculee's healing after the genocide. "But didn't know it back then." Indeed, the Christus Centre nestled in a valley nine kilometres east of the famous *Hotel des Milles Collines*, (otherwise known as Hotel Rwanda), was regularly frequented by Immaculee prior to her role at the United Nations and her migration to the U.S.A.

Francis was driven through the three-metre-high midnight-green iron gates of the centre that met the red earth below. From outside, the centre, built on eight hectares of land, appeared as many a retreat centre would; a series of brick buildings interspersed by gardens and lawns nestled at the feet of giant native trees that rested on the slopes of a hill. This was not an ordinary retreat centre, however. Francis was now on hallowed ground.

The first Rwandese born Jesuit, Fr. Mahame, once strolled past the gardens, actively welcoming Tutsis refugees fleeing the sporadic violence against them that had erupted increasingly since 1990, in a long-standing tradition that had begun even further in the past, ever since the first massacre of Tutsi in 1959. Fr. Mahame was one of the enlightened Church pastors in Rwanda. He was unlike the clergy who first came with the German and Belgium colonisers. Together with the colonists, the clergy, ironically, helped blow the smoke of social Darwinism across Rwanda, supporting the rule of the Aristocratic Tutsi who were considered racially superior. Over time it was not difficult to see just how this could have sown resentment among the Hutu majority.

Fr. Mahame was also unlike those that followed in the Sixties, when, inspired by the social revolution sweeping across Europe, strengthening the voice of minority or oppressed people, Belgian clergy promoted the independence of Rwanda and the installation in power of the Hutu majority. Instead, Fr. Mahame, like his Jesuit brothers, refused to count race as a factor determining the pastoral care of their flocks, and he paid the ultimate price.

"This is the room where our brothers and sisters were killed," said one of the hosts, inviting Francis and other delegates to experience their first taste of the blood lust that infected the Hutu like a rancorous virus. Here, Christus staff were led and exterminated. Immaculee had visited that room. Francis refused. He did not see the stain of dried blood still coating the ceiling and walls, which had flowed through the seventeen priests, seminarians, sisters and lay people slaughtered by the Presidential Guard. The clerical and religious cloth provided no immunity from genocide, just as the waters of Baptism, which bound Hutu and Tutsi, had not.

"Quite a few survivors shared their story," Francis told me somewhat a little reluctantly. "Do you know I could not speak publicly about my experience of Rwanda until this year," he confided. For a period of 19 years!

"I didn't want to deal with Rwanda," he continued. "I put it aside, closed the box and left it alone." As we talked further and I immersed myself in survivors' stories, like that of Immaculee, I slowly came to understand more deeply what Francis meant.

17

Vultures

"Can you see it, Francis?" a fellow delegate asked one morning at breakfast, sitting with other participants from the Refugee Studies Unit in Oxford and workers associated with the Jesuit Refugee service. Francis glanced at the bush outside, his eyes searching for anything peculiar. When he saw it, he wondered why he hadn't seen it sooner. Human remains stared blindly back from behind the bush, long forgetting the burning hatred that fuelled the flames of their demise.

Once I had become acquainted with stories of Rwanda, I did not need to imagine for too long how the person Francis had seen, had died. Perhaps the remains were once a woman who had been raped, mutilated and thrown into a ditch? Perhaps it was an old man who, after being stopped at a roadblock and having shown his identity card identifying him as Tutsi, was mercilessly clubbed to death and discarded? Perhaps this person, like so many Tutsi, took their last breath knowing that the person killing them was a life-long neighbour, after having been hunted down like a frightened animal, too poor to buy the bullet that would have given them a speedy death?

Francis had walked to and from the venue for five days and hadn't even noticed the remains. "It's amazing what the mind just blocks off," Francis explained to me. "You would go to breakfast every day and only notice, once pointed out, the parts of a body near a bush. The vultures had plenty to feed off." It was government policy to leave many of the decomposing body parts precisely where they rested the day of the genocide.

"The government wanted to make a statement," Francis recalled. Francis now understood why he had seen vultures hovering in the sky above Kigali. The new Rwanda must never forget their holocaust. It would take until the summer of 1995 before most of the remains were eventually buried.

How could anyone forget? How could *he* forget? The thought that he could come to Rwanda and even attempt to avoid evidence of hell on earth seemed foolish to him now. Francis may have avoided the caked blood on the walls of the room where Fr Mahame and his friends had been killed. But he saw much more, and in a place that was inconceivable, in the most sacred of places, not too long into his sojourn.

"It wasn't until Fr. Emmanuel came to Perth that I actually realised that I couldn't escape the memory of what I saw that day," Francis declared.

"Perth? I never realised," I replied, surprised that I should be interviewing Francis about Rwanda only a few months after he had lifted his 19-year ban on the subject.

"Catholic Mission sponsored him to come and speak about the appeal of raising awareness and funds for the project of reconciliation and healing in Rwanda. So much struck me about his story. He spoke of the parish he is pastor of in Rwanda, and how it had been the scene of a massacre. He spoke about the nightmares he had, just knowing he would be speaking about it." The admiration Francis had for this priest was palpable. "You could see the pain in his eyes as he spoke of the forgiveness that had blessed his parish. But what touched me most was that Fr. Emmanuel was now the parish priest of the same parish I had visited that day."

Francis had approached the remains of the Church building of Nyamata with dread, and then made his way in cautiously. The Church walls still bore the scars - casualties of the grenades and gunfire that enabled the carnage to bear its ugly fruit and which accompanied the ever-present machetes like instruments in a diabolical symphony.

Where Francis presently stood, Rwandans had rushed past begging for sanctuary as the genocide raged on. The *Interahamwe* surrounded the Tutsi, preparing their burial ground. Now, emaciated bodies, skeletons, some still clothed, lay in various postures, their death pangs memorialised for all to behold.

In previous bouts of ethnic cleansing nobody had been killed in a Church. But things changed in 1994.

18

Entombment

It was in the Nyamata church where the Hutu mayor called Tutsi to hide, pretending to be their saviour, only to betray them to the *Interahamwe*. The Church, the place where Heaven and Earth met, became their tomb. "It was a desecration," Francis recalled. "Bodies were still there. Bodies hacked. Under the Tabernacle. Over the altar." Francis' soft and calming voice gently tempered the memory he retrieved dolefully, in order to share it with me.

He spoke softly and his gentle eyes attempted to deny the pain that the memory evoked. "You don't even need to imagine," he added. "But, when I heard Fr. Emmanuel speak of the stories of forgiveness and healing he had witnessed, it made it possible for me to contemplate the genocide with some sense of civility. If the lady who forgave the man who had killed her whole family could forgive, then I too could heal and share my own story."

If it weren't for the divine forgiveness that had been able to rise from the ashes of the massacre, nothing about the genocide would make sense. I found it difficult to accept that once-close neighbours murdered their friends from their own parish, their children in the same Holy Communion preparation classes, brothers and sisters in Christ coming together to the Eucharistic table. That those professing belief in Christ could all join in the hunt and murder of their Tutsi brothers and sisters was unbelievable. In fact, catholic churches, like that of Nyamata, had been one of the main venues of the many mass killings that occurred throughout the genocide. And the parish priest at the time was certainly not like Fr. Emmanuel. Instead, the former parish priest gave up his collar for a gun and remained faithful to the Hutu cause.

Nyamata had not been unique. In the Kibuye region for instance, with the largest number of Tutsi in Rwanda, neighbours and militia hunted down Tutsi seeking protection in the Kibuye parish Church, Gatwaro Stadium and Kibuye hospital. At times they were lured to such places with the promise of protection only to be surrounded by exploding grenades and gunfire or butchering machetes. That some Hutu risked death to remain faithful to Christ's commandment of love, saving in whichever method the lives of their Tutsi neighbours, is the only evidence that the Holy Spirit's presence in Rwanda had not been completely extinguished. That some Hutu clergy participated in the carnage, absolutely defies belief!

Walking away from Nyamata, Francis, like so many others, was left traumatised, needed time to absorb the horror that still echoed in the silence of the building. In time, the world would come to know of those Rwandans who made it out alive, and forgave those who had murdered their family, witnessing to a power stronger than death.

Their faith, like the faith that had called Francis to join the Jesuit Refugee Service, has a more radical nature than its expression in the comfortable West. This faith is itself most powerful when the spiritual warfare that St. Paul speaks of is manifested in real time and when it conquers in Christ's strength and in Christ's manner, hands extended, crucified, seemingly abandoned and crying out, "Father, forgive them." This faith is that of a rebel, the only faith that made sense in the Rwandan killing fields.

I began to understand why Francis tried to avoid the memory of Rwanda. I had struggled with other evil events in our history. But genocide?

Before the genocide, and more shockingly during it, the international community represented at the UN Security Council all but abandoned the people of Rwanda. Cost, ignorance, denial and indifference led to one of the greatest showcases of the sins of omission in history. Details of the incumbent genocide, that had been provided to the council by UN peacekeeper Dallaire, were side-lined. His requests for permission to confiscate stocked weapons piled up in preparation for a government-sponsored genocide were denied. And yet, as streams of Hutu power extremists, and *genocidaires* made their way to refugee camps in the diaspora following the genocide, foreign aid was quick in coming. While the 800,000 Tutsi killed in the carnage had received no more than lip service, one million Hutu refugees, including killers and *Interahamwe,* were fed and clothed and their weapons not confiscated.

So much evil. So much injustice. But the paradox remained.

I think of those known to Fr. Emmanuel, such as Concile Mukarutsinga, who came to not only forgive the very man who led her children to slaughter. They even became firm friends.

I think of Frida Gashumba who retells her story in *Frida: Chosen to Die, Destined to Live*. Frida knew that her family had already been listed on one of the death lists even before the massacre. Even her old school master had been involved. For almost four weeks, her family spent their days sleeping out in the forest for fear of being burnt in their homes, fleeing to the mountain, finding further refuge, and ultimately returning to the decimated home of their grandfather where they prepared for the bright yellow, green and red of the *Interahamwe* to complete their work. When the day finally came, after days of taunting, Frida and her family were led to a trench, the key organiser being an elder in the Seventh Day Adventist Church.

Surrounded by killers, her own neighbours, Frida witnessed her mother and grandfather's slaughter before she received a blow with a club. She was buried alive, only to live to be delivered many hours later by a Hutu friend of the family who happened to hear her cries from her subterraneous shelter. Frida too, after much healing and prayer, forgave her father's killer.

Rwanda was indeed a cacophony of paradoxes. Francis came to learn of yet another. In the hell that Rwanda had become, an ambassador of Heaven had made, and was making, her appearance in what would come to be known universally as the apparitions of Our Lady of Kibeho. There, ten years before the genocide, the Blessed Virgin Mary had visited a number of Rwanda teenagers asking for hearts to be turned to her Son, prophesying that rivers of blood would flow in the streets if Hutu and Tutsi forgot who they were as brothers and sisters in Christ.

Rwanda did not listen then. Eventually it did. Through Francis, I was reminded that the story of Africa defies the stereotype. The Africa that is exported to the rest of the world is often the wild tourist Africa. If not, it is the beleaguered African continent, a haven for terrorism and for refugees, and an ancient land torn apart by the ongoing effects of colonial greed and blood lust, war, famine, and genocide. As Immaculee Ilibagiza has taught through her witness and her dissemination of the message of Our Lady of Kibeho, the power of forgiveness can transform a whole nation. She witnessed to this, ten years after the genocide, when, following a new life in America, Immaculee returned to Rwanda.

Immaculee discovered a Rwanda very different from the one she and Francis had witnessed. Rwanda was in the midst of a renaissance, a baby boom. And as she glanced across the landscape, she saw that the beauty for which Rwanda had once been known had made its comeback. It was not because of the revitalised economy. It was something deeper that Francis understands as well.

She writes, "If the evil that was unleashed here could be conquered with love, where could evil not be conquered? If the hearts of Rwanda could be healed through forgiveness, then what heart couldn't?"

Love. Forgiveness. Somehow these two phenomena are compatriots of the less pleasant phenomenon of pain. It took Francis a long time to remember the Rwandan version of this lesson, when he finally chose to open that box of memories from which he had hidden for so long. Perhaps it was only then that he could also understand the lesson on a more personal level and aid me further in my own search. Escaping death after staring down the barrel of a gun is no mean feat. Repeating it when the barrel actually fires, is cheating death.

THE REBEL AND THE CHILD SOLDIER

⌘

To make a difference in this world you need to be a rebel. Countercultural.
- Francis Leong

⌘

19

The Call

Mary Street in the old suburb of Highgate in Perth, is arguably one of the most picturesque streets of Perth and remains a vision of beauty. The Moreton bay fig trees that bow towards each other, forming a silk green canopy over the vehicles which use the street as a thoroughfare to the nearby café strip, are simply magnificent. It was on this street, in what used to be a convent and was now home to a number of organisations belonging to the Perth Archdiocese, that I met Francis.

"If one is not ready for the dots to be joined, well they won't be," Francis said, pondering the path his life has taken since his birth in New Zealand, and since his return from Zambia where he had worked for eight years. He had not thought he would leave Zambia; just as he had never thought of becoming Director of Catholic Mission in Perth.

In Zambia he had met his wife, a native Angolan of Portuguese decent who had fled the war-torn country. Those in the camp were like family to him, both fellow Catholics working with him, as well as the refugees. When he accepted a promotional position as country director some years into his stay in Zambia, however, administration replaced the relationship with people that energised him. "I was still involved with other projects of course. Attending UN meetings. Advocacy." And, still being the rebel, Francis challenged certain practices and raised issues that concern the church. "But I was removed from my first love. It was time to start afresh," Francis continued. It seemed that the path that God had laid out for him would be a series of new beginnings.

And all in God's time.

Francis had already moved a number of times before ending up in Zambia. From New Zealand, Francis first moved to Perth. After completing his tertiary degree in physiology, he ended up in France in the Moselle, working in the Chamber of Commerce, setting up training programmes in the areas of English Language and Stress Management. Soon enough, a holiday in the Eternal City determined his fate and his die were cast.

"I met with a Jesuit who had once visited my school, St. Louis College, to speak about the advocacy group he had set up for East Timorese refugees."

"I have never heard of that school."

"That's because it no longer exists. It amalgamated some time ago with a Loreto convent school. Now, it's John XXIII College." This was a college I *did* know, one of Perth's more affluent Catholic schools situated in the leafy suburb of Mt. Claremont.

"Anyway, this Jesuit introduced me to the Jesuit Refugee Service, or JRS in Rome. And almost instantly my Sunday Mass faith took on an *option for the poor* significance," he said.

"I knew I needed to offer the poor something," he said, "just like those working as volunteers with the service whose stories inspired me – from El Salvador where Jesuits had been massacred not long before, for instance. I was deeply impressed that volunteers working with the service remained with the people. They didn't disappear," he emphasised. "Like the workers of Sierra Leone, they stayed during the civil war, planting themselves in the heart of the people in their great need."

This desire to serve was like a reawakening of a sensitivity that had been instilled in Francis many years before in Perth. "In hindsight, I think the seed was sown by my high school principal, Fr. Daven Day. In 1970's Perth society he responded to the aftermath of the East Timor invasion by opening the school's doors to these refugees. It was actually the first school to accept refugees in Perth. Quite radical, actually!"

I was somewhat surprised by the implication that my own childhood society of Perth had been generally less than welcoming of refugees or those of migrant heritage. I certainly hadn't noticed it but then again it was probably because my own school, just a stone-throw away from the room we were in, had been visibly multicultural. My best friends growing up were Vietnamese refugees fleeing the aftermath of the Vietnam War, or Italians, children of migrants like myself, together with a mix of Indian, Greek and Macedonian to make it even more colourful. Perhaps, multicultural North Perth had somehow been preserved from an engrained racism, taken over as it had, or at least it seemed to me, by Europeans of the gesticulating, loud and very down to earth kind, aware of the struggle that came with making it in a new country.

"Fr. Day said, 'Let's give them a place in our school'," Francis recalled proudly, "and, despite parent uproar, he had taken on and fought for these children's right to remain. I got to know them as friends and heard their stories – of torture, of families killed."

I remembered two of my own friends then, both Vietnamese, and wondered if they recalled the suffering accompanying their escape from Vietnam, even though they had never really talked to me about it. I remember only one conversation with one of them, whose family had come by boat. I wished now that I had asked him more about that.

"By the time the last school Mass came along," Francis continued, "I was struck by Fr. Day's final words. 'Be rebels' he said. Fr. Day meant, of course, rebels of the Gospel kind – the kind that is countercultural. Somehow the message stuck.... And in the true spirit of Jesuit spirituality, I knew that it is through the most difficult path that one finds the right path." It was a path that took Francis into the heart of the Angolan civil war.

20

Meheba

Sitting in the auto service centre waiting room, shortly after I began writing this chapter, I knew I would have to wait a while. The hour ended up being on one level pointless – my Honda Civic, my mother's old car, was simply incompatible with the cruise control I was attempting to have fitted to help me avoid those speeding fines that I had accumulated! But the visit wasn't completely wasted. As I continued waiting, laptop out, I just happened to come across a QANTAS magazine with the following title pasted on its front cover – "Wild about Africa." It was a Joe Yogerst article on Zambia of all places. By the time I left, the apologetic would-be installer let me have the magazine as a consolation prize, after telling me that in ten years of fitting cruise controls, this was the first time he hadn't been able to work out why he couldn't exactly make my car cooperate. (I wasn't surprised. My history with cars and their suitability for technological enhancements has not been the best. So much so that I totalled my following car, and called yet a later car my ReTARDIS!)

Yogerst gave me an insight into the terrain Francis worked in. Zambia, as a land of spectacular contrasts, home to the awe-inspiring Victoria Falls, as well as host to dangerous animals, alligators, hippos and buffalos, is quickly becoming the "next big thing" in African tourism, states Yogerst, its untainted wild the new "go-to safari."

Its capital city – Lusaka - is currently undergoing a construction boom replete with western style shopping. Things have not always been this way, though. Zambia has had its fair share of corrupt governments and has faced the ills that plague a nation transitioning to democracy. But one thing that has not changed is its unique position in southern Africa. Somehow, despite being surrounded by nations riddled with the plague of war, Zambia has retained its neutrality. This Anglophone nation has provided shelter to a host of refugees from surrounding nations, especially those from Portuguese speaking Angola, representing the vast majority of refugees, and French speaking Rwanda, Burundi and the Congo.

Francis was spiritually uplifted in his work at the Meheba Refugee Camp in northern Zambia. By 1992 it had already been in operation for twenty-one years. His work in the pastoral team of the JRS, operating out of St. Mary's parish in the centre of the camp, primarily consisted of the coordination of education and health services.

"Did your day follow a particular schedule?" I asked.

"No, there was no typical day," Francis said. "I prefer to entrust my day to the direction of the Holy Spirit, with no set agendas. Of course, there were the projects but for me there was also much more. The real work, in a sense, was whatever we did to build relationships with people, and to find Christ in them." In a camp over 700 square kilometres in size, this meant much travel - via mountain bike, past UN vehicles that routinely covered everyone with dust, and out in various directions with no particular goal other than sitting with whoever welcomed him, listening to their wisdom, engaging in their story. Most of the camp dwellers were women and children, their husbands and fathers either killed or fighting in war, or working in townships to support their families.

Demographically, the camp was a potpourri consisting not only of different nationalities but different religions, from Christianity to Islam, and ancestral worship to witchcraft. Alcoholism was rife in the camp. But Francis was not there to judge anyone, just to be present, and contribute to the development of the camp which, even by his time, had the infrastructure that heralded an incipient modernity – open-air schools with minimal teaching resources, minimal police presence, a poorly supplied clinic, rudimentary dirt roads ill-disposed to comfortable transport, and agricultural plots to encourage self-sufficiency farming.

Part of the JRS outreach work included supporting a Franciscan mission west of the camp adjacent to the Angolan border. Francis marvelled at the ambitious dam they had managed to construct which provided hydro-electricity for the entire community. The natural beauty of the place out there in the middle of nowhere impressed him deeply; the Franciscans had made it look like a picturesque Swiss landscape, replete with pine trees around the lake, and grazing cattle. Their mission included the preparation of catechists from Angola, who risked their lives to cross the border and obtain the formation they needed to re-enter their war-torn nation and minister to the people. Some had already been martyred.

"Theirs were the true stories of heroism," reflected Francis. The Angolan war had been flaring for nearly forty years, and had wreaked havoc on the Church, not to mention causing a humanitarian crisis that has become all too common for the African continent, repeated in war after war.

"These catechists, in many ways, replaced the priests who had been killed – some parishes in Angola had been without a priest for twenty years," said Francis. Appointed by the community, the catechists also did what they could to protect the women and children who sought to cross the border into Zambia. Without the help of JRS supporting the mission, they often faced a daunting task, even during periods of peace.

There was the danger of the crocodile infested Zambesi River. There was the worse threat of UNITA, the paramilitary forces that patrolled the border, at times using intimidation, physical violence and even intense questioning before allowing Angolans to enter Zambia.

Francis and other members of the pastoral team, made up of Jesuits and Sisters of Charity, were not normally involved with UNITA negotiations and with child rescue operations. So, there was seemingly nothing out of the ordinary, that day in 1992, when, during a relatively long lull in the fighting, Francis ventured 80 kilometres into Angola, based on a hunch and as an extension of the team's pastoral outreach.

As his normal company was otherwise preoccupied, Francis obtained the help of one of the catechists who became his guide. Setting off in a pick-up truck, Francis and Alfredo headed across the border to the village where orphaned and other children from the Kazombo region had sought refuge.

The two men drove on the clay earth through landscape that, to Francis, was reminiscent of the Western Australian bush. Eventually, they found the village. Children, aged between five and fifteen years of age, came out from their shelter to meet the men who promised a future filled with hope. For those whose family members had been separated, already safe in Zambia, it heralded a reunion that would soon come to pass.

In Luvale, the local Angolan language, Francis, with Alfredo's assistance, chatted and smiled with the eight children, helped them into the truck and set out once more for what would be a routine journey.

It was only some distance from the border when he saw them – the UNITA patrol of about ten soldiers. Francis instinctively began slowing the car down as fear gripped onto his soul and played to the terrible tune of his pounding heart.

21

Suspicion

The truck came to a halt and the company exited the car as the soldiers approached them, wearing what could only be described as a military uniform suited to soldiers of the lowest rank – army green or tracksuit pants, with mismatched hats and t-shirts. They all carried a threatening guise that matched the weapons they held effortlessly. The children, who were now seated on the ground behind Francis and Alfredo, seemed used to this. They had been hardened in many ways; their eyes beholding scenes that most western children wouldn't even have nightmares about. It was Francis who was not used to it.

"Is there a problem?" asked Francis brazenly but in a tone that clearly respected, with due deference, the chain of command, just before the 'leader' began to interrogate the men in broken Portuguese. *So, he has had some education*, thought Francis. He was already thinking of ways to communicate with these young men, on ways to affirm them as human beings made in God's image and likeness, even though he could see only suspicion in their eyes.

As the patrol periodically pointed their weapons directly at the men and children, they got their message across clearly – *we are in charge*. The movement of their weapons was strategic. Francis had to maintain eye contact and not show any reaction, and conveniently sought to put in the back of his mind the fact, as he now remembered, that he had left the car keys in the ignition. Should these soldiers wish to, they could easily ambush their only get-away.

"These are my passes," said Francis, relying more urgently now on Alfredo's assistance. He handed the papers over to his main interrogator, who took them, shuffled through them with disinterest and returned them.

"Where are you taking these children?" the young soldier demanded.

"I am here to take them to Zambia," Francis replied keeping his voice controlled but calm, with a sense that if handled correctly, this could be a moment for transformation, in whichever guise that would appear. The fear was not leaving, but neither did a growing awareness that he was not alone.

"They need to stay here," the soldier instructed, obviously intent on maintaining control in his discussion with Francis.

"These children are my responsibility. I cannot leave them behind," Francis replied.

"No! These children are *our* responsibility, not yours. This is *our* place. Don't they have parents?"

As the *to-ing* and *fro-ing* continued, in words exchanged in Portuguese, Luvale and English, Francis realised that the soldier thought Francis was kidnapping the children.

Barely had the soldier finished speaking when Francis heard himself say, "You don't understand. Fr. Agostino is expecting them in Zambia. So, how can you not allow this to happen?"

Francis had not intended to speak those words, like others that he just put out there hoping to make some connection with the soldiers – such as his reference to St. Benedict's mission in Kazombo. But now, the words sounded like someone else spoke them. Francis did not even know where Fr. Agostino was or whether he even knew any of these children. *Why did I say that?* Francis was astounded at his false admission.

The leader's face softened, and he asked, "Fr. Agostino? Is he still alive?"

"Yes, of course," replied Francis, still recovering from the shock. "Why do you ask?"

"He used to be our parish priest. We were altar servers for him before the war."

"You were an altar boy?"

"Yes," he said, an air of nostalgic excitement lighting his face. Francis could see the pride shining through as his own sense of relief marvelled at the unanticipated turn of events.

For almost two hours the conversation continued while the children remained seated, patiently. It was a deep conversation about the war, their forced recruitment with UNITA, an admission that the child soldiers had known that the war was evil, and that they feared it, because of what they had been involved in, but also because of what they might have to do in the future.

"The conversation became like a dance," Francis told me. "It was a giving and a taking, a sharing of our stories." And then he asked them directly.

"Will you let me take the children to Meheba across the border? They need an education," Francis continued. "Why don't you come with us? What is the point of running around like this? There is a future there. But if you want to come, you must leave your soldier's uniform and weapons behind."

They began to mumble among themselves. Five decided to remove their uniform. Moments later, with four others in the patrol, the rebel soldier joined Francis and the children and made it across the border.

"These five joined the camp and continued their education," Francis told me.

"Did they end up seeing Fr. Agostino?"

"I don't know. I am not even sure where they ended up. Some may even have gone back. But what I do know is that someone was working through me that day. I still can't work out how it all happened. The children and I could have been killed."

After a pause, Francis continued. "Have I told you about the time I was shot?"

"What?"

I had known about the child soldiers. But I was taken aback by Francis' sudden revelation – about that night when the cost of working with the poor became all too apparent.

22

Gunshot

The warm air danced around Francis as he blew out the candles just before midnight and lay down for the night. Francis did not sleep in the camp's headquarters and was therefore not privileged with the only source of electricity known in the camp. The moon, however, shared its light with Francis as his eyes adjusted.

It was 1997 and the memory of both his near escape on the Angola border and his Rwandan pilgrimage were still fresh in his mind; the one providing hope and the other a source of trauma in the face of pure evil. There had been many a night when the vision of death brushed across the landscape of his nightmares. No sign of goodness could yet do away with the strain that those memories brought with them.

But there *was* goodness.

That very day would have passed by like so many in the camp; training people in the art of reflexology in order to diagnose major illnesses (the camp having run out of traditional medicines), or setting up another educational programme. Francis had taught his new students what to do with vegetable seeds instead of pills, helped husbands learn how to provide treatment to wives so that all in the community could learn to heal themselves. Wasn't there goodness in that? In the eyes of those whose feet Francis massaged he had also seen gratitude and humility.

But the memories of man's inhumanity to man remained, of a callousness that knew no boundary. As sleep beckoned him, Francis closed his eyes, only to be violently opened a short time later. Gunfire! As the nocturnal peace was suddenly extinguished, Francis' bedroom door burst open.

"Get out of bed," yelled the gunman looming over Francis' bed, repeatedly cocking his AK 47 as Francis froze. Barely had Francis registered when the crazed man began firing indiscriminately. The first shot missed him. *I know him*, thought Francis. It was a man who lived in the camp.

Immediately, the intruder began firing again, the second shot entering Francis' upper thigh. With adrenalin pumping, Francis recoiled from the shocked impact but felt no immediate pain. It was *annoyance* that first came to mind. He had just recovered from a wounded arm!

"Where's your money?" the assailant demanded. "Get out of bed and get me the money!"

In pitch darkness, Francis managed to roll off the bed, holding his wounded thigh. He began to comb his bedside drawers looking for whatever money he could find, handing it over to the thief, who was obviously drunk or stoned.

"Is that all?" asked the intruder, assessing the quality of cash in his hands.

"Yes …..... that is all I've got," stammered Francis. Penetrating the darkness in broken English, another man's voice called out in desperation. "Don't shoot Brother Francis! Shoot me," he begged as Francis heard stones being thrown at the roof of the house in a futile attempt, presumably by the second man, at frightening the would-be assassin. Surprisingly, the gunman turned around and ran out of the room while Francis examined his increasingly painful wound.

Francis recognised the second guest even before he made it into his bedroom. It was Roger, a camper of twenty years, the intelligent man who spoke four or five languages, and whom Francis regarded as a pest. His alcoholism and its effects were all too well known among the others and even Francis had found it a challenge to love this man. But this night it was Roger's sobriety that led him directly into Francis' room.

"C'mon Francis. Let's go to the sisters!" he exclaimed in a panic. He helped Francis off the floor and then across the compound. The sisters, having heard all the gunshots, were already awake.

"Quick, Roger! Take him to the car," one of the sisters directed while Sr. Alice got in to drive the sisters' only car, and Francis, bent over in pain, tried to get in, assisted by Roger. If it weren't for the pain in his leg, Francis would have thought he was still asleep and in one of his nightmares. For a long time to come the acrid smell of cordite would haunt him, even in waking hours.

It was 2 a.m. when they drove off, heading for the nearest health clinic some fifteen kilometres away. Francis held on to Roger at his side, the irony of it all not lost on him. All this time in the camp, Francis had seen Roger as an irritant spending most of his time fulfilling that expectation with everyone at the camp. What would inspire compassion, for Roger's traumatic past, in even the harshest critic, had somehow not been enough for Francis; not even the trauma Roger must have faced surviving a village massacre in Angola as a child.

Now, staining Roger's clothes with his blood, Francis felt shame, summoning his strength to speak.

"Roger, why did you do such a foolish thing, screaming at the gunman like that? You could have been shot too!"

"I was frightened for you. I wanted to help you. You listen to me a lot, Francis!"

"Roger, when you are drunk, everyone listens to you," replied Francis, the throbbing in his leg continuing, his speech halted.

"It's different."

"How?" Francis asked, still confused, each bump in the road agony for him.

"Well," he said, adding without embarrassment, "I know … that you love me."

Francis fell silent. How could anything shock him more than being shot? But it had. The tears formed flowing rivers down his cheeks as the significance struck him with more force than the bullet. This man holding him now was the *least* of his brothers! Roger, far from being the village drunk or pest, had become Francis' meeting place with Christ.

Francis was still bleeding when they arrived at the clinic only to be told by the clinician that he had to be taken to the police first. They drove on to report to the paramilitary, for whom they waited yet another fifteen minutes.

"We don't have any vehicles," they revealed finally. "You will have to take him back to the clinic." *You have got to be kidding*, thought Francis.

Continuing to hold his wound, with not even as much as a bandage administered, Francis made it back to the car, Roger still by his side. He tried to sleep as they drove away, again incredulous at the third world care he had received, even by Zambian standards.

"And after all that, I was only given paracetamol when I got to the clinic again and was just bandaged up," Francis told me as I listened, stunned. "The next day we went to the hospital at Solwesi and I was told that it was a spiral bullet which missed all my arteries. Luckily, it had been fired at close range so the normal effect of a spiral bullet was avoided."

"What was that?"

"A huge exit hole!"

"Wow," I said. The image was disturbing enough but then he told me the rest. Anaesthetic, he was told, would halt the healing process, so salt baths would suffice, together with the paracetamol that was generously provided and happily accepted!

But despite the tremendous pain that Francis endured with each salt bath and each cleansing and repacking of the wound, the main event of this story was something else – or rather someone else. Roger!

"God reveals himself to you in situations you least expect." Francis had learnt that a key way God speaks to us is through the poorest of the poor. Once again, I was reminded that the effects of evil can be overcome by love. Love can bring meaning to personal evil.

Could it truly be that simple, though? Does love *truly* have the power to conquer all?

IS LOVE ENOUGH?

⌘

We are all born for love.
It is the principle of existence, and its only end.
- Benjamin Disraeli

⌘

23

Viktor Frankl's Beloved

Can love truly be the answer for everything? I needed more convincing. And so, I turned to one of the most evil-filled events in history to investigate; the same event that inspired my first real extended piece of writing at the age of 16; the Holocaust. Perhaps I would be convinced if a survivor of the holocaust, one such as Viktor Frankl, could answer this question for me more directly, beyond mere platitudes?

One of the most interesting insights into the human response to evil is Frankl's recognition of the possibility for even the vilest evil to lose its power before human will. Humans can endure greater evil with a focus on the notion that bliss, as brief as it may be, could still be found in "contemplation of his beloved."

Does this power of love truly help bring meaning even to the most horrendous circumstances? At the end of the day is it love alone, both human and divine, that will conquer the power of evil and bring its mystery to light? I can see how this might be the case when a person endures suffering out of love for another or to retain his integrity and to stand up for what he believes in. But is every form of suffering, in order for it to have meaning, somehow an invitation to focus our gaze on an ultimate Beloved?

Take, for instance, the suffering of a martyr. He is willing to endure torture and death so as to not renounce his faith in Christ. He is inspired by the memory of the love given by this Beloved! He has the hope that this love will never die and will be experienced again when he meets Christ in paradise. His suffering is a witness to love, both God's for him, allowing him to share in Christ's own suffering, and his for God.

Or again, take the example of one who accepts death after a long illness, with dignity and courage. In her dying moments all that matters to her now is knowing that she is surrounded by those she loves, that she has loved enough, that she has forgiven and been forgiven, and, if she has a faith, that her life in fact is not ending but being completed. She too has set her gaze upon love, both earthly and heavenly, because love for others and from others is all that matters in the end. She has contemplated love, and acknowledged its ultimate power by submitting to death – a total detachment from things that will pass away.

And isn't love what we are invited to remember and celebrate with every single form of suffering, as nonsensical as it may seem, if only we acknowledge this Beloved who created us?

Perhaps, if for no other reason, evil and suffering are a constant reminder of what Australia's first saint, Mary of the Cross MacKillop once said: "Remember, we are but travellers here." The longer we forget that this life and world can never provide the love we long for, the more the world's rejection of love and its attachment to hate and evil will surprise us. The more we accept that everything is passing away, the more we too will understand "how a man who has nothing left in this world still may know bliss, be it only for a brief moment, in the contemplation of his beloved," the longing for whom can only be satisfied in death.

As I continued my journey through the "valley of the shadow of death" that our shared human experience can be, I needed some "relief" from the reality of suffering, notwithstanding the macabre beauty that can nonetheless exist in knowing that love, despite ultimate death, can still be stronger. I needed to be comforted by the knowledge that sometimes, love can do more than just be balm for wounds already inflicted. Love can also prevent the wounds from occurring in the first place, protecting the innocent and giving life a chance.

24

Turning the Tide

Walking into the sonographer's office in March 2012, Therese and I were excited about meeting our new baby. This child was a surprise unlike our others who had been planned. Twenty weeks into the pregnancy, we discovered we were having another little boy (and there was no mistaking it either)! We named him Josiah.

As I sat there glued to the screen and witnessed each part of my child's body being measured, named and analysed, clearly discernible through modern technology, it was difficult to forget that while many like us watch in awe at the miracle of new human life, a great many mothers around the world are placed on an operating table, surrounded by so called nurses and doctors, with an attitude that could not be further away from awe and wonder. Instead, with absolute disrespect for innocent human life these "doctors" betray their oath to protect it and wantonly extinguish it.

It was not the birth of my children that first made me sensitive to the plight of the unborn child. I was a young teacher when in the small hours of May 21, 1998, the Davenport Bill passed through the Western Australian parliament effectively making abortion legal and on demand. Perth's abortion laws were some of the most liberal in the world, until they were surpassed by the law in Victoria of 2008 which is even more heinous, allowing partial birth abortion and denying a child the right to aid if born alive after an abortion.

Back in 1998, standing in the crowd at Parliament House about a month before the law was finally passed, I reported on what I saw and heard, sharing it with my students in the years following. The speech, by now retired Hon. Barbara Mary Scott MLC, said it very well. Eloquently exposing the fallacies spouted by many of her colleagues she proclaimed:

The oppression of women relied upon politicians not interfering in so-called personal and domestic issues. So does abortion.

The oppression of women relied upon the argument that the Church should not impose their values on the rest of society. So does abortion.

The oppression of women relied upon the argument that the victim did not have rights. So does abortion.

The oppression of women relied upon the argument that the victim did not have a voice. So does abortion.

The oppression of women relied upon the claim that it led to the common good. So does abortion.

We will stand for life. This is not just a legal issue. This is not just a political issue. This is not just a moral issue. This is not just a religious issue. This is not just a women's issue. This is a human rights issue.

In the Western world we pride ourselves on the freedom our nations claim to possess. We consider ourselves highly civilised, having reached the peak of human evolution, having done away with a barbarism that our textbooks bemoan and our leaders would be embarrassed to recall.

Yet, the world continues in many ways to turn a blind eye to the great elephant standing smack bang in the middle of the room – the great infanticide. The Kermit Gosnells and Planned Parenthood reincarnations of the world, with their houses of horror and sale of harvested baby organs will be around for some time it would seem.

But there are signs of hope - signs that the tide is turning, seen dramatically in the closure of abortion clinics across the United States or the passing of new laws restricting access to abortion. These signs first begin in the personal individual stories of regular people, occurring in the most unexpected ways; and chance meetings strung together like a fine pearl necklace have a tendency to blow you over with their curious synchronicity.

At least that was what Leanne, as I shall call her, discovered.

Leanne was dropping off a friend, with her two young children in the car, when she was distracted by what looked like Buddhist monks. They were just standing with their backs to the road. Their grey robes were quite odd looking though – not exactly what Buddhist monks would be wearing, she presumed! *They must be praying.* The picture on the banner held by one of them clarified their purpose soon enough.

Leanne had heard of abortion clinics. The "monks" were obviously on a prayer vigil outside this particular clinic. But what struck Leanne the most was not what was on her mind but the sensation that swept over her like a wave. Goosebumps and a compulsion to get out of the car and join them in prayer nearly overwhelmed Leanne, but her children's presence, and an appointment she had to keep, prevented her. Driving home, however, the experience remained with her, consuming her thoughts.

Leanne had herself contemplated an abortion in 1998, just as the Perth abortion debate was raging. She would never have gone through with it. She used it as a strategy, hoping that the threat might knock some sense into the child's father who was unsupportive and left the choice completely to her. Her hopes that he would come to the rescue like a knight in shining armour had been dashed back then. She just wanted to hear him tell her he loved her, that she shouldn't do it and that he would support her. But he didn't.

Leanne had not made the second mistake – perhaps in part courtesy of her conservative Westminster Presbyterian background. Who would have thought that she would find herself years later working alongside Catholics in the same pro-life movement?

It took Leanne a while to realise that those Buddhist monks were Catholic ones, especially since Leanne knew very little about Catholicism at the time.

After suffering a miscarriage at the age of 20, Leanne attended a seminar on pregnancy loss where abortion was also discussed and where she met with women working in a pregnancy crisis centre. Like a moth to a flame, Leanne was drawn to voluntary work at the centre. After a training camp and another chance meeting with women who wanted to bring the *40 Days for Life* campaign to Perth, the point of no return was passed.

Two years after seeing those at the prayer vigil, Leanne ended up joining her Catholic brothers and sisters outside the abortion clinic. She lives and breathes pro-life; her work helping pregnant women and young mothers is not an act of penance, but her calling.

"I wish sometimes …" Leanne hesitated. "It just makes me want to cry that right across the road from where I am shopping, babies are being put into bins. I am still trying to understand how something like this can't unite all Catholics and Protestants."

It was during one of the mornings in Lent when Leanne found herself outside the clinic where the 'Buddhist' monks had prayed five years before. The 40 Days for Life campaign was in full swing.

Leanne watched as a young girl approached the clinic during a silent prayer vigil. One of the prayer team members routinely handed her a brochure, turned back to his prayer and continued his meditation. The girl, faltering briefly, did not walk off straight away. It looked like she wanted to talk, but she proceeded to walk on in the direction of the clinic. Leanne could imagine the talk the girl had already received from the clinic staff about the *crazy* Catholics outside who would, of course, tell her she would be going to hell if she went ahead with her termination!

The desire to walk up to the girl gripped Leanne, as tangibly as a memory of certain words that had touched her on the training DVD. "One day God will actually make you witness a save outside the clinic that will keep you going with the mission." Was this the one? The one she would witness change her mind? She had to talk to this girl. *This is it*, she heard with the ears of her soul.

Slightly uncomfortable that she could be mistaken as stalking the girl, Leanne stopped praying and approached her gently.

Then, she spoke.

"We have been praying for women coming into the clinic. We are here because we believe abortion hurts women. What brings you here today?" The question may have seemed ridiculous after that opening but Leanne asked it anyway.

"I am having an abortion," the girl said without moving off.

"What can we do to help you?" Leanne sensed the girl's fear but also her desire to share her heart. "Would you like to sit in the shade over there and talk?" The girl did not hesitate.

Leanne led the girl away from the prayer vigil. As they sat on the ground near the road, Leanne learned many things about the girl. She was only nineteen years of age. The father of her child had been a long-term friend who had abandoned her once he discovered her pregnancy. Hadn't even offered to take her to the clinic. She had lost her job. "I have lots of friends," she said. "But I am here alone...I wonder what the other girls in the clinic are going through?"

"It's a sad place," Leanne told her. "There are women crying. Not a nice place to be in. I know you are afraid to have this baby, but I can assure you that many women have been in this situation before you. I have been one of them."

Leanne began to understand why she had felt drawn to this girl and was reassured when she remained, listening, and not running away. "I also felt abandoned... But I am so glad I chose not to go through with it. My son is now 15 years old. Things change you know. They can get so much better. I am now married and have other children. My son is a talented sportsman and goes to a private school. And I grew up –

learnt independence. I learnt that I was strong enough even without the help of his father," Leanne continued, buoyed by the girl's attention and openness. "You can do this. You are already a mum. The decision has to be about you and your baby – nobody else."

As Leanne inspired the girl with what *could* be, she saw the weight of the girl's burden literally collapse like a house of cards.

"The most precious jewels you can have are your child's arms around your neck. But if you go through with it, you come out with nothing."

A smile radiated across the nineteen-year-old woman's face, erasing weeks of fear and tension, and with a sigh of relief, her shoulders dropping, she nodded in agreement.

"It's funny you know," said the girl. "I was actually scheduled to come to the clinic yesterday but my friend who was meant to take me had trouble starting her car. I cancelled and rescheduled for today. I got here after catching two buses and walking from the train station."

"Do you want to get out of here?"

"You can't do that for me!"

"Yes, I can. I would love to do that for you," beamed Leanne. The girl agreed, and as they embraced, tears swam down their faces; the joy an unbelievable blessing.

When the unlikely friends reached the girl's home, they exchanged numbers. At least on this occasion, one young girl had been given the compassion required to see her through the fear of the unknown with the knowledge that someone would be there to support her in her vulnerability.

Leanne continues to fight for the rights of the unborn and their mothers. The girl's story continues to inspire her, beyond the birth of her little son which taught the proud mother, in her own words, the meaning of love. Presently, Leanne does not hesitate to tell the women she meets, who are willing to listen, that those praying in vigil are not there to condemn. She has never stopped being surprised at what a difference it makes for a woman in crisis to hear of the help that is offered – free ultrasounds, support during pregnancy, accommodation. Often, she has heard women say, "I didn't know you offer that!"

But so many organisations do. And it's the genuine love and compassion of these organisations – made up of Catholic and Protestant Christians and the 40 Days for Life programme - that is making all the difference around the world. If stats provided by Lifesite News are correct, as reported November 27, 2019, over 14,000 babies have been saved from abortion as a result of the prayer, fasting and witness during the 40 Days for Life campaigns.

You may know someone who did not have a Leanne to speak words of love and compassion to them the day they chose to walk into a clinic. They may have continuing wounds from which they desperately seek healing. If the message of this book was only to reach one group of people, I choose that it reaches the wounded hearts of such women first.

God's mercy is unlimited. His desire for you to know his love, and the child you lost, is equally so. In Him, and through the organisations ministering to women and their male partners who have experienced the loss of a child in whichever manner, you will find the pledge of peace.

INTERLUDE

"Sir, I don't believe in God anymore!"

A number of answers have been given to the problem of evil. "Theodicy" is probably a term that is not familiar to many even though its subject area is, namely, that of the "justification of God," or the attempt to reconcile a good God with an evil in the world that often appears insurmountable.

Having been coined in 1710 by the philosopher Leibniz, the term "theodicy" has had airtime for over 300 years. As a teacher, the problem of evil is one I have attempted to tackle a number of times in the classroom. It is a perennial question which has no doubt set the background for many a philosopher's sleepless night and many a mid-life spiritual crisis. Notwithstanding the insights I have obtained in my life, through personal experience of suffering, or that of others, the mystery of evil will remain this side of Heaven. Only from the perspective of Heaven will we be able to truly plumb its depths.

I suppose that explains why I am still caught a little by surprise when students ask me about it, as did the question of a teenage student in my class some years back. It was the first day back after break and it went pretty much like this.

Student: Sir, I think I don't believe in God anymore.
Me: Why?
Student: If God exists, then why is there so much poverty and suffering in the world?
Me: Okay. Let me tell you what I think you are saying. How could a God whom we call all good, powerful and loving, allow such suffering to occur, appearing as it does to contradict his power, goodness and kindness?... Well, this is something I grapple with too. It is a good question. How about looking at this another way?

Student: Okay.

Me: There is no *one* answer to this problem. I have found some guidance in the following thoughts though. We may not fully understand why God allows for this evil to occur, but we can understand that he must not be indifferent to it. He himself suffered it and allowed himself to feel the effects of it by dying on the cross. He himself became a victim of this evil. Does that make sense?

Student: Yes.

Me: So, even though we can't explain it and perhaps feel uncomfortable with the fact that evil still exists and is such a tragedy in our world, there must be a reason we can't fully grasp. He redeemed us through suffering and so perhaps there is a hidden purpose to suffering. Perhaps we need to trust God and say to him, "Lord, I don't understand what is happening. Please help me to understand."

This student had probably been dwelling on the topic deeply for a while. Perhaps something had occurred to him over the term break? I was grateful that I could tell him that I too have struggled with the exact same question and that I had been thinking about an answer for a long time.

"We can't understand it fully, but what we *can* say is that God is not indifferent to it and has entered it himself."

And I don't see my last sentence as a cop out either – the Catholic Church, after 2000 years of reflection indicates as much in the *Catechism of the Catholic Church* (CCC).

324 The fact that God permits physical and even moral evil is a mystery that God illuminates by his Son Jesus Christ who died and rose to vanquish evil. Faith gives us the certainty that God would not permit an evil if he did not cause a good to come from that very evil, by ways that we shall fully know only in eternal life.

PART TWO

"I will do Wonders"

(Exodus 34:10)

INTRODUCTION TO PART TWO

While it was true that the existence of evil had featured as one of the characteristics of my developing faith, it thankfully did not occupy the main place after my conversion. After all, Christianity is a religion of hope, and it testifies to the miraculous even more so than to the demonic. Evil can indeed be transformed into good. And God does step in at times in ways that can be both ordinary as well as quite spectacular.

There are countless testimonies, both published and anecdotal, demonstrating that God has indeed intervened in nature on many occasions throughout history. We have heard of protection from natural disasters such as the two catholic churches in India protected from the rising flood waters that devastated the surrounding region on December 26, 2004. We marvel at the healings and miracles evident in Charismatic communities. Marian apparition sites such as Lourdes in France, inspire us with hope when healings are declared miraculous after intense scrutiny. In Lourdes alone, 70 healings have been officially declared as supernatural in origin, by the end of 2018. And let's not forget the miracles witnessed in the scriptures, both in the Old and New Testaments.

Then, there are other amazing events testified to through the ages. Many people have recounted quite believable stories that can only be explained by the existence of angels who have protected people from harm. Myriads of grace filled moments have touched the earth over the centuries. (Most recently I was mesmerized by the story of Captain Dale Black, a plane crash survivor, whose miraculous recovery and conversion are perfect examples of this amazing grace). And all this even though Christ had testified that the only sign we should really need is the sign of Jonah (Luke 11:29), that is, his own resurrection, rising after three days in the metaphoric belly of the whale.

While the miraculous is not the norm it still occurs. And it has nourished me – again – from that same day in Year 8 when Roma introduced me to the reality of God.

For a while after my conversion, the experiences I had heard or read of were only second-hand ones – too distant to make any lasting impact on me. As the proverbial sands of time slipped down the hourglass of my life, however, these experiences came close to home, shared with me directly by those who had been touched by grace, and eventually, as experienced personally, in ways I could never have imagined. Finding out that such experiences had actually been part of my extended family's story, as well as those of people I knew, or would come to know, was humbling.

THE UNLIKELY CONVERT

⌘

*And through the hands of the apostles many signs and wonders
were accomplished among the people.
- Acts 5:12*

⌘

25

The Upper Gallery

The Concert Hall on St Georges Terrace is a landmark of Perth, Western Australia. What has been aptly described as its *Late Twentieth Century Classical* style complements its elevated terraced platforms from which one can glimpse the calm waters of the Swan River. Once upon a time I would have called them pristine waters. Even though Perth still ranks as one of the world's most liveable cities, the waterways have been affected by the collateral damage that comes with becoming one of the fastest growing capital cities in Australia.

According to Limelight Magazine, the iconic Concert Hall has one of the best acoustics in Australia. It has hosted the likes of Sting, Michael Buble', the now late B.B. King and even Ray Charles. With its spectacular 3000 pipe organ, the Hall has delighted audiences since it first opened in 1973, and was unique at the time as the first of its ilk to employ closed circuit television for latecomers. The venue has been used continuously since its opening and its main auditorium is easily remembered for the double tier of boxes that elegantly climb the side walls, the ivory white of their frame contrasting with the ebony of the walls.

Into the Cloud of Knowing

I have some vivid memories of the Concert Hall, which has been "twinned" since 2006 with its sister Concert Hall in Perth, Scotland. A number of schools in which I have taught have used the venue for their presentation nights and I have witnessed amazing performances by talented students in between less exciting award presentations and speeches. I even enjoyed a date night there once with the dulcet tones of famous Australian singer Tina Arena as a backdrop.

However, my most vivid memories of the Concert Hall would have to be of the day I decided to give my three eldest children, then eight, six and four, what I boasted to others would be a cultural experience of epic proportions. My very demeanour exuded excitement at the notion that my children would be exposed to something sophisticated – nothing less than a concert with the Western Australia Symphony Orchestra. *They would love it*, I told myself, and the cost would all be worth it. They would soak up all the beauty of orchestral music and bathe in its nourishing springs!

Matters could not have been more remote than the torturous reality.

Within ten minutes of the performance I knew that I had made a serious error of judgement. I was literally held hostage in the Upper Gallery.

I can see now that what my most loving children did to me was nothing short of sweet revenge for the day when I made the different mistake of taking the two eldest children, then under five, through a car wash! I mean, how could I have known that something as simple as a car wash would be akin to an act of terror? I admit, it had been actually quite humorous at first – for about ten seconds – while I took a photo of the horrified expression on their face! But when I saw that the car wash instruments were to them like monsters bearing down on their very soul, annihilation their only goal, I mourned the fact that I had no choice but to see it through as the boys screamed in horror for what seemed like an eternal moment. It actually took my boys two years to forget the experience!

Indeed, it was now payback time, in a grander arena, and even my little princess, Marie Grace, the youngest of the three, joined in for the ride.

The first major panic came when I realised that Joshua had been terrorising the poor couple two rows above us. I didn't know what he had inflicted on them because I was too busy engaging in damage control with one of the others at the time. But the fiery eyes that met mine when I glanced up sheepishly to meet their gaze, gave me the clue I needed. I figured that what Joshua had done was not as important as what *I* needed to do urgently, especially since it was I who had sent him to the next stall to separate him from his brother. Suffice it to say, Joshua only had to look at my equally foreboding gaze to know that his safety, and indeed his very life, depended on a prompt 'prodigal son' like return to his father!

For a further forty-five minutes I cajoled, threatened, and stared down my three reprobates who disregarded my every plea to sit quietly, while the intense music of Vivaldi's *Four Seasons* and other classical compositions provided appropriate backdrop to the drama being played out in my box.

I discovered just how versatile seats could be. You can wriggle in them in fits and starts like a prodded worm. You can even slide off them, lay under them, crawl away from them under your father's feet and swap them with a willing rebel-sibling; and all in the space of a minute! The phrase "ants in your pants" just didn't do any justice to the spectacle I was witnessing. At least Jacob, two years Joshua's junior, decided a change was in order about half-way through the hour – he decided to begin impersonating the conductor with his mock baton as he stood dangerously close to the edge of the box. He was pretty chuffed with himself, while I hyperventilated. Visions of his thin frail body lunging over to a certain premature death, flashed before my wide and frantic eyes!

Checking my watch regularly with eager anticipation, I rejoiced as the hour crept closer to its end. I had forgotten a simple truth: Keeping still and remaining silent are not natural for children, one of whom acted more like an excitable Tigger overdosed on caffeine!

Not able to bear the trauma any longer, my heart racing and my blood pressure increasing exponentially, I packed up while the lights were still off, and left five minutes before the end, my offspring trailing behind.

"Dad, why are we leaving?" Joshua asked me sincerely. *Are you for real?* I thought incredulously as I grabbed Joshua's hand, trusting the others would follow, and made my way to the exit, like a child, eyes to the ground, afraid of reprimand by other offended parents.

The torture was finally over!

Fortunately, the Concert Hall has been the scene of more significant drama than that which I experienced. I am not speaking about drama of the musical kind, either. In 1979 a particular event would usher in a spiritual renewal that would spread through Perth for years to come, surpassing the impact of both the 1979 Perth earthquake and the crash landing southwest of Perth, of *Skylab,* the first U.S. Space Station. (And that is saying something! I remember lying awake at night wondering whether a good chunk of the Skylab would land on my house!) Rather, the event in the Concert Hall was a mass gathering of Christians of the charismatic kind that was more powerful than a seismic calamity or falling celestial debris!

And seated amidst the Concert Hall crowd was a nervous young man, not exactly sure why he was there.

His name was Reg.

Perth, Western Australia, 2020

26
Invitation

Reg and Janny Firth

It all began for Reg Firth in the early Seventies after a parish meeting, when he received and accepted an invitation for coffee with a young couple that had welcomed him into the parish community. The following weekend, Reg's wife Janny, not yet Catholic, also made the couple's acquaintance. More coffee followed; the first of many interactions over a six-year period, and which began to include invitations of a more spiritual kind. Like minions of the Hound of Heaven, the couple repeatedly invited Reg and Janny to events of the Charismatic Renewal.

Soon enough, the Firths accepted their first invitation to attend *Group 50*, a charismatic prayer meeting at a retreat house which formed part of the North Perth Redemptorist Monastery community. Attending with Fr. Chris Ross, Reg and Janny soon heard something they had never heard before. Were these sounds words or just gibberish? Reg was not sure. Whatever it was, the mystifying sound filling the room left Reg and Janny feeling deeply unsettled. They were experiencing the phenomenon of tongues, a controversial occurrence for some Christians, which some believe is the language of the Holy Spirit, citing biblical references as evidence. Acts 19:6 for instance recounts the following post-Pentecost event:

And when Paul had imposed his hands upon them, the Holy Spirit came over them. And they were speaking in tongues and prophesying.

Reg and Janny felt like weary travellers in a foreign land having no idea what would happen next. It seemed bizarre, to say the least, and they soon left, disturbed. Yet, for some strange reason, like a moth that is drawn to the proverbial flame, so too were the Firths drawn to return for more.

The social events to which their close friends had invited them had softened them towards what Reg called the "God things." Friendships made in Heaven are difficult to resist, and so the Firths eventually returned to *Group 50*, the meeting now held in the monastery church. Perhaps they could cope with the *praying in tongues* business if nothing was expected of them other than being mere spectators. However, sometime later, they found themselves on their knees, surrounded by people laying hands on them, feeling the same unease as during their first session, especially when the presiding priest approached Janny and posed her a question.

"Which gifts do you want?" asked the priest. Taken aback by his pointedness, Janny responded bluntly, holding on to some semblance of pride and integrity.

"None of them," she said with defiance.

Reg also felt unrest in his spirit. He had been prayed over already, but nothing had happened. Yet things were happening to the people in the line in front of him, kneeling and receiving something that resulted from the prayer of the priest. The discomfort increased and Reg began to wonder why he and Janny had come at all!

Years passed. The invitations kept flowing. The couple was obviously not giving up. Social events were warmly accepted by the Firths, while the "God" ones were merely tolerated. Reg and his wife still managed to swallow their pride and give them a go from time to time, especially when their friends' honour was at stake.

By the time he discovered that his good friends had organised and invested their finances in a major charismatic conference to be held in the then state-of-the-art Perth Concert Hall, Reg saw crippling bankruptcy on the horizon. Quizzing his good friends, hoping they would not regret their bad business decision, Reg was surprised once more when they quipped, "The Lord will provide." And they were smiling too! *They must be going loopy,* concluded Reg. But his loyalty was stronger than his unsettling doubt.

The idea of their inevitable fate played on his mind. Taking some time out from his work in the city that day, Reg did what he knew was foolish but what seemed the only thing he could do in the circumstances; he registered for the conference. If reason alone could not prevent his friends from financial ruin, perhaps his own loyalty and friendship might – even if to some small extent. After all, what harm could it do?

Upon arrival at the Concert Hall ticketing booth, Reg's fears were being realised right before his eyes. Reg saw only half a dozen unfortunate souls registering for the conference. That night, Reg had a revelation for his wife.

"I don't have any intention of going, Janny, but I bought two tickets for that conference that goes for a week," Reg confessed. "I felt so bad for Kevin and the guys. If this thing flops, they are going to be in deep debt."

"Reg, you realise we are going to have to go now, don't you?" Janny knew that buying a ticket - and then not attending - would be an affront to their close friends, no matter how strange their beliefs and activities might be. Janny's reasoning won out and with some trepidation in their hearts the nervous couple found themselves making their way to the first day of the conference, only to discover that far from empty, the Hall was jam-packed, sending a shock wave down their spines. The Concert Hall, it seemed, had become the place to be in Perth. The only viewing area remaining was from the foyer. Reg was astonished. His good friends had pulled it off.

Walking into the auditorium with trepidation, numb, and silent, Reg and Janny sat in the front-row seats their friends had 'kindly' secured for them. *They really thought of everything*, Reg mused. *Everything!*

27

The Healing Touch

When Reg spoke to Janny at the end of the first day of the conference, he found himself once again summoning the strength for another confession.

"Janny, I have decided to take the whole week off work and attend both day and evening sessions of the conference".

"Reg, I think you should," Janny replied supportively. And Reg's desire to return and to experience more of the first day's strange peace and joy was overwhelming. From the moment a priest with an American accent, began to speak, the more he captured Reg's attention. It was his first exposure to Fr. Francis McNutt and he had never heard of the mercy of God spoken like that before. And then came another American priest, Fr. John Bertolucci, speaking so beautifully on God's love that Reg felt an unexpected sensation in his soul. As if illuminated by a powerful light his soul, Reg was convinced of God's love for him; no, not just love, but mercy too.

The hard wall that Reg and his wife had put up to guard themselves against the seemingly bizarre spirituality was slowly toppling all around them, as mysteriously as the walls of Jericho, but with a great deal less clamour.

With the theme of the following day being *healing*, a spirit of expectancy was in the air. Soon a sea of outstretched hands rose in the auditorium united in the power they invoked as those seeking healing responded to a call that had just gone out to the crowd to come forward for prayer. Many made their way to the stage. Others remained in their seats as delegates seated near them offered to pray over them.

Sitting next to Reg was a ten-year-old boy with a degenerative eye disease, diagnosed as medically blind, the nerve ends at the back of his eyes atrophied. His parents, Reg's fellow parishioners, knew that there was no cure at this time for that sort of thing!

Reg, a novice who had never prayed with anyone before, quite out of character, and shocked, found himself instinctively placing his fingers on the boy's eyes. He uttered, "God if you are here, there are many people who are sick. If you are not too busy could you come here and make this boy see?" In what seemed like an eternity but really only lasted around thirty seconds, Reg felt his fingers become very warm. *Uncomfortably* warm. *Was this what all those people 'falling down' had experienced? Could the little boy feel the warmth too?*

Reg's thoughts were interrupted as he listened to the preacher calling for testimonies of divine healing. "Who has been healed?" the preacher asked, apparently sure of a rapid response. The boy, to Reg's utter astonishment, was among those who raised hands, while his parents sat motionless. The session ended and Reg heard the boy's parents indicate they were going home without any hint of a reason.

Did any of it mean anything? Reg could not deny that something had happened to himself. He had prayed and in direct response to his prayer he had felt an unearthly power, and raw energy soaring through his own body.

The conference continued. At the night session, the boy's father approached Reg with jubilation written all over his face. "Reg, you won't believe it! Each night I read to my boy and as usual I did so tonight. My son was behind me looking over my shoulder. At one point I began skipping words on the page wanting to finish the book and get my boy to bed. You won't believe it, but he said to me, 'Dad, you read the wrong words' and he continued reading the page himself. Reg, your prayer worked!"

Any doubt that may have still been plaguing Reg regarding the willingness of God to heal, and to use mere human instruments to do so, left him instantly as he stared at the face of the healed boy; healed *through* his own hands, although not *by* them. The once *doubting Thomas* could no longer deny the intimacy of God, an intimacy that would come in to even sharper focus by the Thursday evening when a further event was in store for Reg, at Perth's, St. Mary's Cathedral; one more personal and a final piece of a puzzle that had plagued him since the death of his mother, seventeen years earlier.

28

Slain

The Mass began at 7pm and ended around midnight. With around 1000 people in the crowd on fire with love for God, or desperately in need of God's healing power, the energy was electric. Reg watched as many went forward for healing. He knew he had to do the same.

As the minister laid his hand on Reg, a force overwhelmed him, propelling him onto the floor of the gothic cathedral. And the words that penetrated his soul were as sweet as honey. "I have never left you!" The tears welled up as Reg soaked in the amazing feeling of knowing and feeling God's presence and love. It was more than the realization that God had indeed never left him and that he had a plan for his life beyond women, beyond sport, and beyond a career. These words of absolute love had transported him back to the most vulnerable time in his life, at the age of sixteen when he had found himself outside the doors of the same cathedral, while his mother lay dying a stone's throw away in the hospital which overshadows the cathedral like a death veil.

Rushing out of Royal Perth Hospital that dark summer night in 1962, Reg ran towards the Cathedral, its locked and ancient doors hovering over him. The same anguish with which he had begged his mother not to die a few minutes earlier, still hung around him. Falling to his knees, he had cried out, "Please don't leave me!" Seventeen years later, despite years of abandoning a true faith and just attesting to a nominal Catholicism, Reg realised that God had answered his prayer. "I have never left you," he had told him.

From the day he was 'slain' in the Spirit, Reg has embarked on a spiritual journey that has spanned more than three decades. By 1987, after years spent in Sydney's first Disciples of Jesus Covenant Community branch - inspired itself by the universal Charismatic movement - Reg and Janny returned to Perth and established another branch, of which he became Senior Coordinator. Over many years, Reg has witnessed the greatest of all wonders – the conversion and transformation of the soul – but has continued to witness miracles of the more physical kind too.

AND THEY SHALL BE HEALED

⌘

*For this reason, I say to you, all things whatsoever that you ask for when praying:
believe that you will receive them, and they will happen for you.
- Mark 11:24*

⌘

29

Cup and Spill

The idea of faith healers is laughable to some of us. You may have come across supposed faith healers of the *hyped-up televangelist* type. Dressed in a white suit, the healer parades past a line of adult men and women and proceeds to "slay" the expectant infirm merely by raising his arm. At times he even slays a few at a time very dramatically. Somehow, despite the presence of his team of "catchers" who are helping the Holy Spirit along a little (visibly doing more than "catching"), the faith healer's credibility remains intact, his wealth growing.

Fortunately, these frauds cannot fully discredit the real deal. Rather, for Christians such as Reg Firth, the Charismatic gifts are indeed the 'real deal'. I have been a witness to them on a number of occasions – words of knowledge, gifts of healing, speaking in tongues, interpretation of tongues and others that are mentioned in 1 Corinthians 8-10. I have seen men and women, young and old, experience resting in the spirit as the force and love of the Holy Spirit literally blows them to the ground - and without being harmed - after a believing Christian lays hands on them. Experiencing the energy and warmth that charges through your body after 'resting in the spirit' as I have, is enough to help one realise that this is no mere natural phenomenon.

As I became more acquainted with members of the Disciples of Jesus Covenant Community, as a friend and at times colleague in my role as retreat facilitator at one particular Perth catholic school, I realised that the demonstration of God's wonders is not as rare as some may think. One of the first healings that Reg recounted to me occurred at one particular Summer School organised by the Community, which is held annually in various locations throughout Australia, and which has come to be a key vehicle for the healing touch of Heaven. At the 1994 event in Perth, a lovely young lady named Sandra, a member of the community, attended.

Suffering from a severe 'cup and spill ailment' for a long while, Sandra had somewhat grown accustomed to the debilitating symptoms of the disease such as a stomach that slowly enlarges over the course of a day caused by a retarded digestion. For years Sandra had to wear baggy clothes so as to make the daylong gradual expansion of her stomach less noticeable. Each day she had to physically aid her digestion by lying on her stomach.

"There is someone here with a digestive problem," Sandra heard during a healing session, as one of the leaders proclaimed a word of knowledge. Sandra saw a few other hands go up but she knew better. "It's mine," she thought. "I'm claiming this."

Rising from her place Sandra came forward for prayer.

Nothing happened. Naturally disappointed, Sandra turned and walked back to her place, while stubbornly holding on to her claim.

Before thinking any more about it, Sandra felt like a hand had forced its way down through the top of her head, grabbing her stomach and then pull it up. Sandra was totally healed.

30

Tumour

When Reg decided to invite Marist priest, Fr. John Rea, to Perth for the first time in 2008, he knew that this faith healer was not a fraud either. This internationally renowned priest from New Zealand had already been an instrument of a number of fantastic healings including the total healing of a child violinist's crushed hand, the "replacement" of ovaries and tubes that had been removed in surgery, the gift of a child to infertile couples, as well as cancer cures.

Shortly before the scheduled Healing Mission in Perth had begun, however, Reg received the shocking news about his son as he sat beside him in the hospital. CAT scans and an MRI had revealed the undeniable truth. Mark had a tumour. Fr. Rea's visit to Perth suddenly took on a more urgent and personal significance for Reg.

Michelle prepared for whatever was to come when she learned that her husband would need to undergo surgery. When the day came on February 19, 2008, surgeons broke Mark's collarbone in order to remove the tumour that had wrapped itself around the brachial plexus, nerves that supply the shoulder, arm and chest. A six-hour operation had not succeeded in removing it completely but enough had been removed so a biopsy could be performed.

"If we fail to remove the complete tumour soon, it will lead to it crushing the surrounding nerves. Attempting to remove it completely could lead to the severing of those same nerves," the doctors told Michelle.

Pain relief had been relatively ineffective since the beginning of February when Mark had entered hospital. Something had to be done. This type of tumour was normally situated inside the bone and not the "very rare" location in which it found itself. Mark needed further surgery. It was scheduled for February 28.

"Reg," said Steve as he prepared to give his old friend a reminder. "I want you to remember a very important promise Christ made to his followers. 'Truly, I say to you, whoever says to this mountain, 'Be taken up and cast into the sea,' and does not doubt in his heart, but believes that what he says will come to pass, it will be done for him. Therefore, I tell you, whatever you ask in prayer, believe that you receive it, and you will.'" This expectant faith that Steve was inviting Reg to remember and take into his very soul was a gift and not something Reg would be able to "conjure" up himself.

By February 22, when Fr. John Rea touched down at Perth Airport, Reg and many others had already begun taking Christ at his word, by claiming a healing, vocally and in faith. "Lord, thank you for healing Mark. We claim his healing and bless your Name." This prayer of faith was repeated the night of February 26 when Fr. Rea ministered to Mark in the hospital.

"Lord, please remove this tumour. Please do this within twenty-four hours!" It was just enough time before the scheduled operation two days later. As always, Fr. Rea expected a healing, even if the healing never came. And the prospect of a "no" for an answer, as always, did not faze him. "It's all in God's hands," he told me when I met with him during his 2014 visit. As he told me, physical healing this side of Heaven or not, "ultimately there will be healing when we see him face to face."

It was now February 28. Mark was wheeled into surgery as his wife and their children, parents and siblings waited anxiously. The surgeons made their incision and began their attempt to locate the deadly tumour.

The tumour they expected to find choking Mark's brachial plexus, was nowhere to be found! Another CAT scan confirmed the phenomenon, and the event, soon became the talk of the entire hospital.

"I take a record of healings and then forget about them," Fr. Rea explained. "Since I have been in Perth here this time, a woman has regained her hearing in her left ear. Another woman suffering with migraines for 30 years was healed of them." Sometimes, Fr. Rea has the privilege of meeting those he has healed, many years later.

"In 1975 I met a woman with a melanoma who had been given at most a month to live. I met her again this year – still well. And then there was the case of the woman down south named Leanne, who was told, right up until just before the birth of her child, that he would be a Down's Syndrome baby. The baby was born perfectly normal after she had been on our prayer list. I had no doubt that the baby would be normal."

"Fr. Rea, are you describing the charismatic gift known as a Word of Knowledge?" I asked.

"It is what is called an *expectant faith*; the third type of faith mentioned in scriptures – it is not there all the time. It is not the commitment faith that we choose," explained Fr. Rea. I understood what he meant. It was the same faith that I had only been graced with perhaps three times in my life. A supernatural knowledge that what you were about to ask for would be granted.

His words reminded me of one of the healing stories posted in the Disciples of Jesus community bulletin board; the story of Joanne who had suffered a painful hand for months. Fr. Rea had spoken a word of knowledge during a prayer meeting. "God is healing hands," he claimed. Joanne, in an act of faith, claimed that healing for herself. Her pain instantly dissipated. And so did her addiction to caffeine as well as her emotional suffering.

"God is a God of miracles," Reg testifies confidently to this day. "Our challenge is to believe His promises." Reg has been privileged to see how definitively situations can be changed when God is allowed to captain the ship of people's lives. Sometimes the change is subtle and other times it is quite dramatic. Reg shared his belief with me that "God is not about performing to impress but about drawing us into his love. It is God's love which is at the heart of the healing of every embittered body, the rejuvenation of every broken heart."

Reg's witness to God's work in his life and in the lives of so many others inspired me to continue finding traces of God's footsteps in Perth.

I didn't have to look far.

TOUCHED BY GRACE

⌘

Have courage; the good seed will grow up in the children's hearts later on.
-Blessed Edmund Rice

⌘

Brian Clery, (on the right), with siblings, Woodman Point, 1950

31

The Calling

He had wanted a brief escape. Some time alone to breathe deeply, in a location *away* from the reunion. And now he stands in the middle of it, sauntering down a remote street which runs parallel to the ocean only one hundred meters away. The fresh air that caresses his tired face seems to have come by express post from the South Pole. It only serves to intensify his obvious delight at the vision of the beautiful Norfolk Pines that dance before him in the wind, forming a royal guard of honour to their Creator.

His meditation is presently interrupted as the rush of a delivery truck passes him noisily, halting abruptly seconds later. Stopping in his tracks, the man stares as the driver, probably in his sixties, clambers out with a slightly perplexed look, and as if propelled by a distant memory. The driver approaches the man tentatively.

Risking sounding like a fool he asks, "You wouldn't be Brother Clery, would you?"

"Yes, I am," Brian replied confidently, much to the driver's satisfaction. "And you are Francis Lane, aren't you?"

If there were onlookers that day, they would have had the pleasure of seeing the shock absorbers of Francis' face strain as Brian Clery demonstrated his elephant-like memory of a pupil he had last cast eyes on over 50 years previously.

"How could you tell it was me?" Brian asked a little perplexed.

"I could tell by the way you were walking." The man had recognised Brian's distinctive sprightly lope!

The way I walk? Nothing else would amaze Brian after the roller coaster ride of that week, months after he had first received the call that had been completely unexpected; a surprise invitation to a once in a lifetime event that a teacher only gets to visit in his dreams.

"All expenses paid, Brother! Will you come?" Peter McMurrick had asked expectantly, hoping that Brian would make the trek across the Nullabor to the country town of Warmambool in Victoria.

For Brother Brian Clery, at seventy-six years of age, this would be too good to refuse. It is not every day that you get to mingle with students you taught in the late Fifties. Coinciding as it did with the famous Warrnambool May Race Carnival, the event promised to be even more of a celebration. So, it was in Warrnambool, at the special breakfast on the second morning of the Race carnival, where Brian met near-on eighty enthusiastic past pupils and saw breakfast end past midday.

"Brother, do you still teach religion classes, tell stories and draw on the blackboard? Do you still coach football, cricket and athletics?" The questions came fast and Brian was enjoying every moment, although the unexpected exclamation by some who thought he was dead amused him a little, and understandably so. When Brian found time to reflect on the special week's events, his thoughts were gently touched by the words of Edmund Rice, founder of the Christian Brothers' religious order.

Have courage; the good seed will grow up in the children's hearts later on.

Here they were, both children and seeds, witnessing to the difference that God has made through this giant of a man on so many people over the decades. Few, if any, perhaps, knew that Brian had also been the recipient of other graces, flowing through the conduit of love.

I had the privilege of working with Brian during my 7 years at Aquinas College in the Perth suburb of Salter Point. Nestled on the Mount Henry Peninsula, in one of the most beautiful corners of Western Australia, the college is surrounded by stunning river and spectacular cliffs. Its sloping glades, landscaped garden beds and sweeping plains are peppered by an army of jacaranda, eucalyptus and gum trees; their leaves, of various shades of green, serving as a canopy of protection against the Australian sun's offensive heat. In this beautiful setting, I spent some time meeting with Brian, learning about events in his life that few in the school knew about, unless he included them in his many story telling sessions that students had come to love, whether boarders or day boys. I learnt that his path to the religious life, God's calling on his life, had begun in a setting similar to that of the college grounds. Not too far away!

Canning Highway, the main artery of Perth snaking its way alongside Point Walter, is connected to the cliffs and bays of the Canning River via major roads that house some of the most beautiful homes in Perth. When Brian and his family made their home in Point Walter, so that his father, Jim, could commute to Fremantle each day, his house was only one of four in the entire area. The distance between it and the river was marked by bush more than suburbia. It was through that bush that Brian began his seven kilometres trek each day, come rain, hail or shine, to get to school.

Over time Brian grew enamoured with the raw beauty of the bush. Its sounds and silence resonated with his developing sense of place and being. With the sound of twig crunching under his feet and surrounded by the fragrance of giant eucalyptus and gum trees, Brian never tired of it. In the afternoon, returning from school, and while his father was still at work, it was the young boy's job to take the Billy cart into the bush, collect the dead wood, fill the cart with it and return home.

Later, watered by the influence of charismatic religious who taught him, Brian's spirituality was deepening in that bush, sowing the seeds for a religious vocation. At just 9 years of age, Brian knew he would become a Christian Brother. By the time the Vocations Director had visited Brian's class in Grade 6, Brian had already made up his mind.

And so, the day finally came for Jim and his wife to farewell their son, at the tender age of 14, just before he boarded the steam train that would take him across the Nullabor, back to the Eastern States, to Sydney, and to the Juniorate of St. Edna. There had been no fanfare. No tears. No wailing. And even the back-injury Brian had sustained 3 weeks prior his departure from Perth, that had made it difficult for Brian to walk, had not been an impediment. It is only temporary, Jim thought. Brian would be okay. Yet, on arrival in Sydney it was clear that Brian's recovery was not as imminent as his parents had hoped.

The pain and discomfort continued, and so did the emotional pain of not being able to join his friends in playing his beloved cricket. Once again, as at his previous school, Brian was seen as nothing better than the cricket equivalent of a golfer's caddie! "They probably thought I was just a crippled kid," reflected Brian as he recalled the scorer's job he had been given. To make matters worse, homesickness and depression were crouching at the door of his soul.

It was then that *he* came to Sydney all the way from America. The famous Fr. Peyton.

32

The Rosary Priest Down Under

Known for his famous "Family Rosary Crusade", the Irish-American Fr. Peyton, also called the "Rosary Priest," had been spreading the key message around the world that the family that prays together stays together. His devotion to the Blessed Virgin Mary and the Rosary had been consolidated when he was healed of tuberculosis in 1941. He then came to learn of the Virgin's intercession in the 1571 Battle of Lepanto, when Europe was preserved from invasion. For years Fr. Peyton had received the support of Hollywood celebrities as he brought the Gospel to radio. It is almost impossible, with the secularism and militant anti-religious sentiment in vogue in the Western World today, to conceive of there even being a time when a Catholic priest would be able to obtain the endorsement of Hollywood in his promotion of the Rosary. Regardless, this was what Fr. Peyton had managed to do, with the support of actors like Bing Crosby, Jane Wyatt, Lucille Ball, Natalie Wood, Ronald Regan and William Shatner just to name a few.

It was 1951 when Fr. Peyton, who could be called a Catholic Billy Graham, made his way to Sydney to conduct another Rosary Rally. Brian Clery, and around one hundred and twenty or so other young men in the Juniorate, all dressed in their navy-blue uniform, set out from St. Endas and made their way to the Rally on foot. Brian, with his aching back in tow, began his painful trek from Strathfield to Lewisham oval.

As others kept a fine pace, Brian found himself lagging behind. It wasn't long before he no longer saw his peers as he turned a street corner. Brian was lost. Sydney was not a small city even in the early Fifties, much larger than the Fremantle he had grown up in. To his mind, Sydney was much more "old fashioned" too. Despite his pain, and now being alone, Brian prepared himself for the remaining, lonely journey to the Rally.

Brian finally arrived alone, his peers nowhere in sight but presumably already comfortably seated. He made it in time for the recitation of the Rosary, led by Fr. Peyton. "The first sorrowful mystery," he announced, "is the Agony of Jesus in the garden." Brian joined in as the Our Father and Hail Mary prayers were prayed meditatively.

The second mystery followed with the crowd meditating on Jesus' cruel scourging at the pillar. The third and fourth mysteries ensued until the fifth when Fr. Peyton expressed an invitation. "All of you in need of healing, pray now for healing through Mary's intercession! Raise your arms like Jesus on the cross," he directed. Brian joined in, his arms raised in the manner of the cross, his back killing him. He wanted to drop his arms - but it was a *no brainer*. He would rather endure the agony of the odd posture than the humiliation of giving up his pride when so many others had swallowed theirs.

The fifth sorrowful mystery over – *The Crucifixion* – brought the rally to an end. Brian, painfully but joyfully, relaxed his arms, thus relieving some of the pressure off his lower back. As it was time to leave, Brian pondered whether he would find his friends dressed in blue. He feared not being able to get home, but Brian spotted them in the distance. All in blue. All together. With a spring in his step, Brian began his pedestrian passage towards his brothers.

One minute. Two minutes. A total of fifteen minutes or so had passed when it suddenly dawned on Brian that he was walking briskly. This had been impossible for him earlier that day. Reunited with his new family, Brian returned to St. Endas.

"Anyone who wants to play cricket for a while can do so," said the brother in charge to the excited boys as he permitted them to have about an hour of sports before dinner. Brian didn't miss his chance and joined in. By the end of the session, a senior boy came up to Brian with an unmistakable surprised gaze. "Why have you only been *scoring* for us thus far? Why aren't you on a team?" Why indeed! Because the same Brian who had won the Under 13's final for his team against CBC Highgate bowling 6 for 3 runs, and who had recently been injured and presumed "crippled," had now been healed after a Rosary at just one of Fr. Peyton's famous rallies. The homesickness was healed alongside his back to make the victory even sweeter.

For Brian, the God who created the heavens and the earth, who came as a baby and who died on a cross for his salvation, has been faithful. He has asked much from Brian in his many years since his healing that day in Sydney, but he has continued to give him so much more.

Healing would come again for Brian, as well as a second chance of life, worked this time through the hands of a fifteen-year-old schoolboy.

33

Sacred

"That would be great, Brother Clery," said the Year 10 Religious Education teacher when, in 2007, Brian was asked to come and speak to the boys. The shrill of the school siren was his cue to make his way to the speaking appointment.

As Brian neared the classroom, he noticed that his heart rate had increased dramatically. *Oh no*, he thought. He knew what this meant - a heart rate of up to 200 beats per minute. Panic assailed him. As the thoroughfare of students surrounding him became denser, Brian was finding it harder to breathe.

At that moment, a Year Ten boy came by.

"Brother, are you okay?" he asked, noticing the pale hew and fear on Brian's face. "Yeah," muttered Brian, unable to reveal how he really felt. The boy said nothing but immediately gave Brian an encouraging slap on the back, undeterred by Brian's denial.

Immediately, Brian felt like lightning had jolted him. The boy finished, walked off and then turned back and smiled as Brian glanced toward him. Did the boy know what had happened? That his heart rate had returned to normal?

This experience is one of Brian's most tender memories. Seven years later, at the start of the 2014 school year, Brian stood up in front of the Aquinas staff and recounted the experience. "We have these experiences of God's presence all the time," he told us. And he bid all present to reflect on those sacred moments that occur more often than we might think.

As I sat in the audience, I was grateful at how much more Brian could teach me. I was moved deeply when he read the poem he had written about this event.

Renato Bonasera

He Touched Me

The bell had gone to end recess
I was off to class again,
Walking along the well-worn path
To classroom 4A10.

When bang! My heart broke down again.
Pounding at a rate of knots.
Breathing became impossible.
Should I go to class or not?

In total confusion I stopped awhile
To steady my thoughts and pace.
Then a boy passed by and studied me
With concern upon his face.

"Are you all right," he gently smiled.
"I'm okay," I said.
But he ignored my curt reply
And stroked my back instead.

Now when that hand had touched my back
To comfort and assure,
I felt a bolt of lightning strike!
My heart was sound once more.

My breathing was itself again,
I felt my heart set free.
All panic simply disappeared.
No way a fantasy.

What was I supposed to do,
Kneel down, cry out or brood?
Stunned I simply moved along
All full of gratitude.

I looked back at his smiling face,
Did he know what he had done?
I sensed somehow he may have known,
He was no simpleton.

Yet some may scoff when reading this,
And take me for a fool.
But Presence is a mighty force
Yes, even in a school.

So, what's been learnt from these events
That makes it all worthwhile?
The Son of God was once fifteen,
And I think I caught his smile.

Brian has learnt, in the words of Australia's first saint, Mary MacKillop, that gratitude is the memory of the heart. And there is so much to remember with joy; his time away on sabbatical, his finding a spiritual director whom he still sees after nearly 30 years, his retreat experience with Elizabeth Gobbard in Aylesford in England, his healing at the Rosary Rally in Sydney, or his time in Jesuit schools in America that would become the blue print for the retreat programme used in some Australian schools. But Brian also cherishes the way God has loved him and granted him the desires of his heart. Until the Lord calls him home, Brian will continue to tell each generation of young men that God loves them fanatically.

When a child says thank you to him, Brian feels he has been touched by the sacred. When he experiences the special bond with student leaders on retreats, he knows that he has been once again touched by grace. "When someone opens up and talks about their deeper feeling, it is a grace straight away," he told me with conviction. "I just think there is something sacred in the student and something sacred has been happening. The ordinary has become glorified in some way. It is an awesome moment."

Brian has reminded me of another reason why it may be wise to see the sacred in everyone. What I have discovered from speaking to others along my journey, reading books or just being open to the presence of God in my own life, is that you just never know when you may be in the presence of a visitor from Heaven.

Brian Clery, Retreats, 2014

ENTERTAINING ANGELS

⌘

*For he has given his angels charge over you, so as to preserve
you in all your ways.
- Psalm 91:11*

⌘

34

An Angelic Ministry

I have listened to many audiobooks over the past few years. They make my trek to work more manageable and certainly guarantee that any temptation to succumb to road rage is nipped in the bud. As you might gather by now, I am a person who thrives on stories that affirm the existence of the ethereal. So, when I got around to listening to Genelle Guzman's account of one such ethereal experience, I knew it would soon become one of my favourites. Her book, aptly called *Angel in the Rubble* remains the most powerful of my 9/11 survivor and angel accounts.

Those who know Genelle's story will remember that she was the last to be found alive a day after the South Tower of the World Trade Centre imploded and collapsed on her. That she survived the titanic cascade of concrete and glass, over ninety floors above her, is a miracle in itself. But the curious phenomenon that precipitated her discovery by rescuers is equally mystifying; the unexplained help of a mysterious man whose firm hand met hers as she successfully punched her hand through the debris above her head. He had known her name even though they had never met. And then, just as mysteriously as he had appeared, he left, nowhere to be seen by her merely mortal rescuers.

Genelle concluded that this *man* was not mortal. He was, she believed, an angel.

There would be few people alive today who have not have at least heard the word *angel*. Angels form part of the deposit of a number of faiths, including of course the Christian faith. Statues of angels adorn our churches and cemeteries, continuously reminding us that only a thin veil separates this material world from the spiritual. Catholics grow up trusting that everybody is gifted with a guardian angel that watches over them. Other Christians join us in nurturing our children with a smorgasbord of biblical accounts of the presence and work of angels: whether it be those of the flaming sword wielding type who keep Adam and Eve out of paradise, or lead Israel into battle, or those who dine with Abraham and Sarah before providing a message from the Lord. Or again, we delight in the awe of those who protect Sidrach, Meshach and Abednego from the fiery furnace, who appear before shepherds, comfort Jesus in the Garden of Gethsemane or help Peter break out of prison in the Acts of the Apostles.

Some angels are singled out for a special role such as the Archangels: Michael, whose role is to lead God's army against Satan; Gabriel who heralds the coming of the Messiah at the Annunciation; and Raphael, who brings God's healing.

I only discovered this latter archangel once I read part of the book of Tobit in which he protects young Tobias from the spirit of death. The following prayer to Raphael spoke to me of the deeply spiritual battle in which angels are primarily engaged.

Holy Archangel Raphael, you guided young Tobias on his journey and protected him from the Spirit of Death which sought to destroy his life. Protect all from the road that leads to physical and spiritual death, especially those in most danger of despair and suicide.

Lead them by the hand, as you did Tobias, away from the sadness of addiction, to peace and joy.

O Holy Raphael, whose name means "God has healed," bring them the Lord's healing. Amen.

The ongoing ministry of angels is part of the deposit of faith but is, perhaps, denied by those Christians of the more liberal-progressive persuasion who side with an exclusivist rationalist thinking and wish to be liberated from the chains of medieval superstition. Angels may have been active in more primitive times but not so any more, they might argue, even if they do actually believe in them. The New Age movement has perhaps contributed to this decline in the belief in angels of the Christian type, with its redefinition of angels often presented through the paraphernalia of alternative spiritualties, some of which border on the occult. Angels, *a la* the New Age type are more akin to false gods or goddesses than angels in the Christian sense.

Yet, the traditional view of angels persists. Accounts of near-death experiences have for many years now been captivating audiences worldwide with visions of angels such as the one made famous by Colton Burpo. The fact that the book recounting Colton's journey to Heaven and back, entitled *Heaven is for Real*, was a #1 New York Times bestseller, is testimony to the yearning so many people have to acknowledge the existence of angels; and of course the afterlife. The popularity of the *Touched by an Angel* series also witnesses to this. Its nine years in production was certainly a major feat for its time. Far from falling victim to the rationalism of the late Twentieth and early Twenty-First Centuries, belief in the existence of angels, our heavenly messenger friends, has at least retained the vitality it once had, and in some circles even surpassed it.

The question is, why? Is it simply because of a desire to latch on to a distant past, or a form of escapism caused by the brutality of a world which lusts for war more often than thirsts for peace? Is it simply because of the many testimonies we have had about angels?

I have been privileged to cross paths with intangible doctrine and tangible reality through the personal experience of people I know. It is easy to dismiss the testimony of one not known to you. However, the same cannot be said when the testimony is from those one knows more personally.

9/11 Ground Zero – Lest we Forget

35

Angel at the Foot of the Bed

Therese was prepared from a young age to take on the responsibilities associated with the nurture of children. As the eldest child she came to be known as sister-mum by her siblings; a fact I became associated with when we first met. It wasn't surprising then to learn later that she had continued babysitting even after commencing her early childhood teaching career.

During one weekend in the mid-1990s she made her way to the family she worked for in the south eastern suburb of Huntingdale in Perth. The parents (whom I shall call Tanya and Matt) flew to Melbourne on business and left their three young children, the youngest only nine months, in Therese's care.

Eager not to disappoint the parents but aware that she had begun developing flu-like symptoms, Therese took the children on an outing almost as soon as she arrived and the parents had left. Therese drove the three small children to the local pharmacy and wondered what others thought as she stood with one child on her hip and two standing by her side.

Not long into the job, Therese heard the shrill of the phone, picked up and listened. It was Tanya. "Therese, the kids' uncle has threatened to harm them. He is watching the house and we can't get a flight earlier than tomorrow. There are people praying for you all here in Melbourne."

Therese immediately locked the house. There was no question of leaving even if it were to take the children to her own home. Was the uncle truly watching the house? Surely if she even took them out the front door, she would be exposing them to danger? No, the safest place would be inside, she convinced herself.

That night, with the children tucked in, Therese tried to get some sleep. So far nothing had happened. But she would remain awake as long as she could. Exhausted, however, Therese lay face down on the parents' bed without pulling back the covers.

The silence was, after some time, broken by what sounded like footsteps down the hallway. Therese froze and she instinctively prepared for what she feared was likely to be a violent attack. Was this how it would all end? What about the children? But she could not move. Terror gripped her further as she felt the peculiar sound approach her. The footsteps stopped suddenly. Therese felt something descend upon her body.

This could only mean one thing. Her heart racing, Therese waited for the inevitable. What would he do to her? But as the seemingly endless seconds passed on, nothing happened. *Just get it over and done with!* What was he waiting for? Therese braced herself and then, something strange happened. Or rather, didn't happen. What was he covering her with? Something appeared to be enveloping her on both sides of her body as if at the same time.

Blackness enveloped her, only to be broken by the morning. The children were safe. It was as if nothing at all had happened. And if something had, then Therese and the children had been spared.

If relief were the primary emotion Therese felt upon seeing the children in her charge, it did nothing to take away her awe inspired confusion. Where did those footsteps come from? That feeling of being completely enveloped?

For about a month Therese could not get the experience off her mind and she eventually decided to speak to Tanya, somewhat embarrassed.

"I had a really strange experience that weekend you were over east," she muttered to Tanya. She knew she was risking being ridiculed. But when Therese explained what had occurred, Tanya surprised her with the following words.

"Therese, that is not at all strange. When we came back, I asked my four-year-old if he had been scared. And then he said, 'No mum. The angel sat at the foot of the bed and told me that the Precious Blood of Jesus had been poured over the house.' What was truly amazing was that while we were in Melbourne, those praying for us specifically prayed that the house be covered by the Blood of Jesus."

City of Melbourne, Australia

36

The Vaal River

Jacob's home was more modern than those in the smaller surrounding townships in the Orange Free State. Nevertheless, the stone that characterised many homes in this region of South Africa, which came courtesy of the Sandstone Mountains in the northeast, also characterised those in his hometown of Sasolburg.

Architecturally, there was a definite Victorian lineage evident – quite different to the homes in Germany and Holland from which his parents' families had migrated. Likewise, the unique mushroom-like Rondavels, (circular buildings with a conical roof that peppered South Africa), were testimony to the country's rich indigenous past.

Sasolburg was still quite new, only established in 1954, five years before Jacob was born, and named after the Sasol Petro-chemical company that supplied employment to many in the town, including Jacob's father. At 5 years of age, the young boy was not yet aware that Vredefort Dome, home to the greatest visible meteor impact site in the world, was only fifty kilometres from his doorstep, or that the state's capital Bloemfontein was the birthplace of Tolkien.

He may have wondered exactly where the domestic servants travelled to after they left his home by 9 p.m. every night after the sounding of the bell. The servants' township was around 15 kilometres away and Jacob was still too young to understand the complexities of the Apartheid that plagued the nation. He could see that the servants' skin colour may have differed from his own, and yet their faith was that of his own mother's. Jacob remembers the servant named Sophie who was deeply spiritual and who spoke to him about the Christian faith.

The day Jacob had been looking forward to finally came and his parents and siblings set out. It was summer and the dirt road was dry and dusty. As they drove down the road toward the Vaal River, not far from Johannesburg, Jacob glanced at the flat, rolling grasslands and crop fields passing him by. He looked up to his friend Hennie, 12, who was like a big brother and at whose home he often sought refuge. Hennie's parents wondered why Jacob liked to have so many sleepovers at their home. Jacob could never tell them about his father's angry outbursts.

The open lawns of the recreation area on the banks of the Vaal River, rising to the five-metre-high embankment that overshadowed the river below, suddenly came into view as they approached the parking area. Quickly getting out of the car, Jacob soon spotted Hennie as the parents chatted and looked forward to this traditional annual inter-family get together. With soccer ball in tow, the two boys soon ran off and reached the wide embankment that must have seemed like it went on forever to a boy of Jacob's age.

Kick. Block. Kick. Stop. Kick… and chase. And Jacob did, running across the embankment after the elusive ball. Had Hennie meant to send the ball that way? Jacob didn't know but the thrill of the chase was good enough for him, and no match for his young legs.

Perhaps Hennie called out for him when he saw Jacob jump down onto the sloping sand hill just over the other side of the embankment, the ball still out of his reach. Jacob was too busy to even think about it, sliding down feet first and then tobogganing over the edge, and in an upright position, falling, descending rapidly into the murky still waters below.

Jacob sank like a rock. He knew he couldn't swim and yet he mused with childish confidence that someone would find him. This wasn't too bad, he thought.

It wasn't until he had come up for air the first time that he realised that breathing was no longer something he could take for granted. No sooner had he taken a breath, he had been pulled under again … the second attempt a little while later, futile.

As he went under again, his eyes were drawn to his left, to an absolute brightness that was alien in the dirty stagnant waters separating him from his next breath. Jacob felt attracted to the light, and as he made his way towards it, he saw a figure standing on the riverbed, luminescent, somehow imbibing Jacob with the same serenity with which the vision was bathed.

Jacob could not discern bodily features clearly but he knew the vision was not a young boy like himself. The facial features were difficult to define but Jacob saw that the 'man' had begun drawing Jacob's attention away from him and in another direction. As the thick tree root came into his view, Jacob knew he had to reach it even though he wasn't aware what he needed to do with it once he had.

But first he needed to breathe and he found himself instinctively going up for air, gasping as he reached the surface, and hearing his father's voice in the distance above him.

"Jacob! Grab the tree roots!" his father yelled. Jacob reached for the roots whose location he now knew, grabbed onto them and began to rise, above the gloomy Vaal that almost became his cold watery grave.

"I have never told anyone this story," Jacob confessed to me as we spoke 51 years after the event had occurred. It was finally time to tell the story of the man with the halo who marked a path for him to safety.

Vaal River, South Africa
Attribution: tadpolefarm – licensed under the Creative Commons Attribution-Share Alike 3.0

37

Angel on the Roof Top

The day he found himself on the rooftop had not gone the way others had. He sat calmly, his legs dangling over the edge just above the balcony that jutted out from the games room on the second floor of his Johannesburg home. The backyard with its swimming pool and charming garden beds certainly looked different from up there. But his eyes remained fixed on the still pool and the figure of the little boy he could see motionless at the bottom of it.

Mark had lived in this double story home all his life, all three years of it. He had never been on the roof before, though. His sister, about 14 years of age, walked out onto the balcony just beneath him and looked out towards the pool. Her pale blonde hair shone in the sun and contrasted awkwardly with her orange knitted jumper.

She suddenly pointed in the direction of the pool and yelled at the top of her lungs. "Dad, Dad quick! The pool!"

Mark knew his sister was worried about the boy at the bottom of the pool. It all seemed, in some strange way, a little surreal. At least the *Presence* next to him made things a little easier. He didn't know how he knew (as he didn't see him), but Mark had a sense that this presence was a guardian angel. He even had a sneaking suspicion that the angel had been responsible for calling the sister out onto the balcony.

They never went out onto the balcony. Why had his sister gone there now?

Mark saw his father run like a cut snake through the open pool gate, dive to the bottom and frantically scoop the boy out of the pool. Mark wondered what his father was doing to the boy's chest after he lay him down on the ground. He pushed down on it really fast and then listened to something near the boy's face. Then he pushed down again and again. More listening.

As time passed on, for his dad kept pushing and listening, Mark knew the angel was next to him. He could feel his true care and strong protection. He sensed that they were just waiting and watching together.

Mark didn't know that the body his father had scooped from the pool was his own. He had forgotten that he had wandered outside not long before, curious about the waters in the pool. Perhaps he had thrown his pacifier in and now sought to retrieve it? He didn't know his father had accidently left the pool gate ajar.

And there are some other things he cannot remember. That he must have been clinically dead for twenty minutes as CPR was ministered first by his father and then by the paramedics. Or that his pulse rate was detected only after they arrived at the hospital. And yet, it took only a day or so for Mark to return to his usual bouncy self.

"Mark, I think God had some serious plans for you," his dad told him later in life. Mark had the distinct impression his father may even have made some serious deal with the Lord that fateful day.

"I have never asked Dad what that was," Mark told me. "I have no other clear memory of my life this early on. *This* memory is crystal clear."

The memory of the angel on a rooftop.

South Africa – Raw Beauty

City of Johannesburg, South Africa

38

The Brush of an Angel's Wing

I have often wondered whether or not I have come inches away from experiencing the metaphorical brush of an angel's wing. What of all those times I have woken up on the freeway having fallen asleep at the wheel, barely seconds away from making contact with a barrier, curb or pole? These have been too many to count and span decades. How many times I have been millimetres away from coming into contact with another vehicle at high speeds, momentarily distracted but fortunately "awakened" at just the right time! On one particular occasion I managed to navigate my way like an earthworm in *trans warp* drive between merging traffic. Somehow, instinctively, I knew just how far to swerve to the right to avoid the car that sat motionless in my lane, growing in size at a troubling rate, but just far enough back left, to avoid colliding with an oncoming car; one still unseen but which I somehow knew was moments away from impact – and all within seconds of the first evasive manoeuvre!

I could claim superior driving skills, but I don't think that would stick! I remained calm through it all and *that* is saying something!

An incident involving Josiah when he was only four months old, brought me a little closer to seeing that angel's wing.

It was the middle of the night, Therese awaking me in a panic, hardly able to get her words out. I knew this couldn't be good news. She had found Josiah lying flat on his back on the bedroom floor, as if thrown from the pram we sometimes used for his sleep. It was inexplicable. Aided by adrenaline I jolted upright and took him in my arms. "Look, he's okay Therese," I said reassuringly after my initial inspection at his beautiful face. The slight red mark at the back of his neck made it clear that his head had come in contact with a part of the pram's frame on the way down.

As I examined him, fearing the worst, he smiled at me. He hadn't even been crying. I almost laughed in intense relief and reassured Therese. "See he's happy. He's okay." But I wondered. How had he first of all slid out when he couldn't roll yet? How had he not been hurt at all and how could he be laying perfectly flat after having fallen from the height of the pram? It was as if someone had thrown him out of it and someone else had broken his fall.

Whatever the cause, Therese and I were understandably grateful. It is clear to me that daily family prayer to one's guardian angels is a non-negotiable. While we cannot expect that our children will be protected from every fall, scratch or slip, we can and should expect that Christ meant what he said about angels in a passage that speaks primarily of the dignity of the child.

"See to it that you do not despise even one of these little ones. For I say to you, that their angels in heaven continually look upon the face of my Father who is in heaven" (Matthew 18:10).

It is difficult for me to reason away the experiences that have been recounted in this chapter. But perhaps I would have been less likely to believe in the ministry of angels if I hadn't already become aware of other such occurrences following my "second" conversion, while still in my teens, in 1989, when I accompanied my parents on a visit to our Aunt Sarina.

My father was driving, and I was in the back seat, reading enthusiastically. We had just crossed over the Narrows Bridge connecting the southern and northern suburbs of Perth.

Without even thinking about praying, I unexpectedly "heard" the following directive in my heart. *Pray for safety!* Whatever one might call it, a word of knowledge, or an inspiration - I immediately complied. My conversion was still quite fresh, and I was beginning to understand it best not to ignore such requests; so, I closed the book and prayed a very short and simple prayer asking the Holy Spirit for protection. And then, satisfied that I had complied with the request, I returned to my reading.

Within a minute the three of us jerked sideways and then back the other way as my father barely missed colliding with the car that had appeared to his right. Who had inspired me? To this day I cannot say for sure. But I remember the word that came to my mind at the end of the experience. *Angel.*

SICILY:
ISLAND OF SAINTS AND WONDERS

⌘

Vos et ipsam Civitatem benedicimus. (I bless you and your city).
- Letter of the Blessed Virgin Mary to the people of Messina, circa 42 A.D.

⌘

39

Ancient Roots

When I took a DNA test in 2018, I was a little surprised just how firmly my racial identity was rooted in Italy. I was declared to be a whopping 88% Italian (including 2% from the Island of Sardegna), with the remaining 12% comprised of a Caucasian and Middle Eastern mix. My sense of racial identity was finally consolidated with some scientific data about which I could boast. No wonder it resonated with me, in a mischievous kind of way of course, the time I came across a group on Facebook entitled, "No one is perfect, but being Italian is close enough!" Every race enjoys claiming superiority at the expense of others and I wouldn't be a good Italo-Australian if I didn't subscribe to being proud of the many things that are peculiar to the Italian culture, or more specifically to the Sicilian one.

One very obvious sign of an Italian - at least for the more traditional type - is a somewhat inordinate appreciation for food and cooking, and yes, the stereotypes are true. Visit a migrant Italian home and when you are offered something to eat or drink, don't even bother saying, '*No, thank you!*' You might even be given more – and then the cup of espresso!

I recall with fondness the extended family gatherings, replete with great food as I was growing up. But the food was just the icing on the cake! Food for Italians means much more than just culinary pleasure. Eating together is a way of life, an event that marks the confident and proud sense of family and story, which migrants in particular worked so hard to build in their new homes across the seas. And the loud noise and joyous music which accompanied large family gatherings such as wedding celebrations where my uncles' band entertained and the rest of us danced, only added to the joyful mosaic. And by the way, at these events and even when we just meet on the street, you will find that we are not actually initiating a fight when you see our eyes widen wildly and our hands cut through the air impulsively. The drama of it all is the best part. The heightened volume and gesticulations only allow us to ensure that enough passion goes into every word that we speak.

I always have a smile on my face when I hear an outsider retelling the story of the Italians down the road who seem to be fighting even if they are just making random comments about the weather. I had to visit my parents' homeland to truly understand my heritage.

The day I disembarked on Italian soil in December 1997, the icy cold wind at the Fiumicino Airport greeted me without any attempt at disguise. As my parents and I paced towards our connecting flight, I enjoyed the melodious sound of the Italian being spoken by a slender dark-haired woman walking in the opposite direction. The words enveloped me, carried in a crisp accent that I innately identified as unadulterated, native and raw. The Italian I heard back home in Australia suddenly seemed vulgar by comparison. The difference was like switching from analogue to digital television for the first time.

Soon we were on our connecting flight to the Island of Sicily, in particular to Naso, my parents' birthplace in the mountains surrounding Messina, on the island's north-eastern tip. It would be my mother's first trip back there in 35 years.

I knew this trip would be somewhat of a culture shock as soon as we entered the dilapidated arrival lounge at Catania airport and cigarette smoke permeated the small building with its stench. It all contributed to the noticeable haze-like ambience. Soon we became acquainted with Sicilian drivers who demonstrated skills that were quite unique – the ability to drive up steep, narrow, winding mountain roads such as the one leading to Naso, navigating the path with an unnatural dexterity that left me wondering whether we would fall off the cliff at each turn. It would not have surprised me had these drivers not indeed been consummate professional daredevils on some racetrack in their youth!

On one of our first day trips to the surrounding towns and villages, I had the humorous experience of our hired red Fiat 127 having to give way to a seemingly endless procession of cows that were sauntering down the street. My little cousin Vittorio, who had joined us with his family, shouted out with youthful exuberance, "Look at the little ones!" He continued watching as the calves passed by, their jingling bells an increasingly loud clang.

And then there was all that food—the mortadella and other cold meats—and also the use of unlicensed fireworks in the backyard on New Year's Eve. The story that tops it all off, however, is the one my uncle told me regarding a fattened pig that was stolen by the Mafia one

Christmas, albeit in another town. Nobody dared complain for fear of retribution.

Over the next few weeks I would come to appreciate the land that is Sicily. It is a living museum of antiquity and breath-taking natural beauty, Christian and Islamic roots, conquest and culture, the calamity of major earthquakes and of the intrigue of peoples as diverse as Greek, Phoenician, Moor or Norman. And this was regardless of whether I stood in the ancient Greek Amphitheatre at the famous tourist town of Taormina or marvelled at the third world conditions of the public toilet at Messina's central train station, which was merely a hole in the ground. I knew that there was more to Sicily then just great food and the iconic Mt Etna. I also realised why my mother always said that the thunderstorms in Perth were nothing compared to those in Sicily!

In a true sense I came to appreciate my own Mediterranean origins while in Sicily. Both my parents had been born in this land, had met and fallen in love there. I recall fondly the romantic vineyard my father showed me, not for the look of it but for the memories it held. It was the sight of their first kiss! In a real sense that first kiss was the beginning of my own story.

I came to care for the two thirds of my father's family that I had never met who gave me an appreciation of my father's heritage. Some of them did indeed have the stereotypically exotic dark Middle Eastern features of a Southern Italian. The difference between them and my mother's side could not have been greater despite their common Sicilian roots. But that had more to do with a more ancient ancestry than the process of natural selection. As my eldest maternal cousin had discovered, my mother's family could "boast" a Viking ancestry; hence the green-blue or hazelnut eyes or fair hair of some relatives, including my mother. Through the story telling of my relatives, from whichever side of the family it came, I began to learn that the musical notes of heritage are more than skin deep. They also play the tune of the spiritual muses. Sicily had indeed been blessed with a deep Christian heritage.

Mosaic of Sicily, Land of Contrast

40

The Cloud of Witnesses

The Sicily of today may well be just as secular as the rest of the Western world. However, the Christian roots of Sicily remain etched in the fibre of the Sicilian people through at least a culturally motivated devotion to the myriad of saints who have graced their shores. These roots still nourish, in varying degrees, those who left their homes and migrated to foreign lands as my relatives did. And they brought more with them to Australia than just cafés, great architecture, "That's Amore," excess hair, the Mediterranean Diet, kisses on both cheeks, the block-size veggie patch, well defined gender roles, multiple cousins all named after your *nonna*, the notion of "third" cousins, the siesta, wedding receptions befitting royalty, ornate white cement homes with the token lion guarding out front, and of course bocce! Indeed, they also brought with them stories of saints, some well-known and others quite obscure, but nevertheless saints who testified to the wonders of faith.

Often, the names of San Cono, Sant'Antonio, San Calogero and Santa Rita were heard while I was growing up. Grandparents, aunts and uncles recalled their protection and intercession with filial devotion. My mother's family considered these saints the strongest bond to their Christian faith.

The ever-enduring Italian processions held in honour of these saints are not always a spiritual experience. Local Aussies might see them as a manifestation of a merely cultural Catholicism that might be cute but, nonetheless, well, simply weird! Attend the St. Anthony procession in the northern Perth suburb of Wanneroo or the Blessing of the Fleet Festival in the port city of Fremantle and you will see that such processions can be, for some, merely an excuse to get together and share the latest stories about the olives they pickled or how many bottles of tomato sauce they managed to produce on the last Tomato Day. (Okay... I admit I may be exaggerating a bit). I could even say that the Sicilian devotion to saints could be considered a contributing factor in the number of ex-Catholics who have joined the Jehovah's Witnesses. The devotion can easily appear as a form of idolatry, even though it isn't.

However, the stories told by my relatives testify to a devotion that is grounded in experience and in deep faith, more than just a fading attachment to a by-gone era.

41

Conon and the Barbarian

My uncle Cono was named after San Cono (Saint Conon), patron saint of Naso. If you visit Naso on September 1st, you will witness the most important of four feast days associated with the Twelfth Century saint. The daylong celebration is comprised of concerts, fireworks, and of course the annual procession. The town is abuzz with devotees, a sea of faces following the route of the saint as he makes his way from the Sixteenth-Century *Church of the Santa Madre* in Piazza Roma towards the *Church of the Madonna della Catena* at the other end of town. Balloons are released and applause resounds through the autumn air as the band plays.

San Cono's Shrine in Naso, Sicily.

The statue of San Cono is carried on the shoulders of twenty men, as shouts of *Na Vuci Viva, Razzii San Cono*, ('*With one living voice we proclaim thank you, Saint Conon*') reverberate along their path. In much the same way as the *Messinesi* (natives of Messina) celebrate the Blessed Virgin Mary's motherly care, each generation of *Nasitani* celebrates the miracles of San Cono, who protected his people from invading Turks in the sixteenth century.

A close look at the statue that is processed through the town tells us the story. The figure of San Cono is black, his face is round, and his eyes are bulging. He holds a cross in his right hand and the Holy Bible in his left. The somewhat unattractive face of the statue is meant to depict the expression the saint took on when he appeared, with gigantic proportions, behind *Belvedere Grande*, from which a magnificent view of the Timeto River can be admired. Frightened by his size and the look on his face, the invading Turkish forces that were making their way towards this mountain town fled in fear, and Naso was spared another invasion.

Miracles abound in my family's oral tradition, because San Cono is not the only saint who has done great things in the town of Naso. How often have I heard the beloved name of St. Anthony who is not even Sicilian! So well-loved is he that his feast day is still celebrated by the Italian community even in places as far away as my own city where many Sicilians migrated after World War Two. In 1960, my uncle witnessed a wonder associated with the saint, a glorious story that has been passed down through the whole Casilli family and into my own.

42

St. Anthony & St. Calogero

Statue of St. Anthony, beloved by Sicilians and Portuguese alike.

Giuseppe Casilli, my maternal uncle (known affectionately by his family as Pippo), was still in Naso and doing what he normally did for any saint's feast day in the town - serving as a saxophonist in the music ensemble that accompanied the procession of Sant'Antonio through the streets. "It happened before my eyes," my uncle recounts. He had played in the band since the age of 16 and continued to do so until he migrated to Australia in 1961. Everyone knew of the middle-aged woman who had an infirm leg and couldn't walk without the aid of a walking stick. My aunt Francesca, the eldest of my mother's siblings, recalls that the lady "was always in bed." Her name was Nina Catilioti.

When St. Anthony's feast day came around that year, the woman made a special request. She asked the parish priest if he could make sure that a small change was made to the path of the procession so that the statue of St. Anthony could be passed by her home. The priest complied. As soon as the woman heard the dulcet tones of the music approaching her home, she felt a distinctive urge to get out of bed, without the aid of her stick, and go outside onto her balcony to see the statue of the saint. "I am not sure if the church of St. Anthony is still there," my Aunt Francesca continued, "but after that miracle, the walking stick was hung up in the church as a reminder of what had taken place." Not surprisingly, the miracle became the talk of the town and has been remembered to this day.

Other patron saints from nearby towns are also well known to the *Nasitani* as instruments of God's favour and protection. It was around 1953 and my uncle Giuseppe was ten years old. My grandmother Calogera was about to leave for a pilgrimage of thanks to the town of San Salvatore di Fitalia, which borders Naso. San Salvatore di Fitalia originates as far back as the Fifth Century BC and is home to a church dedicated to San Calogero, my grandmother's own patron saint. The church, which was inaugurated in 1901, houses some of his relics, and in it stands his late Seventeenth Century statue. It was to this Church that my grandmother made her way, setting out on a hot August morning. Giuseppe was the only one of Calogera's nine children to accompany her.

The five-kilometre stretch from Naso to San Salvatore di Fitalia can now be sojourned by vehicle and would not be taxing for a ten-year-old. However, in 1953 the journey was a little more arduous and took a little longer, being made completely on foot and requiring a different route. No doubt the pristine beauty of the landscape made it all worthwhile, even for a tired little soul. Departing Naso and taking a quick look north, my uncle and grandmother would have gazed upon the spectacular coastline of northern Sicily, which is cushioned by the famous Aeolian Islands that sleep near the coastal town of Capo-D'Orlando. They saw this beautiful vision until their descent of the mountain slopes west of Naso, where they entered a valley. From there, walking beside primordial forests, they made their way to Cagnano, where Calogera and her son replenished their thirst. Not even the many winding roads and sharp turns that met their path, as they continued their climb up the mountains towards Fitalia, minimised the natural beauty of the Nebrodi Mountains with its extensive forests of flowering manna ash and oak trees.

My uncle recalls how tired he was by the time they arrived at the church, about two hours after leaving home. But it wasn't too long a trip for Calogera, who had to make her thanks for all the graces received through the intercession of San Calogero. She made her way through the city streets, arriving at the Church of San Calogero in the town square.

Giuseppe was captivated by the grandeur of the church and observed his mother closely as they beheld the statue of the saint. But he noted that this saint's statue was black, like the statue of San Cono. My grandmother then genuflected before the altar, prayed silently, and promptly returned to her son, who was wondering what would happen next.

"Let's go, Pippo," she said matter-of-factly.

"What? Are we going home after all that? Why did we come here? Just to see this black man's face?" balked my uncle belligerently. His mother didn't reply but promptly set out once more with her child to face the scorching sun for another two-hour journey home.

Their return trip via the town of Patti was routine except for one event. As ten-year-olds do when they are not so happy, Giuseppe went ahead of his mother in protest, heading down the road that overlooked a cliff face that reached down to another winding road below. He remembers looking back at his mother, who by now was at a distance. He checked his backpack and then, walking around a bend, tripped and toppled down the cliff. My grandmother watched in horror as she rushed towards her young son.

Like the mythical cat that rights itself after being thrown from a deathly height, my uncle landed on his feet without as much as a scratch. Looking up at his mother, he could see the agony on her face and her hands tearing at her hair as she looked on helplessly at what could have been the last moments of her son's life. To this day San Calogero's intercession is claimed as the cause of my uncle's good fortune.

Giuseppe Casilli learnt a very important lesson that day: The power of a saint rests not in the simplicity of his statue but in the mercy of God. It also rests on a personal relationship with these spiritual brothers and sisters of ours who have gone before us and who form the *cloud of witnesses* before the throne of God. And, as my grandfather Salvatore discovered, sometimes these witnesses make their presence felt in even more tangible ways.

Giuseppe, with parents in 1956
(Above) Some years after his near-death descent!

(Above) With his own growing family, two brothers Carmelo
and Cono, and my grandparents (circa 1970)

43

St. Rita and the Police Officer

Growing up, I often heard of Santa Rita, whose incorrupt body can still be viewed in a town called Cascia in central Italy. Salvatore was well known for his devotion to her especially after her intercession in the years between the World Wars. It came as no surprise that a statue of St. Rita came to adorn my grandfather's tombstone after his death. He had good reason not to hide his affection for the saint.

The Sicily of the 1930s was an impoverished land. Various fascist policies at the time were not effective in helping Sicily get rid of social problems, and poverty and illiteracy were common. My grandfather had been a police officer for a time but now found himself earning a living as a hired servant, doing whatever work he could get, including picking the fruit from olive and lemon trees. He did what he could to ensure that his wife and three small children at the time—Calogero, Francesca, and Caterina—kept a roof over their heads, in their rented two-bedroom home with its very small kitchen.

It was the winter of 1937 when my grandfather became ill with pneumonia. My Aunt Caterina was six years old at the time. "We called the doctor to our home, but he gave us no hope," she told me. She watched her father sweating profusely and spouting mostly gibberish in his fevered state. But then they saw him sit up in bed with his eyes looking towards the foot of the bed. "It's St. Rita," he proclaimed as he stretched out his arms as if to grab someone. He then fell back asleep.

When he awoke the next morning from what must have seemed to my grandmother an endless sleep, my *nonno* amazed everyone. He had fully recovered, and he told his family what had happened.

"During the night St. Rita appeared to me wearing her black habit. She stood at my side, on the left side of the bed, and tenderly touched me on the forehead." My grandfather continued, leaving his children spellbound.

"Without saying anything at first, she moved to the right side of my bed, again placing her hand on my forehead. And then she spoke: 'Are you sad that you will die?' she asked me. I said, 'No, except I don't want to leave my wife and three small children.' St. Rita then walked around to the other side of the bed again and told me not to be afraid, that I would be okay in the morning and that I would get up and go to work. But she had a request too and said, 'Have a large candle in my honour placed in the church near the main altar.'" No doubt this was a way for all the townsfolk to remember the amazing grace that had been bestowed on my grandfather through the intercession of the *Beata*.

Salvatore walked through the cobble stoned streets to pass on this request to Monsignor Portale, the parish priest. He told him what had happened, and the priest believed my grandfather and proclaimed it to all the people. However, he asked for money to be pledged to the Church instead of being spent on a tall candle. "If St. Rita wants me to donate money, she will come to me again and tell me," replied Salvatore. The saint did indeed come to him again in his dreams, but she made no mention of it. Instead she asked him to carry an image of her on a holy card under his beret and to keep a medal with her image on a necklace and on a bracelet. My grandfather faithfully complied, but little did he know that St. Rita had another favour in store for Salvatore's family. This time it was for his firstborn son.

My grandfather Salvatore Casilli, in his younger years as a "carabinieri" police officer (left) and circa 1940 (right).

My maternal grandparents, aunts and uncles.
My Uncle Calogero is absent from the photo. Francesca is
the second from the right and Caterina is on the far left.
Circa 1975, Perth, Western Australia.

44

St. Rita and the Necklace

I have few memories of my Uncle Calogero, not surprisingly also named after his mother's patron saint. I remember visiting his modest home in the 70s. The front door was reached after a short flight of stairs and a landing that was probably not as large as it appeared to me at the age of five. His gentleness is what I feel the most.

"Renato, I have something to tell you," my mother said the day of my uncle's death. The words rolled out gently, sensitively as she sat next to me in bed. It must have been a bright sunny day if the light shining through the white-laced curtain that draped down my wall was any indication. My uncle had finally succumbed to asbestosis, as many had, as a result of corporate ignorance about the dangers of asbestos. When I learned about the graces he had received as a young man in Sicily, I was grateful that my uncle's sickness and death would no longer be the only memories associated with him.

By 1946, Calogero had met the love of his life, a tall and slender woman by the name of Sarina who came from a nearby village called *La Rocca*. Calogero wanted to make a good impression on his fiancée but could not afford expensive jewellery. He asked his father, "Dad, may I borrow your gold necklace with the medal of St. Rita?" My grandfather obliged and Calogero wore it proudly on his date, after which he went fishing with his friends at San Gregorio.

The weather soon became turbulent. With a storm raging, the small boat was tossed about like a plastic cup brushed by the wheel of a speeding car on a highway. It mercilessly threw everyone overboard, including my uncle who could not swim. Whereas swimming skills managed to keep his friends from drowning, a necklace with a medal of St. Rita on it managed to do the same for Calogero. The necklace had conveniently draped itself around the boat's pointed bow and kept my uncle afloat until his friends, all of whom made it back to the boat safely, collected him.

Sicily is indeed a land that has had a tumultuous and fractured past, having been invaded by foreign powers and being prone to natural disasters. But as my family has experienced, it is also a land that has been favoured with graces flowing to those humble people who call out for help with an undying faith. In Catholic theology, the saints do not in any way replace God. Some Protestants may still believe that Catholics worship saints, but this is simply not true. The saints are not mediators with God in the way that Christ is, but they do intercede for their brothers and sisters in Christ who are still fighting the good fight this side of Heaven. This is especially true for one particular saint - the Queen of all Saints.

ALL SHALL CALL HER BLESSED

⌘

For he has looked with favour on the humility of his handmaid.
For behold, from this time, all generations shall call me blessed.
For he who is great has done great things for me, and holy is his name.
- Luke 1:48-49

⌘

45

The Madonna

Images have a way of speaking to the heart as we all know, especially when they represent a woman whose impact on the earth has been tremendous; a woman who is not God and yet Mother of God, who is not an Angel and yet Queen of the Angels, and who is a member of the same fallen human race and yet not subject to original sin, saved, as the Catholic Church teaches, from the moment of her own conception.

Posted all over the world, in the aftermath of Hurricane Sandy some years back now, were photos of one such image that came to be known as the *Breezy Point Madonna*. For New Yorkers who experienced the harrowing onslaught of the devastating hurricane, the statue of Mary that survived the flooding and fire that left only the foundation of homes intact in Queens, became a place of pilgrimage. It had become a symbol of hope.

Of course, it is not the image as much as the person behind the image that resonates with millions of Catholics around the world. It may surprise some to know that this devotion is not limited to Catholics or Orthodox Christians. I was intrigued some years ago to discover a book by Dee Jepsen - *Jesus Called Her Mother* - in which the author posed the question, "If we can find Jesus in other people, why can't we find him in Mary?" Or again, I felt much joy when Protestant Pastor Todd Burpo admitted to his Catholic friends that his son Colton, famous for his visit to Heaven as recounted in *Heaven is for Real*, saw Mary standing near Jesus or kneeling before God's throne. (And if you don't believe me, check out the book).

Mary's impact has been felt throughout the world. But, as with Sts. Rita, Anthony, Conon and Calogero, Mary has a special connection to the birthplace of my parents, and so it is back to the Island of Sicily where I begin my search for the myriad of ways the Madonna's affection for God's people has been manifested.

Sicily's history is replete with miracles and wonders wrought through the Madonna. There is the story of the Black Madonna, for instance, a statue of Byzantine origin encased in a glass cubicle, elevated by two winged angels behind the altar in the Shrine at Tindari. This tiny statue had ended up on the shores of Sicily escorted by sailors escaping the iconoclastic movement occurring in the East at the time. Local legend states that the sailors were forced to enter the bay at Tindari due to a storm and were unable to set off again until they had offloaded the sacred cargo into the care of the friars at the local abbey. The Madonna, it would appear, didn't want to leave.

So, it was not surprising that our sojourn in Sicily in 1998 included a trip to this famous shrine at Tindari, about 22 kilometres east of Naso in rural Messina. As the following conversation shows, however, our walk from the car park to the actual Shrine was less than heavenly focused as we traversed an ancient ruin adjacent to the Shrine.

"Maria what do you wish to say?" I teased my Zia, or aunt, in a simulated tone of command directing the bulky old-school style camera on her as she stood near my bemused mother. She stared at me blankly while my uncle Decimo encouraged her facetiously.

"Maria, please tell him a little word or two, won't you?"

As she stared at my uncle blankly - or perhaps it was patiently - she waited for the interrogation to end. I decided I would fill in the expected response for the camera.

"Not a word, right, Zia? Not a word! You tell him now!"

My aunt laughed and gesticulated the expected response (a forearm quickly shot up into the air with flair) on cue as we had rehearsed many times already, aiming it at the camera.

"Not a word!" she repeated emphatically. "Not a word!"

My uncle, of course, had not finished. For an Italian his larrikinism was endearing.

"Just look at how handsome I am," he preened looking directly into the lens. "I am indeed beautiful!" He was unrelenting, oblivious to the lack of response on my part or the ridicule of his wife, which he knew, was forthcoming. They had no children of their own and over the years this fact had strengthened their own soul bond and no doubt their tolerance for each other.

"Where *exactly* are you beautiful?"

"So beautiful," he continued unabated as she struck him on the arm, and I chuckled softly.

The banter over, my uncle and aunt finally led us to the entrance of the Tindari shrine. Staring up at the edifice of the Church was all that was necessary in order to understand the significance that this shrine has for the Sicilian people. The following phrase is etched in gold above the ornate masonry, which arches over the windows on the facade of the Church: *Tutto è poco per Te O Madre,* which can be translated as, *Nothing is too much for you, O Mother!*

I was struck by the ornate beauty of the church's interior, resembling a midway point between Heaven and earth. Time and timelessness seemed to merge briefly, and I lapped it all up as I filmed each moment with the same bulky video camera that I carried around like a rock around my neck. Some type of precious metal, stained glass window, statue, mosaic or inscription covered each inch of the building.

Great columns that held the massive structure in place patrolled the walkways as tourists and pilgrims shuffled past. The walls were tiled with carefully crafted mosaics of each mystery of the Rosary. I stood in admiration of the depiction of Jesus' *Agony in the Garden* with its focus on the angel who appeared and comforted Jesus before he drank his cup of suffering. The grandeur did not end at the height of the walls, though. Latin titles for Mary, *Virgo Potens* and *Virgo Clemens,* again etched in gold and flanked by images of angels, greeted my tilted camera lens as I inspected the cornices above the pews and sanctuary. And just as the words of Christ to Peter circle the lip of the dome floating above the sanctuary in St. Peter's Basilica in Rome, so too do the words of the *Hail Mary* at Tindari.

As the story of Tindari demonstrates, one could say that the Blessed Virgin Mary adopted the Sicilian people as her own. But more stories reveal that this adoption occurred a long time before the statue arrived, dating back to the First Century while the Blessed Virgin still walked the earth.

According to tradition, the apostle Paul introduced the Christian gospel to the people of Messina while *en-route* to Rome, barely ten years after the death of Christ. Inspired by the message of Christianity, the *Messinesi* were ecstatic to discover that the Mother of the Saviour was still living in Jerusalem. They asked for word to be sent to her, asking for her blessing, and the Madonna obliged by writing a letter, around the year 42AD. The letter is commemorated by a magnificent golden statue known as the *Madonna della Lettera* perched atop a majestic 20-foot column on the San Salvatore fort tower just off the shore in the Strait of Messina. (Historically, this is feasible, although not recorded in scripture, as Paul may well have sailed through Messina on route to Rome after being shipwrecked in Malta).

Climbing one of the hills of Messina I soaked up the visual delights of the port, with its vibrant blue waters that once lapped the hull of the ship carrying my parents' tear filled *addio* across the world to Australia. The mountainous terrain of Calabria saluted me from across the harbour, and the *modern* non-cobbled streets, limestone buildings and clay-tiled roofs of Messina itself formed a colourful kaleidoscope, courtesy, ironically, of the rebuilding of the city after the cataclysmic 1908 Messina earthquake.

Wall size mosaic in the Shrine at Tindari, Sicily.

My mischievous Uncle Decimo and his wife Maria, in between my father and mother outside the Shrine.

The Madonna della Lettera statue in the Strait of Messina – up close and in the distance.
Below: My parents and I overlooking the Strait from which my parents originally set on their voyage to Australia.

On this hill I came across the Church and Shrine of the *Madonna di Montalto*. A plaque on its façade tells of another story of the Madonna's motherly care for the *Messinesi* on a particular occasion in 1282 during a war with the French.

Nel 1282 durante la Guerra del Vespro sopra questo Colle della Capperrino apparve la Madonna che in sembianza di dama vestita di bianco copriva di veli le mura della città a difesa dei Messinesi.

In translation it reads, *"In 1282 during the Vespers War on this Capperino Hill, the Madonna appeared resembling a dame dressed in white, who covered the city walls with her mantle, in defence of the people of Messina."*

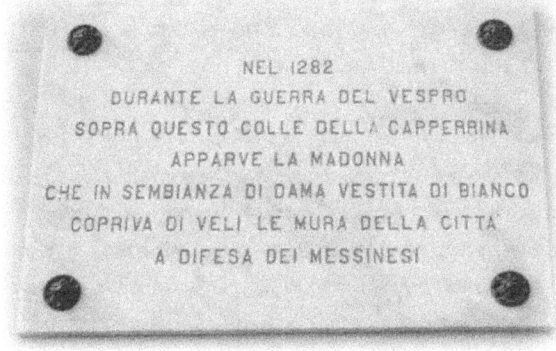

These stories situated in the land of my parents' birth, naturally encouraged devotion for the Blessed Virgin Mary. However, my love of Mary, as the spiritual mother of all of God's children united in Christ, is not of cultural origin. It has its origins the very same day as my conversion when the blond-haired middle-aged woman you have already been introduced to briefly, walked into my Year 8 Religious Education classroom as our guest speaker for the day.

46

Roma

Roma Martino shared her conversion story with my fellow classmates in 1984. It was not just the story of Jesus' love that Roma shared, it was also that of Mary's love for her, who led her to Jesus.

As Roma spoke of her conversion through the love and intercession of Mary my heart was filled with the knowledge that Christ's words on the cross, to his disciple John, were also true for me. "Behold your mother" (John 19:27). The story behind Roma's own meeting with Christ, through the woman she came to know as her own Blessed Mother, is best retold in Roma's own words.

Although my parents were Catholic, and although I was baptised, they never practised their faith. God or religion was never mentioned in our home, except on very rare occasions when my father's friends from the old country, Yugoslavia (now Croatia), would visit, and the conversation would sometimes turn into gossip about a priest and his housekeeper. They had no respect for priests and just could not understand or accept that a man could remain celibate.

I attended a State school, and once a month a priest would visit the Catholic children, teaching us our prayers and preparing us for our First Holy Communion and later Confirmation. They were the only two times that I had set foot in a church.

During my teens I became friendly with a Catholic boy and spent quite a lot of time with his family who were very devout. They prayed the family rosary every evening. I was not impressed! I hadn't a clue about this rosary business. The mother gave me a rosary and a little booklet on the rosary. I learned to say it, hoping to make a good impression on my boyfriend.

Several years later, I met and married my husband who became a practising Catholic. After our marriage, I turned away from God, and he ceased receiving the Sacraments. In 1969, our marriage was going through a bad time. We had four children, the youngest was a one-year-old, and I had become an alcoholic. I had always been a nervous, highly-strung person, even as a child, owing to the fact that my father had been an alcoholic. We owned a vineyard and he made his own wine. Many a time my mother would let the wine out of the barrels, which drove my father crazy, and grabbing his rifle he threatened to kill us. We'd have to run down the vines and hide for many hours in the night.

I had begun taking pills for my nerves at the age of 14. In 1968, I was taking 6 Librium and 6 Laroxyl per day, plus the alcohol. I was a complete mess. It was a miracle that I had survived. Towards the end of 1968, I spent a few weeks in the Mount Hospital, Perth, (Australia) recovering from a nervous breakdown.

My health or marriage did not improve. One night towards mid-1969, my husband told me that he could not stand it anymore and, if I didn't try to change my ways, he would leave and take the children. I felt so helpless, hopeless and useless. That night, lying in bed, I remembered Our Lady and the rosary of years gone by. I can recall saying that if she really existed to help me, because I didn't know where to turn. I could not help myself.

An unknown lady

Meanwhile, my husband had turned back to God, and had started going to Mass on Sundays. He also began a novena to St. Anthony by attending Mass on Tuesday mornings at another parish named after that Saint.

Several weeks into this novena, he awoke very early this Saturday morning. He then woke me, saying that he couldn't get back to sleep, and had this great urge to attend Mass at St. Anthony's that morning, but could not explain why. I, personally, thought he had lost his marbles and told him so. Regardless of my opinion he went. After the conclusion of Mass, a lady unknown to my husband approached him and said that he needed help, that his wife was ill, and that the Blessed Virgin would help! Then she handed him a leaflet on the Apparitions of Garabandal.

My husband was quite astounded by the whole thing and was afraid to tell me about the episode when he returned home from his business, for fear of an argument and ridicule. But that evening, God gave him the courage to tell me what had happened that morning, showing me the Garabandal leaflet. I can remember reading it, saying that maybe it could be true that Our Lady had appeared to four girls, but that did not interest or concern me! After much difficulty he eventually persuaded me to say at least one decade of the rosary with him. It ended up being five decades.

My condition still remained the same, except now, I was experiencing violent headaches and I couldn't get this Garabandal thing out of my mind. It never left me in peace. I also kept thinking about that unknown lady who seemed to know about our personal lives - that really irritated me!

My husband continued with his Tuesday Masses. After about two weeks of these violent headaches I decided to ask him if this strange lady attended Mass. She *did! I was determined to get to the bottom of all this and asked my husband to get her name and address. Several more weeks passed by. I decided it was time to visit this woman. When I arrived on her doorstep, I felt rather foolish. What would I say? But when this stranger answered the door, she immediately said that she had been expecting me!*

I was completely taken aback. I could not understand any of this! The lady said that she knew it was my husband to whom she had given the Garabandal leaflet. She explained that, after she had attended the Tuesday Mass for a few weeks, on this particular Tuesday when the priest approached my husband to give him Holy Communion, Our Lady told her that my husband needed help, that his wife was ill, and that she was to give him the Garabandal leaflet and all would be well!

She always carried a leaflet in her bag, and intended to approach my husband after Mass, but he had rushed out before the Mass had ended. Then Our Lady told the woman that this man would be back on "Saturday morning", the morning when he awoke so early!

I was even more bothered and bewildered. I knew and understood nothing about religion. I was utterly confused!

A piece of kissed Missal

I found myself going back to see this lady again and again. Each time I received more knowledge about the Catholic religion, she even told me about Padre Pio. I couldn't grasp anything at the time about his stigmata!

On one of my visits she gave me a piece of Missal from Mari-Loli's prayer book that had been kissed by Our Lady at Garabandal. I didn't understand when she explained that this relic had cured sick people, that I was to buy a locket, place this bit of paper therein and wear it around my neck. Rather strange I thought!

At this time our one-year old child had a very bad infection on the palm of his hand, being red, swollen and full of pus. The doctor had been treating him with antibiotics, but without success. He advised me to take Neville to Princess Margaret Hospital for children.

When I arrived home with this piece of paper, the Garabandal "relic", my husband suggested that we place it on our son's hand and ask Our Lady to cure the infection. I thought it was ridiculous, what could a bit of paper do for our child? But my husband insisted, and we said three Hail Marys.

The next morning, while preparing the table for breakfast in the dinette, I suddenly noticed our young son, standing in the lounge room looking up at a statue of Our Lady that my husband had recently purchased. I could not understand why Neville was standing there, smiling up at *Our Lady*. Then I remembered his hand and the relic. I rushed over to him. I was quite shocked to discover that all the redness, swelling and pus had completely disappeared. In fact, his hand looked quite normal except for a piece of dried scab that I removed, revealing a small scar. That scar remained for many months. After that day the "little piece of paper" took on a new and special meaning for me. I purchased a locket and chain and placed the relic therein. I am still wearing it to this day.

My life began to change. I wanted to know more about my Catholic religion. I received instruction from a Franciscan priest. I was amazed to learn that Jesus was present in the Blessed Sacrament, also about Heaven and Hell, the Angels and the devil, and especially about Mary. I began to pray every day, eventually receiving the Sacraments and attending daily Holy Mass.

I still wanted to have a drink, but it just would not go down my throat. The 12 nerve pills per day became a thing of the past! I don't remember exact dates nor exact numbers of weeks. I only remember that my conversion and cure occurred after July 1969, and that it was over a period of 6 - 8 weeks.

God is so merciful and good, and I cannot express in words what Our Blessed Mother means to me.

47

The Scandal of Mary

Perhaps no practice in the Catholic Church is as clear an indicator of the division that exists within our own ranks, let alone in our relationship with other Christians, than devotion to the Blessed Virgin Mary. For some it may even be a stronger force than the scandal of the Protestant Reformation, the Enlightenment, Darwinian Evolutionary science, two world wars, the sexual revolution, the errors of Communism, clerical paedophilia, hedonism, atheism, the unsustainability of a cultural Catholicism or simply a crisis of faith. And even when staunch anti-Catholics begin thinking of *crossing the Tiber* and coming into full communion with the Catholic Church, difficulties with Marian devotion is usually one of the last strongholds of resistance. It takes a while for the false idea that Catholics worship Mary to be finally exposed as indeed false.

When I heard the testimony of Dr Scott Hahn, famously known in Catholic circles for his conversion story, it was once again Mary who posed a major stumbling block.

Hahn's testimony regarding his final acceptance of Mary as his spiritual mother had, until my mother's death, only been something I appreciated intellectually. But after her death, waiting patiently at a set of traffic lights, and lost in thought, I reflected on how I wanted to tell people all about my mother; how kind she was and how she always put others first. I literally wanted to *glorify* her and highlight her generosity, love and goodness to all. It all made sense then, what Hahn meant, when he spoke of it being only natural that a son should want to glorify his mother. We only glorify Christ's mother in imitation of Christ who glorified her first.

Personally, I could not fathom having written this book without somehow highlighting the role that this special woman has played in my spiritual life. Her motherly love is pivotal to my pre-conversion at the age of twelve, (and then my conversion, properly speaking, at age fifteen), through the prayers of Roma, who always included me in her Rosary. It is the Mother of Jesus who keeps calling me back to her Son, especially through times of struggle. How often have I returned to the Lord on days especially dedicated to her after somewhat losing my way or doubting my devotion for her? How many times I have felt her motherly mantle spread across the anguish of my life, when at Lourdes, Medjugorje, Fatima or when praying the Rosary, although I struggle even now with this prayer.

In 1998, it was in Lourdes, France, a major shrine of the Blessed Virgin Mary, where I obtained my own little miracle for my ailing mother, after telling my parents that I would only go to Europe with them for our family trip if a visit to Lourdes was included in the itinerary. My mother had been away from the Sacrament of Reconciliation for many years and I had been praying that she would gain the courage to go. So, when I saw my mother making her way to the confessional at Lourdes, my heart thrilled. Should I have been surprised? This was, after all, the town in the Pyrenees where the Mother of God herself had descended from Heaven to appear to a peasant girl named Bernadette. It was there that Mary led Bernadette to a miraculous underground spring that has reminded the world of the transforming waters of baptism. It has been the catalyst for countless graces since 1858. Seeing my mother go to confession there was indeed *my* miracle. It would be her last time as well.

With my mother, in Lourdes, January 1998

INTERLUDE

Blog: Conversation with an Agnostic

Some time ago I became entrenched in an interesting dialogue with an agnostic/atheist Facebook friend after I had posted a link regarding a mystical phenomenon of some sort – I think it may have been a cure at Lourdes or some other healing or inexplicable occurrence. Doubts were quickly expressed by my friend and some others about the reliability of a "miraculous" and "inexplicable" explanation for the phenomenon.

The discussion that ensued was very enlightening and a catalyst for further thought. The response from my friend, let me call him "Anthony," reminded me of why I used to enjoy sparring with him in the past. Anthony is honest; honest about his convictions and about his love for science and the wonder of the human body and mind. His scepticism about matters of faith is borne not from following the crowd but from a genuine desire to not accept what he would consider akin to fable. He told me that it would be honest for one, when faced with so called "mystical occurrences", to adopt an agnostic attitude of "I don't know" instead of "well it must be God then." He asked for the evidence, without which, he claimed, there could be no logical support for God being the cause.

I could see what he was saying and to a great extent I would agree. Believers can all too easily claim God to be the cause of an event without necessarily thinking through the validity of their claims. I guess that's why Catholics accept that the Magisterium is ultimately responsible for discerning truth in these matters. However, the more I read the more I wondered if his bias for scientific truth prevented him from seeing any other source of reality as valid. It seemed that for Anthony, as for famous atheists like Dawkins, only "evidence-based, logical analysis of our world" will do. Why? Because the system we base our life on is that of "physical processes," he said.

I do not think intellectual honesty is only the domain of a scientific naturalist. While a non-Christian or a seeker of truth will express their open mindedness by saying "I don't know and I can keep exploring,"

I believe that a person of faith can still unashamedly claim God as the source of a supposed miracle, when the "baffling event"(or miracle) has occurred within the context of a faith experience and when it is attested to by multiple sources. When more than one source, and in fact many, from different periods of the world's history and in various continents, all profess the same experience, then it should make one sit up and wonder.

Throughout history, amazing deeds have been worked in the "Name of Jesus." Since the agents of scientific rigour have absolutely no wisdom to bring to the table in such an event, then which is it more logical to assert – that the miracle has come by chance or that it has come by the one in whose name the miracle was invoked?

But ultimately, I do not think one can win arguments through logic. The older I get the more I realise that a phenomenological approach to truth and reality has the greater merit; namely that of appreciating the value of subjective human experience - and the desires and truth that spring from deep inside this experience.

Let me explain! The reality is that even though the scientific naturalist will only see only physical processes as being a valid window into our life experience, the reality is that the human heart says something else.

Can you imagine telling a medical doctor, for instance, that their only job is to provide a summary of the physical processes that have led to the condition of their patient? Will you just examine your patient, diagnose as best you can and then sign a script? Now, if this is the approach that doctors have towards their patients, don't we soon note that there is a problem? No, a good doctor brings more to the table than their scientific knowledge. What he brings is a truth which attests to ethical, spiritual and experiential realities that remain standing long after the yardstick of "scientific rigour" has been tested against them; knowledge of the innate dignity of his patient, of the need for compassion and respect, for instance.

Or again, can you imagine a father telling his son that the reason he loves him is because of the hormones that force him to, which have come from random evolutionary processes, and which somehow are initiated even when the son is a right-out loser and the father would be better off without him? I don't think that would go down too well. I do not think it reflects human experience at all. Human experience says that at the heart of our moral and ethical sensitivities is a spiritual core that cannot be explained by "physical processes."

Once an atheist accepts that a logical analysis of our reality is not the only window into our world then their world can truly open up. This was what blogger, ex-atheist and 22-year-old Yale graduate Leah Libresco discovered in 2012. It was the study of "Truth" itself which was her window. It was not long before moral truth became self-evident to her – in fact it was after a Yale alumni debate during which the penny dropped. It would appear that the connection between the moral law and humanity just simply did not compute through logical analysis alone. A higher truth was at play.

For Christians this higher Truth is none other than a person: Jesus Christ. In him alone does any of this reality we call human life mean anything.

PART THREE

"I will establish My covenant
between Me and you
and your descendants
after you"

(Genesis 17:7)

INTRODUCTION TO PART THREE

The pre-Christmas school holidays in 1987, began like those of the previous few years. I would awake, bitter and alone, hating my life, disconnected from my family and with hardly any friends. Growing up had been unkind to me. So had the first few years of high school generally. I had abandoned my Catholic faith for about two years – it frankly felt too hard to live by while I navigated the murky waters of adolescence, isolation, rebellion and health issues that saw my weight plummeting about 30 kilograms until the fat little 10-year-old had become a stick of a figure. The crisis had affected my schooling; I failed Eleventh Grade and didn't really care until it was too late to do anything about it.

It would have been hard for those who knew me to imagine that the boy who had once almost become Head Boy of his primary school had now become anything but a model student. At least some sense began to return to me by about October of 1987 when I decided that I would repeat Eleventh grade in another school. Since I had started school at the age of 5, I was a grade ahead anyway, so it didn't really matter, I thought.

I was beginning to remember the power of hope. And another intuition, like a shooting star from a distant galaxy, began to cross the trajectory my memory was taking me on. "I know what I need," I told the school counsellor with confidence when I met him before leaving school. "I need to pray", I said. Ironically, the Catholic school counsellor basically discounted my solution, but not to the detriment of my confidence which remained as I left his office. There was a way out of the mess. I could find my way again.

Then, not long before Christmas, something greater than hope literally changed me overnight. One morning, a few weeks shy of my 16th birthday, I simply felt a peace and joy I had not experienced in years. Far from hating the world, I now loved it. Instead of hating myself, I found much to love. And, over the next month my greatest joy was spending time with my sister and her family who had come to Perth for Christmas, playing with my 9-month-old nephew, and returning to the Sacrament of Reconciliation. I still remember the priest's joy when I returned to God after the two years that had passed since my last confession.

For the following 9 months, God's presence continued to fill my life. I was a 16-year-old boy and I felt like I was floating on clouds every night as I meditated on spiritual readings and felt Christ's presence. And for a while, the source of my sudden return to God had been a mystery, until I finally got through to Roma Martino once again and she told me that she had not stopped praying for me, even for a single day, since meeting me 3 years earlier.

"Those 9 months were like being reborn," another saintly and elderly friend told me some years later when I shared my conversion story with her one Sunday night after a prayer meeting. Those 9 months of joy were like the 9-month gestation of an unborn child, she told me, smiling. And when I reflected on the meaning of my name, Renato, which in Italian means "Reborn", I knew my friend Anne-Marie was on to something. I had been given a rebirth – a second chance to respond to the graces I had first received in that Year 8 Religious Education classroom, and which I had walked away from like a Prodigal Son for a while.

For over 30 years since my conversion, I could safely say that my immediate post-conversion experience of spiritual joy and of God's tangible presence and love, would never be repeated. In fact, the 9 months of being reborn, was a honeymoon period. I was a new-born child being led by the hand, assured of God's loving presence and sharing my new-found joy with many whom I met, oblivious to how crazy I may have sounded. Good news naturally begs spreading!

The honeymoon was soon replaced by a much longer period, however, when my faith began to undergo a process of purification. There have certainly been times of joy since then, but more commonly there have been times of testing, as with all who claim to be followers of Christ. Together with my brothers and sisters in Christ, I too have had to carry my cross, trust with a blind-yet-tested faith, and continue to fight the good fight with all the spiritual weapons at my disposal; even when the Lord removed his presence and gave me the opportunity to prove my fidelity – not because of the tangible graces he might give me, but rather in spite of their apparent absence and simply out of love and obedience.

In those darker moments, such as the death of my mother, the same pattern of God's fidelity and unfathomable mercy emerged. While, like to the apostle Thomas I would hear Christ say to me, "blessed are they who believe without seeing" (John 20:29), I would, also like the apostle Thomas, receive the signs that make this pure faith much easier to attain, and, in the long term, easier to understand.

THE PROMISE

⌘

And after this, it will happen that I will pour out my spirit upon all flesh, and your sons and daughters will prophesy; your elders will dream dreams, and your youths will see visions.
- Joel 2:28

⌘

48

Mystery Unveiling

Standing guard before the monstrance, the silent candles flickered warmly. I sat in the Adoration Chapel of Sacred Heart, a Nineteenth-Century gothic church that my family had made its parish. The surrounding night quiet was an oasis in the desert I traversed that day. My sixty-two-year-old mother was buried, and I dared for the peace I could not find.

Images of the funeral were wild children needing taming. It was a day of contradictions, of raw emotion. Friends and family gathered together, the black of their funeral attire set against the native green of the cemetery lawn. Tear-streaked faces and heartfelt embraces had softened the anguish of seeing the deliberately ornate oak casket lowered into that deep hole in the ground. None of it made sense. It was Easter Tuesday, a day that celebrates the resurrection of the body, not its interment. That hole was such an unsuitable resting place for a woman who had loved me, her youngest child, unconditionally, for thirty-one years.

The moving tones of Andrea Boccelli's *The Prayer* gently swept over the crowd of mourners as my siblings and I comforted our father. By then, my own well of tears had dried up, shed bitterly during the requiem Mass. I had made it through the hymn I had sung in my mother's honour, when, with the last note barely out of my mouth, I had fallen to my seat and sobbed like a child. My mission to comfort those present and remind them that only a thin veil separated us from this much-loved woman, was finally over.

I no longer remember how long I remained in the chapel. But I do remember when *it* happened—the moment it all started making some sense.

Kneeling in prayer I decided to read a passage from an ancient sacred text. I read from the Book of Isaiah. Only a day before my mother's death, a friend had asked me to read it. As I read the opening verses, my eyes began to dance. The proverbial penny dropped - and my jaw followed suit.

Incredulous at the significance of what my eyes fell upon, I savoured the sweetness of it all. There in black and white was my message from

Heaven, the answer to a prayer and the unveiling of a mystery hidden in a cryptic dream two nights before my mother's death. That evening in the chapel, the Lord finally joined the missing pieces of the puzzle and revealed the bittersweet meaning of the fateful event that had begun five days earlier.

It was a beautiful autumn morning when three best friends set out for their morning walk. Gianna, Sarina, and Grace, my mother, visited Perth's historic Hyde Park once again, just as they did each day. With its swaying branches of Moreton Bay fig trees and Jacaranda giants, winding paths and rising lawns, landscaped gardens and gorgeous glades, Hyde Park still appears somewhat out of place in the inner-city suburb of Highgate where it delights its visitors. Its magical setting seems more reminiscent of a land inhabited by Tolkien's hobbits than a modern inner-city hub—excepting, of course, the relatively new water playground constructed for twenty-first-century families.

The park had once been more a paddock than a lovely landscaped garden, like the ones developed in Eighteenth-Century England. Though surrounded by a combination of colonial-style homes, Italian homes built in the Seventies, and Twenty-First-Century apartment buildings that sprang up during the area's demographic renaissance, the park retains its anachronistic old elegance and natural charm.

On Holy Thursday morning, April 17, 2003, Hyde Park once again welcomed the three migrant women as they came together for their weekday morning rendezvous.

Migrant family life bonded these three women. I had often driven past them on my way to work, beeping the horn as they waved back at me, diminishing in view as I drove on. They greeted familiar faces as they circled the two central groundwater lakes shaded by the drooping leaves of the plane trees. Chatting and laughing while they warmly greeted fellow fitness enthusiasts, they may have noticed the coots and black swans, or possibly other *early birds* of the humankind, executing their fitness regimen. The three women completed their walk in the park via the path on the northern hill towards Vincent Street, passing the quaint gazebo on their right. To their left, the rising lawn and the majestic trunks of the fig trees, blanketed with verdant undergrowth, rose almost all the way to the edge of the street beyond the glade.

On her steady ascent to the gazebo, my mother suddenly stopped. "I'm feeling very tired," she uttered. Sarina could tell that something was not right. "Let's rest a while," she suggested. "Let me phone Bruno." Not wishing to disturb my father, my mother insisted on the contrary.

Only a moment later, gasping for breath she whispered, "I'm dying." Sarina took my mother in her arms. Her head rested on Sarina's breast while Gianna frantically phoned my father. Rubbing my mother's chest, seeking to ease her pain, Sarina lay her friend down on the grass near the top of the hill, beside the lamppost that lights the path for evening visitors. My mother's heart raced out of control and a terrible gushing sound could be heard rumbling in her lungs as they filled with fluid. By the time my father arrived, it was too late. My mother had already passed away in the arms of her best friend.

49

Final Sojourn

Mum at City Beach, Perth

Sand under my feet. City Beach. Our family's favourite beach. Avoiding the offensive Perth summer heat, we enjoy the refreshing breeze gifted by the infamous elixir known in Western Australia as the Fremantle Doctor. I glance towards Mum as she pauses on the incline, puffing. She is almost absorbed into the distant darkness that fills the expanse behind her. It's a little strange that she should be so challenged by the climb. In a few weeks, death will take her from me. Do I somehow sense it already? I walk towards her. "Mum, just wait a while, take your time. Let me push you up." She gives her permission. I place my hand on the middle of her back as if to prop her up. We saunter quietly and carefully to the less stubborn terrain of the stony path leading to the car park. She struggles. Despite the sound of the wind and of the waves crashing against the shore, I can still hear her chest heaving.

It had been a number of years since I became preoccupied by my mother's well-being. I guess I had always been concerned, especially since that day at age nine or so when I watched my parents argue about something and I panicked. Struck as if by a dark premonition, I cried out in anguish, "Mum, stop getting so upset. I don't want you to get a heart attack!" I somehow knew even as a young boy that stress couldn't be good. I don't know why I thought of her heart then. She embraced me, then immediately reassured me she would be okay as she calmed down. The irony is not lost on me now. I had announced the precise cause of her death.

For as long as I could remember, mum's diet had included a smorgasbord of tablets to help manage a litany of ailments. Difficulties with sleep and her diabetes, glaucoma, arthritis, and anxiety, were well known. Her back was slightly humped, and she suffered much tension in her legs. In 2001 she'd had a first heart attack. It happened only two weeks after I left home to consider religious life. I felt so guilty. Was it the stress of me leaving? We sat in the doctor's office, waiting anxiously to find out her test results. "It looks like you won't need an operation," the heart specialist told Mum, "just a blood thinner." Mum didn't smile when she heard but I knew she was relieved too. I think she was even more relieved when I decided some months later that religious life would not be for me and I returned home.

The morning of her death, Mum came into my room to say goodbye before her walk. I had awoken feeling dizzy and unable to get out of the single bed that still rests in my old room with its creaking floorboards, as if a monument to times gone by. "Do you have a fever?" she asked me, checking my forehead tenderly. I guess a mum's tenderness knows no boundaries, even when it is targeted at her adult son. She then left the room, her rushing legs the only thing I could see. She moved quickly that morning, not wanting to be late for her rendezvous.

About forty minutes later my father picked up the phone. He came into the room, trying to conceal his concern. "Mum's not feeling the best," he told me. I didn't respond apprehensively as I characteristically did when it came to my mother's health. I still felt sick and couldn't get up. I decided that Dad going would be enough. He would bring Mum home.

Barely ten minutes passed. The phone shrilled. Dad's exasperated voice echoed hauntingly. "Renato," he whimpered, failing to keep his composure. "Your mum is not well." His euphemism betrayed his sheer despair.

Arising in a panic, my nausea and dizziness suddenly evaporating, I rushed to the car, and sped onto Norfolk Street, which ended in a T-junction at the park. I dropped the car at the side of the road like a madman and took to flight. A crowd was now gathering on the sloping lawn around my mother's body, which lay almost at the top of the hill and in view of motorists and pedestrians along the busy street.

It was the second time I had run towards my mother in distress from that same street.

A fading memory. Our second car crash. Nightmares lingered for weeks, perhaps months. This time I am in the front seat. My body convulses forwards, or perhaps sideward—as our conversation comes to an abrupt stop. I see it—a huge truck descending on my brother Mel's tiny car. The redness of the stop sign evades his field of vision. We are only one minute from home. The joy of going out with my big brother is replaced now by shock and fear. The car's bonnet, once facing northward, is now facing towards the west. Such was the force of the impact.

My brother anxiously checks if I am safe and then exits the car. The graze on my neck burns slightly, an unwelcome product of my seatbelt's saving intervention. Better this than my head propelled through the windscreen. Mel tells me to run home and tell Mum. Yes, I will run. I run as fast as my ten-year-old legs will let me. I run up the slight incline of my street, calling out as I approach our backyard and enter through the kitchen. "Mum! Mum!" She will know what to do. It will be okay. I see her proudly shining the imitation antique cupboard that had just arrived, humming a joyful tune. She wastes no time comforting me as I share the news.

How could I comfort my mother now? Mum, I am coming. *Dear Lord, please let her be okay.* I bounded across the busy street falling hard on my knees near my mother's feet. Someone had placed her in the recovery position.

Her body appeared lifeless, fluid excreting from one nostril, her lips quivering and dark blue. Yet they were quivering. There was movement. *How can she be dead?* I took her hand, began praying, and pressed the relic against her leg as everyone milled around. *"Pray with me"*, I begged her, believing that she could hear me even though in my heart of hearts I knew such a hope to be foolish.

Our parish priest arrived and administered the Last Rites. It all happened in a blur, but I remember the look on his face as he finished. He knew. As a Catholic priest he had seen the signs so many times. But I resisted. Surely, she was still alive? Her lips were still twitching and the spasms in her legs meant that she was still moving, right? Surely, the blue shade of her lips was not important? I had seen that shade before, perhaps not as dark, but blue, nonetheless. 30, 000 feet in the air.

The turbulence periodically interrupts my thoughts but does little to avert my fearful stare fixed stubbornly on my mother's closed eyes. I know other passengers are watching, but it doesn't matter. Mum has had trouble flying before, but not like this. Hadn't we done this countless times, ever since Tina married and moved to Sydney?

"I can't breathe very well," she explains. Thirty thousand feet in the air, perhaps still flying over the black waters of the Great Australian Byte, we are but a spec in the black sky. Will we need to land prematurely? I try to hide my panic as I keep dabbing her forehead with the moist cloth given to me by the flight attendant. I ignore his irritated request for me to stop dabbing Mum's head. I am not sure why he is so annoyed. The oxygen mask on her face tells me I need to distract her, comfort her.

Kneeling before my mother now, I was aware of more bystanders gathering. Thinking she still might begin breathing again, I kept praying, hoping and denying. Dad's exasperated cries, and those of my mother's friends as the ambulance officer tried to resuscitate her, pierced the air. The CPR did not last long.

"Sorry, there is nothing more we can do." The medical officer's announcement sounded so routine, so heartless. *Is that it? Aren't you going to try again? You could have tried a little longer,* I screamed interiorly. But *they* knew too! Not able to be denied any longer, the truth penetrated my soul violently. I stared at the body that once housed my mother, then bowed my head as my bottom and heels met.

Near mum's final resting place, Hyde Park, Perth.

50

Gutted

The moist grass cushioned my knees, comforting me in vain as I heard Sarina tearfully call my name. She rushed towards me, almost knocking me over, embracing me as she tried to console me for the loss of the woman whom I loved the most. Mum had spoken to her friends often of her love for her children, and Sarina knew how much we meant to each other.

I remained in a kneeling position while chaos swept over me without mercy. So, this was what the death of a loved one felt like? Yet, one thought gripped me.

Mum won't have to suffer anymore.

Seeing your mother's dead body pulled into an ambulance, hearing your father screaming, seeing him pressing his hands to his head while walking in circles aimlessly, lost, is so difficult to process. I had never seen my father like that. His open display of despair and anguish were a stark contrast to my stoic silence.

I watched the ambulance take my mother's body away. The lifeless body! Silence. Her soft voice and affectionate hugs were already evaporating, metamorphosing into now distant memories like clouds beyond the fading horizon. I hadn't had a chance to say goodbye, to tell her I was sorry for the times I hadn't been a good enough son, and to remind her I loved her.

"Why didn't you dance with me?" she asked me a few months earlier when I uncharacteristically refused while at a dinner dance which my family was attending.

"I wanted you to dance with Dad," I told her. They were having a tiff and mum had dug her heels in. I hoped my refusal would lead to an opportunity for reconciliation. I didn't mean to reject her, and I found her emotional response a little unsettling. Maybe she knew. Did she want to dance with me just one more time?

Her sister knew it too, that last time I saw her, just before she died. Just a few years before my mother's death, I had walked into my Aunt Maria's makeshift bedroom, trying to smile at her as she summoned enough energy to raise her head slightly off the pillow that provided a semblance of comfort. She returned the smile, but it was an act of courage intended for me. The strength of her kisses was instinctive, borne of her love for me. Four kisses in quick succession told me this would be her last sign of affection for me this side of heaven. The cancer that riddled her body was already consuming her.

As I watched the ambulance drive off with my mother's body, the call to duty took over. I suppose it was logical that it should fall to me to be interrogated by doctors at Sir Charles Gairdner Hospital. Mel had arrived after me and my father was in no condition to answer questions. I explained what had happened to my mother as if I were reporting a stranger's death, while out of the corner of my eye I saw relatives arrive. *Address? Yes, that's right. Medical record: heart condition, diabetes. Yes, that's right. North Perth.* It was all so routine, almost heartless, and yet unavoidable.

Then I saw my mother again, on a sterile table covered with a white sheet, only her face exposed. But she didn't look the same. How much time had passed? Just a couple of hours? Her stomach was so distended that it seemed as if someone had pumped it with gas. I still did not cry. The protective armour I had donned was still in place.

There was a Mass booklet to prepare with the help of cousins. And of course, messages accompanying my mother's death notice had to be sent to the local paper. Mine read as follows:

Mum, I thank you for being the most precious mum one could have asked for, loving me right until the hour before you died. You always gave till you could give no more, teaching me how to love and forgive. I am so proud to be your son. I want to tell you what I would have said had I been there before you died. Mum, I'm here, holding you. Don't be afraid. Rest in Jesus' Heart. He wants to bring you home for Easter.

One thing kept me going in the days that followed, perhaps more than anything else. I sensed a keen call to comfort my family, to hold the family up and to witness to the faith which I clung to. I was the one for whom faith reflected much more than that of a cultural Catholicism. There was one family member, however, I would find it most difficult to console. My sister.

51

Dreams & Visions

My sister has been described as a cross between American performer Paula Abdul and actress Valerie Bertinelli, with the dark olive complexion of one and the youthful round face of the other. It is a beauty that she does not flaunt but that she protects all the more by her modesty. We have shared a special bond ever since the age of seven when she became my big sister.

She would often remind me how she used to change my nappies when we were growing up. I have many photos of us together in which her maternal instincts are verified by the tenderness with which she holds me. My favourite memory is a cassette recording of her helping me sing "row, row, row your boat gently down the stream", while Dad took the mickey out of my husky, congested three-year-old voice, which emitted a strange dialect of Sicilian English. (And yes, who can forget the day she dressed me up as my cousin Carla and had me walking awkwardly around the house with lipstick on, wearing the high heels she had conveniently given me, while she and another cousin thought it quite amusing. I guess it was funny watching some people think I actually *was* Carla since we looked alike).

Tina was a vivid storyteller and would entertain my cousins and I with her detailed plot summaries of various novels she had read. One night, long before she married, she took us for a walk around the block with the moon and the sporadic street lamps as our only light, a reprieve from the many shadows that activated my wild imagination. How I longed for more moonlight as we neared home! I guess hearing the story of Stephen King's vampire epic *Salem's Lot* would be enough to impress on any child's mind a few things he would rather forget!

But what Tina lacked in prudence she made up for with her generosity. She spoilt me. Each payday I would wait for Tina on the footpath outside our home. With my eyes directed towards the horizon, which blurred into the small opening at the top of our street, I would see a small figure turn the corner and return my wave. I grew excited as she drew closer. I knew what was coming; a gift for her little brother, the recipient of the first fruit of her hard labour.

I remain her baby brother although I was taller by the age of 15. Once, when she took me for a driving lesson on one of her visits to Perth, she called me a "good boy" and got excited when I reached my milestone. It was very embarrassing but endearing at the same time. It was sometimes hard to believe that such a generous person could also be so tenacious in battle. One thing we still share is a thirst for righting wrongs, with the lethal combination of a strong sense of justice and traditional unrestrained Sicilian passion!

It was our brother who informed Tina that our mum had died. She would have to catch a flight and return from Sydney just three months after her last visit! When she ascended the garage stairs the night of our mother's death, her head buried, her heart torn, she seemed defeated. For the first time, after almost twenty years of countless joyful arrivals in the QANTAS lounge at Perth Domestic Airport, Tina, her husband Phil, and their three children, would not be greeted with Mum's joyful embrace. Etched in her swollen eyes was the pain of loss, but also a false hope. As she walked through the silent house, flanked now also by our brother, Mum's absence became palpable. "I can't believe it," she kept repeating between episodes of weeping.

My siblings and I sat on our mother's bed, the same questions in our hearts: *Where are you Mum? Are you happy? Will we see you again?* We needed so desperately to know.

We finally tried to get some sleep. The heaviness of the day's events held a dark cloak over us. Mum, for the first time in years, didn't need the light on in the bathroom to light her way during her sleepless nights. Neither would she be waking up regularly despite the medication smorgasbord she feasted on each day, or maybe, *because* of them.

That night, or the following—I no longer remember exactly—strange things began to happen. I woke up at around 4 am thinking about Mum and what she might want to say to us. I heard, unexpectedly but unmistakably, a message in our mother's voice, addressed to my sister. *Tina, sugnu tanta cuntenta.* (Tina, I am so happy).

The signs continued.

"Tina, what's wrong?" Phil asked after he was awakened by Tina's restlessness one morning prior to the funeral.

"Mum was here. She was here in the bedroom and—I could feel her," Tina answered. I knew the experience was real when she walked into the kitchen and spoke of her vision. I say *vision* because I do not know what else to call it. I trusted that this was not some fanciful self-effected apparition. It was not the first time Tina had been gifted with a significant dream that was clearly not delusional. Four years earlier she had dreamt of a coffin a few days before the death of our dearly beloved neighbour. So, I listened.

The action she "saw" occurred in the old kitchen we had prior to the extension. "When I came back into the kitchen, I saw Dad at the table," she began. "You were at his left and Mum was standing between you with her back to me, rummaging through a bag. I walked past Mum, who was wearing a beautiful long-sleeved blue top." A black button on our father's shoulder traditionally worn by Italians in mourning also caught Tina's eye. In the vision, Tina walked past our Dad and brushed the black button with her hand. It was then that she understood. She was not witnessing a past event. The Mum in her *vision* had in fact died. This was mum in the present.

Without seeing Mum's face, Tina embraced her as Mum turned around. Looking over towards Dad and I in the dream, Tina cried out, "Can't you see Mum?" We replied, "No, mum is dead." Tina began crying and asked mum repeatedly, *"Sini cuntenta Ma, sini cuntenta?" Are you happy, Mum? Are you happy?* Mum didn't answer but she stepped back. "There was one tear streaming down her face," Tina continued. "Mum was younger, peaceful, and healthy looking, with a full, round face. I touched Mum's face to wipe her tear away and Mum answered by nodding and smiling."

The gift of visionary dreams runs in the family, it would seem. Mum would often say she didn't think she would live very long. "Don't be silly, Mum," I would reply, though I didn't believe her intuitions were just laments about her struggle with daily illness.

"I had a dream last night," Mum exclaimed one morning, a little mesmerised.

"What was it about?"

"It was strange. I have often dreamed of family members who have passed away, but I have never had them all in the same dream." I began to feel a little on edge. "This time they were all in the dream, coming out of the church to welcome me." I knew then, though I chose immediately to ignore it, that my mum would be the next family passenger on the death barge. She was!

My mother, with my sister Tina in the mid-Sixties.

52

Weeping

Easter lunch was bittersweet. It was surreal sitting all together around the dining table, eating the meal our mother had made just a few days before, for us all to share at Easter. No lasagne had ever had so much meaning, and the silent conversation our family shared was accompanied only by the clanging of knives and forks against ceramic bowls. On the one hand, it was like having her with us, but on the other, it was so difficult! Our mother was the invisible guest at the table.

Visitors kept coming, bringing food, washing dishes, providing a distraction, or taking my niece and nephews out and about. And late one night all of us were in hysterics without a clue as to how it had all started. My father was cracking jokes and laughing so hard we were all in tears. I guess there is only so much tragedy a person can take.

How I miss my mum's laughter! Of all her lovable foibles, this one was the best. It was the silent-movie infectious type. She laughed so hard that her eyes would disappear and even though her lips mouthed something, nothing could be heard. If it weren't for the regular heaving of her chest you wouldn't even know she was taking a breath!

It was something I used to enjoy mocking tenderly as only a son can do, though she reprimanded me each time, slightly embarrassed. Her laughter was all the more precious to me because she hardly ever laughed except with my Aunt Adele or other close friends who helped her forget all her problems for a short while. She was otherwise timid, shy, and melancholic, not daring to laugh lest things would go wrong—a fearful attitude common among my mother's family. After all, *hope for nothing and you won't be disappointed when you don't get it,* she would say often. "Laugh too hard and tomorrow you will cry!" Fortunately, I managed to capture a smile on her face not long before her death, when she heard someone joke about her and Dad kissing for a particular photo that I was about to take to commemorate Dad's Sixtieth birthday. I captured that smile, and this particular photo, along with her youthful Hollywood actress style portrait that I had framed. These are the memories I treasure most—along with other, more ancient ones.

It is just two days before I return home to Perth from my first teaching position, in the mining town of Kalgoorlie-Boulder. The train station will soon be packed.

My pensioner neighbours dismount, and they approach. Their decision to use their free travel passes to visit me, touches me deeply; a glimmer of light in the failed experiment which was my country teaching post. I smile as I embrace the woman who held me as a child and whom I affectionately called "Signora." Over her shoulder I see another woman as she carefully steps onto the platform. She has faced the eight-hour train ride and travel sickness to be with me. Mum is smiling, half giggling, and says to Signora, as she sees the expression on my face, "Look at his smile. He can't stop smiling." We embrace—one of the leech-type hugs Mum would give me at the airport when I began to take interstate and overseas trips on my own. They are the clearest sign that Mum loves me, because she never tells me so.

Tears indeed seemed to be the main item on the household menu that long Easter weekend in 2003, especially the first time we visited Mum's body. Still plagued by fear and doubt, I continued to ask. *Where are you mum? Have you been saved?*

Entering the Purslowe funeral home, I acknowledged close members of the extended family who had also arrived and began making their way into the small viewing room. I wasted no time kneeling next to my mother's frigid right hand. I grabbed it before anyone else could, bowed my head, and began to weep silently, my tears joining in the torrent that had already begun in the room. My brother's wife, Carmen, affectionately laid her hand on my shoulder, seeking to comfort me. I remained in that position for as long as it took me to pray a whole rosary and a little more, all the time picking up on what others were saying, including their reminiscing about Mum.

Where are you, Mum? Have you really been saved? I kept asking. And remembering. The priest had gotten there too late. She hadn't been to confession for so long—five years, to be precise—and not for at least fifteen years before that. "I don't need to confess to a priest," she would often say at the mention of it. "I haven't killed anyone!"

"Mum, killing someone is not the only sin," I would retort arrogantly, not meeting Mum where she was. I was more simplistic then, not reading between the lines or, rather, misjudging what I read between them. I think I now understand that not judging others is a key feature of the Christian. We simply can never know the heart of a person or understand the conversation between them and their Creator.

In that claustrophobic room at the funeral home, my mind wandered as I covered my mum's hand with mine, warming hers considerably. A string of ideas flashed across my mind: Last week she visited her sick friend, Rosa. Mum visited the sick often. Didn't Jesus promise that when you show love to the least of his brothers you show it to him? *Lord, are you telling me that Mum has been judged on her love?*

I recalled 1 Peter 4:8 - Love *covers a multitude of sins* - and then another distant and sweet memory draped across the window of my mind's eye.

53

The Promise of Jeremiah

The Redemptorist Monastery Church. A weekday in January. A year before my mother's death. I look around at what could arguably be called the most majestic gothic church building in Perth. Its impressive edifice, masonry, creaking floorboards, artwork, and beautiful shrine to Our Lady of Perpetual Help, plunge the faithful and visitors alike back in time. What manifold spiritual treasures have been experienced within its walls by countless numbers of the faithful since its completion in 1903?

My knees fall roughly onto the cushioned pews on the left-hand side of the church, beneath one of the Stations of the Cross. I pray: Lord, please look after my mother. The following words pierce my soul audibly, gently: "My plans for you are peace, not disaster." I recognise them instantly. Words from the Prophet Jeremiah. You are referring to my mother, Lord, aren't you? As Mass starts, the reader, a woman, comes to the lectern. "A reading from the Book of Jeremiah," she announces. "I know what plans I have in mind for you, Yahweh declares: plans for peace, not for disaster, to give you a future and a hope." You have got to be kidding! She is proclaiming the same words I was given moments before.

About five months after God's promise I wrote the following in my journal:

Spiritually, mum is afraid. She refuses to go to confession. Physically, mum has everything wrong with her and it is so sad. Lord, when you revealed to me that your plan for her is peace and not disaster did you mean physically as well as spiritually? Jesus, I trust in you.

No. She was dead, and we were preparing for her funeral! I couldn't yet see how the Lord had kept his promise about her, either physically or spiritually. She hadn't gotten better. Instead she had died suddenly!

As we entered Sacred Heart Church for her requiem Mass on Easter Tuesday, I avoided as much as I could the eyes of friends and family. The colour of the shirt I wore was non-traditional burgundy, my mother's favourite colour and the colour of the funeral director's company. Reaching the front pew, I looked across at the closed casket and then towards the chapel to the left of the sanctuary, where Therese was sitting, unseen by the congregation. We had been dating for only two months and nobody knew about us.

The Mass began. I sat alone at the end of the pew. My brother and sister sat with their families and with my father. I prayed and waited for my time to witness, to let what I truly felt and believed be heard by all. I had been a mess at the funeral home, but I knew, somehow, that I would make it through the song I wanted to sing in our mother's honour.

It would be strange to lead the singing again here in my old parish, which I had left some years before, in order to join the choir of St. Mary's Cathedral in the city. It was a homecoming of sorts, but not the homecoming I had planned.

With my heart pounding and hands shaking I stood up after Communion, my back to the congregation. I signalled for someone to press the play button, glad that I would have some accompaniment, even if it were just a recording.

I opened my lips, wondering whether I would carry the first note. As I sang, not only did I carry each note, but I felt as if someone was carrying *me*. This was what I was waiting for. Now, I could comfort my family.

"*Like a Shepherd, I will feed you,*" I sang. "*I will gather you with care.*" The song, *We Will Rise Again* by David Haas would say what I could not speak and which I wanted so much to trust. That we would all see my mother again.

Managing to complete the song without a tear, and in a clear voice, I reached all the high notes as the Communion line continued to stream in front of me, still feeling carried as if on the wings of an eagle and as the hymn proclaimed. There were so many people, so many who knew and loved or at least respected my mother, listening to what I wanted them to know in truth. We *will* rise again. Death is not the end.

As I intoned the last note in harmony, I turned to sit down, and simply could not hold back the dam that burst from deep within. Weeping openly, I buried my head in my hands. Out of the corner of my eye I saw the pianist gesture for Therese to come to me. She hesitantly came out and cradled me, as mourners continued to process past us, returning to their pews after receiving communion. I did not look at them. Even as I was focusing on my own mourning, I couldn't help see as ironic that the day of my mother's funeral was the day everyone came to know about the woman I would one day build a family with.

54

The Italian Lady

Memories of the funeral and burial accompanied me that night as I returned to the Adoration Chapel just metres away from where I had been comforted twelve hours earlier. I settled in for an indefinite period of time of quiet reflection.

Picking up my Bible I turned to the fortieth chapter of Isaiah, the precise section of scripture my friend Claudelle had asked me to read just one day before my mother's death.

"Good morning, Claudelle," I had muttered the previous Wednesday morning, glancing sideways at the secretary behind the desk in the school's main office.

"Good morning," she replied in her soft-spoken South African accent. Claudelle, a charismatic Christian, was yet another woman gifted with prophetic dreams. She came out from behind her desk and followed me into the staff room where I proceeded to prepare my morning coffee. It is staff rooms such as these, and not my Italian heritage, which initiated me into the world of the coffee bean.

"Renato, I had a dream about you last night," she proclaimed. I was intrigued and listened intently. "In the dream an Italian lady came up to me and asked if I could pass you a note with a message on it. I took a peek at the note before I handed it to you and it said Isaiah 40. I think you should read Isaiah 40." I knew by the tone of her voice that the suggestion was more like a motherly directive.

"Okay, I will read it," I assured her before I walked to my classroom across creaking floorboards in the hallway. Sitting at my desk, I flicked through the Bible and read the ancient words of the Prophet Isaiah, who penned his book more than 2,500 years earlier. The message appeared to be twofold. Know who God is. He is bigger than all of it.

As I read it that morning, I hadn't really understood the relevance of the passage. Now, six days later, I read Isaiah 40 carefully, humbled by the events of the past 6 days.

My eyes fell upon the first verse. "*Be consoled, be consoled, O my people,* says your God." Immediately, I was captivated. This directive mirrored the desire I had fulfilled that very day, witnessing to my mother's life after death through song. I had wanted to comfort my family and the message I had been guided to give was precisely one of consolation. It was intriguing. I continued reading.

"Speak to the heart of Jerusalem and call out to her! For her malice has reached its end. Her iniquity has been forgiven. She has received double for all her sins from the hand of the Lord."

What! Could it be? Sins forgiven? Mercy shown? Saved? It was like hearing the answers to the questions that had plagued me for the previous week, or confirmation of what I knew I had to do. Questions about Mum being forgiven; my relief that mum didn't need to suffer anymore! It was *her* warfare that had ended! *Exactly* as I thought as soon as she had died.

If someone had come and punched me across the face I would not have cared at that moment. I felt like someone being let in on a secret. *Lord, are you talking to me? And is Jerusalem representing my mother?* I knew from my studies that Jerusalem could mean the whole people of God, the earthly city, the Heavenly Jerusalem, or an individual of faith. It was as if the passage had been written solely for me all those centuries ago. *Are you telling me that she has been forgiven all her sins, Lord? That she is saved?*

The revelation continued—that sweet surprise of a God who knows even before we ask and allows the eternal to pierce the mundane or painful in our lives. The verses that followed spoke of the mercy of God and the inevitability of death: "All flesh is grass ... truly the people are like grass... but the Word of our Lord remains for eternity." My mother had taken her last breath on grass. Claudelle had been given a dream directing me to read an ancient text that was about the hope of everlasting life despite the ugly scandal of death. Isaiah tells us why. "*Lift up your voice with strength! ... He will pasture his flock like a shep—*"

I froze! The darkened room of my soul was suddenly illuminated by a flurry of lights as the significance of those last words hung in the air. It all made sense now. God wasn't speaking to me just through Isaiah. It was the song I had sung at the funeral, directly inspired by only one place in Scripture.

Isaiah 40!

All the lyrics of the song were rephrased or paraphrased from the verses in Isaiah 40.

(40:11) He will pasture his flock like a shepherd. He will gather together the lambs with his arm, and he will lift them up to his bosom, and he himself will carry the very young.

(40:12) Who has measured the waters in the hollow of his hand, and who has weighed the heavens with his palm?

(40:26) Lift up your eyes on high and see who has created these things. He leads forth their army by number, and he calls them all by name. Because of the fullness of his strength and robustness and virtue, not one of them was left behind.

(40:29) It is he who gives strength to the weary, and it is he who increases fortitude and strength in those who are failing.

(40:30) Servants will struggle and fail, and young men will fall into infirmity.

(40:31) But those who hope in the Lord will renew their strength. They will take up wings like eagles. They will run and not struggle. They will walk and not tire.

'Read Isaiah 40' Claudelle had told me. What graces we receive when we open the ears of our hearts! In the early hours of the morning of April 16, 2003, God had remembered me. For a reason I do not understand, God chose to send me a message through a woman I trusted. It was as though he had warned, "Your mother will die tomorrow. You will be plagued by doubts about me and about her salvation. But I will inspire you to sing for her the theme song of the words with which I inspired my prophet Isaiah more than two thousand years ago. The message is the same: death must come, but there is so much more than death. My Word will comfort you and others. Trust me!"

I now understand why I felt *carried* as I sang. The more I scrutinised the words of Isaiah 40 after Mum's funeral, the more I realised that I had kept a divine appointment. My desire to comfort family and friends had been confirmed. My fear that she had not been saved had turned to ashes. Her warfare with Satan, with illness and depression, and the struggles that had come with starting a new life as a migrant in a foreign country, had come to an end. And I hope to this day, that a dream I had about the song in June 2005 was not just a product of my desire.

"Mum, do you remember how I sang that song for you after you died?" I asked a youthful mum, delighted to 'see' her again.

"I remember," she enjoined with a smile on her face.

This dream particularly edified me. But that was not the only one. Another was of particular significance - my Aunt Adele's dream in which my mother gave her a directive: "Adele, go outside and see the potted flower I bought you. It is blooming." When my aunt awoke, she went outside. The flower my mother had indeed bought her was very much in bloom. Death, it would seem, had not severed the bond that Mum shared with her beloved sister-in-law, with whom she was very close.

Being Catholic I knew that I could not presume that my mother had completed her journey towards God's "holy mountain" or that she had definitely bypassed Purgatory despite the signs that might indicate the contrary. I knew from Scripture that it is a "holy and beneficial thought to pray on behalf of those who have passed away, so that they may be released from sins" (2 Maccabees 12:46). I knew in faith, however, that my mother had begun to rise "with wings like eagles" towards the Holy Mountain of God, the day she died. I testify with joy to the hope that she now dwells where God will wipe away 'every tear' and destroy death forever (Revelation 21), finding the place that Christ has prepared for her in the Father's house (John 14:2).

My mother and I, 1972

Final photo taken of my mother, April 4, 2003

55

17th Day of the 7th Month

Over the years I have shared my mother's story countless times with family, friends and students alike, of how God kept his promise to me, and how he still inspires his people through his Word in surprisingly distinctive ways. I marvel at how the Lord continues to make known his will as he did of old, through dreams and visions and other manifestations of His Spirit.

But in 2014, eleven years after my mother's passing, it dawned on me that I was only just beginning to understand what God had done for me. There was more that God wanted to reveal to me. And the first clue that was conveniently dropped in my lap came from the lips of a most unlikely source - a former model.

A snippet of a Joanna Lumley special caught my eye on the ABC one evening after the birth of our fifth child, Jonah. *The Search for Noah's Ark* was a title that drew me in immediately. I often teach about Noah in the context of the major covenants God established with Israel and with all humanity. The inevitable question about the historicity of the flood and Noah's Ark always rears its cynical head when I do teach it and I wondered if Lumley's investigative work would offer some valuable insight to my existing knowledge of Noah and his historicity.

One of Lumley's incidental references in the film drew my attention on a more personal level. One particular scene thrust me instantly back in time to the saga surrounding that fateful seventeenth day of April 2003. My antennae were extended when I heard Lumley quote Genesis 8:4.

"And the ark rested in the seventh month, on the seventeenth day of the month…"

I was taken by surprise. The adjective *seventeenth* (alongside the well-known biblical number *seven* signifying completion, perfection and sanctification), was not one I had ever heard referred to in Scripture. I was intrigued that a number holding personal significance (my mother passed on the 17th of April) should suddenly find itself in the scriptures too, especially since I could join this "dot" to another that had come just weeks earlier while Therese was still recuperating in two different hospital rooms after Jonah's birth. Both rooms were numbered seven and seventeen! And in order to get to her room when I managed to visit (a little difficult with the other four children to look after at home), I had a choice of three lifts, numbered, not one, two and three, but sixteen, seventeen and eighteen!

Does God use such signs? I wondered! And the more I investigated, the less dubious I became.

The birth of a child in the Bible is often associated with God's covenant promise, as with Abraham and Isaac. Was there something in all this that God wanted me to see? First came the revelation of Isaiah 40, of God keeping his promises, and now the notion of covenant?

I conducted a digital search revealing that the number seventeen occurs twelve times in the entire Bible and, more specifically, that the phrase "seventeenth day" occurs only twice, both in the story of Noah, a covenant story, where the word "covenant" is used for the first time in the whole of scripture.

Genesis 8:4 quoted by Lumley detailed the arrival of the Ark of Noah on dry ground, signifying God's fidelity to Noah's family. Genesis 7:11 provides details of when it all began; the "seventeenth day of the month [when] all the fountains of the great abyss were released, and the floodgates of heaven were opened."

I like to imagine the Lord feeling a little chuffed as I began to discover the clues he was laying at my feet, as when I found myself sharing the Noah and Maternity ward link with a group of Year 9 students, just before taking the class roll and seeing the date as I stared at the laptop screen in disbelief, yet again. It was the *seventeenth* of the month!

For over eleven years after my mother's death I thought I understood everything there was to understand about what God had shown me in his merciful love. This God, who as Isaiah proclaimed centuries earlier "extends the heavens as if they were nothing," was a God whom I could trust to keep his promise, even though his wisdom remained 'inscrutable.'

It took a series of seemingly random events, strung together by prophetic dreams, numbers, a maternity ward, a class roll, and a former model's documentary on Noah's Ark, to teach me an even deeper lesson about the nature of his promise. It was nothing less than the fulfilment of the very same covenant promise he has been making with his people since the dawn of creation. Nothing less than the one perpetual covenant: "to be God to you and to your offspring after you" (Genesis 17:7), made with Noah, (Genesis 6:18), with Abraham, Isaac, Jacob, and through them with all the "sons of Israel" (Exodus 2:25), sealed first in animal's blood (Exodus 24:8), and then in the Precious Blood of his Son, the "blood of the new covenant" (Matthew 26:28), present at the Last Supper on Holy Thursday, before the gruesome events of Good Friday.

And this mystery, this "communion in the Blood of Christ" (1 Corinthians 10:16) the Catholic world celebrates at every Mass, beginning with Holy Thursday, was celebrated liturgically the *day my mother died.*

In 2003, April 17 was *Holy Thursday,* the dawn of the new and *everlasting* covenant.

COVENANT

⌘

This is my [covenant] with them, says the Lord. My Spirit is within you, and my words, which I have put in your mouth, will not withdraw from your mouth, nor from the mouth of your offspring, nor from the mouth of your offspring's offspring, says the Lord, from this moment, and even forever.
- Isaiah 59:21

⌘

56

Out of the Mouths of Babes

Entrusting one's life to an invisible God is not that easy for many of us. The journey to the *Land of Trust* can be more like a hazardous marathon with steep mountains to climb and dangerous terrain to traverse. It is one thing to know that God has entered into a covenant relationship with us, promising to be with us always, but it is another for us to remember our own covenant promises, to abandon ourselves to his will, to trust him with our very lives.

In the language of mystical theology, the periods of purgation replete with desolation can be plentiful, while those of illumination and consolation can appear scant as we begin this journey to intimate union with Christ. I have found that travelling along the path to union with God also involves retreating back into past habits, depending on old crutches that appear very attractive but which I know will provide only a fleeting diversion.

Perhaps this stems from the need to remain in our comfort zones? Instead of addressing what is holding us back from seeking perfection, we fill our lives with distractions, our shopping baskets with treats, our time with meaningless talk and, as in my case, our wallets with multiple loyalty cards at various cafes.

And so, it was on one fine morning, having dragged my feet to the car ready for another trek through traffic to work, when I was sustained by a single thought!

Coffee! Rich, percolated and aromatising coffee!

As I had left home uncharacteristically early, I was already crossing the Narrows Bridge by 7.50 a.m., glancing at the attractive city skyline to my left. I survived the long crawl down the Mitchell Freeway courtesy of my music and audiobook compilation. The irritating traffic was now an increasingly distant memory, and it wouldn't be long before the *Barista Lady*, otherwise known as Jan, was preparing the warm beverage for me.

My excitement increased childishly as I turned into the only parking space available just in front of the BP "convenience store" which housed the *Wild Bean* café. Fortunately, there was nearly always a space just for me, as if the station's employees were expecting me. I hardly ever purchased petrol there. Just the coffee.

Closing the car door behind me, I shuffled past the magazine stand and main cashier console and on towards the Barista Lady, always looking forward to seeing her,

"Morning, Jan," I managed to mumble despite the effort it took. Jan greeted me with her broad smile, her blond hair larger than life as usual.

"Good morning, Stefan," she called out joyfully, forgetting my real name once more. I let it go – again. "So, it'll be the usual?" she queried as I made it to the front of the queue. She didn't know that today was *not* a normal day. Today was a day when the sticker that had a central place in my home office wall spoke powerfully for itself. "Give me coffee and no one gets hurt!"

Facetiously, and looking forward to the friendly banter I knew would occur, I cut to the chase. "The most maxi soy mocha you have," I ordered. This day it would be chocolate plus coffee with full fat to boot.

"It's like that is it?" Jan asked me with a glimmer in her eye as a chuckle escaped her mouth.

"It is one of those weeks," I replied.

It was with the same mega size coffee in hand, but on a different day that week, when I exited the store in the same frame of mind, dragged my feet to the car and attempted to unlock the door only to realise the door belonged to a different customer's car. That explained why the key didn't really fit the lock!

Fearing imminent accusations of theft, I made sure to exclaim in a melodramatic tone loud enough for a nearby witness to hear, "That's not my car!!!" while he cracked up and I sheepishly found my own car three parking bays down.

It was indeed one of those weeks. The catalyst was the birth of a new baby. The time of hibernation, and the time when parents are blessed with a weird blend of enamoured glances and fitful sleep, great joys and frayed nerves, deep thanks and fearful anxiety. Or, to put it once again in terms of mystical theology, when the Lord invites you to progress along the stages of deeper union with him through exercise in charity.

The gift of children can indeed be an instrument of great sculpturing. The joys of children are of course delightful. The sweet hugs of a child. The many instances of "I love you" and excited acclamations upon seeing Daddy return from work, are too precious for words. "Daddy, Daddy," followed by a bear hug, or "Look what I made today, Dad," simply obliterate the angst of the day.

I hope I will never forget the unabashed excitement in my children when, as infants, they greeted me at their first waking moment with a beaming smile, their limbs jerking in excitement as I picked them up in a deep embrace, or those times when "aba" or "dada" was their first word. Eventually, each of my children knew that I was more than just the strange guy competing with mum for their affection.

I think also about my children's innate inability to keep a secret. In the days leading up to Father's Day in 2012 I came home to the inevitable, "Dad, we wrapped your present today. We can't tell you what is in it but maybe you can guess." By the time Father's Day had come, I knew exactly which gift their mum had them all conspire to hide from me. "It starts with *First* and the second word is *Aid*. Can you guess?" Jacob asked me.

I have had many adorable conversations with my only daughter Marie Grace. One, in particular, stands out: when I had a backache after holding baby Josiah for too long.

"Oh, my back. It still hurts," I complained.

"Stop it, Dad!"

"Stop what?"

"Holding Josiah."

"I can't stop holding Josiah."

"Yes, you can!" she retorted authoritatively.

"You want me to stop holding him so I can hold you more, right?" I could tell. Marie Grace nodded and immediately, knowing she was caught out, smiled sweetly and endearingly.

On another occasion she threatened me. "If you want me to eat the breakfast, I am not going to because you haven't given me the biscuit." And again, "I will never eat again if you don't...." I waited stubbornly for ten minutes and then saw a little hand collect the bowl to my right where I had deposited it after removing it from her silently. Then, with an equally stubborn air of authority, Marie Grace said, "If you want to make my breakfast tomorrow you have to put a cookie in it." *How cute*, I thought before she continued. "I am just going to eat it, without one, just this once."

At times, children are sweet but in a much more masculine way so to speak. I knew this the day I opened my eyes after a restful sleep and saw *him*. The Amazing Spiderman was standing before me. He was a bit shorter than usual. In fact, he was so short he was the same size as my six-year-old Jacob! Noticing me awake my own *Spidey* came over and lay down next to me for a morning cuddle. But it didn't take long for the mission to start. The battle for supremacy began.

"Dad see if you can push me off the bed," he commanded. I complied. It took about three seconds. Defeated but not out for the count, Spidey came back for more.

"Try again!" he demanded. He would persevere until he had shown his muscle. I simply laughed a little, admiring his determination.

Once again, Spidey found himself out of the bed. "Try it again, Dad!" And each time I pushed him off, Spidey came back for more, confident that the following attempt would go in his favour. I recalled at that point the iconic mantra of the alien species known as the Borg whom Star Trek enthusiasts would know well. "Resistance is futile."

With each attempt I could see, or rather feel (owing to the Spiderman mask that he was wearing), the excitement in his face which spoke of his dogged determination to beat his father. And even though he lost the wrestling match, the tickle competition and the game of human hand snap, my son Spidey never lost his spark.

The opportunities to see in my fatherhood an invitation to understand more deeply the Fatherhood of God, have been plentiful. So too have been the opportunities to see that the gift of children is a double-edged sword. It can become the greatest tool used in the Potter's hands to teach a parent unconditional trust. To really come to depend on the Lord and to see that, ultimately, our children do not belong to us. They belong to him and he is moulding them as well, often in ways that blow our minds.

Again and again I have come to see that if we let him, God can not only use our children to nudge us on the way to holiness; he can also fashion them in such a way that he can console us with his wisdom and insight, transforming our fearful gaze with the grace to trust.

Marie Grace, age 4

57

Jonah's Song

It was coming to that time again. Labour. It was our fifth child. As the time got closer, my imagination was beginning to be plagued by doubts. The same had happened before the birth of Josiah, our fourth child. It was like developing an irrational fear of flying after having flown a thousand times. Suddenly, that which once seemed familiar and commonplace, now seemed once again threatening and unknown territory.

Before Josiah we had already become proficient in the art of childbirth. I say *we* because even I had scars to prove it. Three puncture wounds in my arm where Therese gripped for dear life as she gave birth to our beautiful little girl, our third. And yet, I was afraid like I had never been, just before Josiah was born.

He had to be induced because he was a big baby. I guess that was enough to do it. We began hearing about all that could go wrong with inductions. Thankfully, I kept the terrible fears of death of either mother or child to myself, telling Therese about it only after delivery. And there I was again, only days before the birth of Jonah, and the fears were clawing their way back in.

There should have been no reason to doubt. I *knew* that with my mind when the Lord had set yet another series of "God-incidences" in motion regarding the naming of Jonah a few months prior. Jonah was meant to be John Paul, after John Paul II, but one day Therese expressed her doubts.

"I have been thinking about the name John Paul and I am not sure. I've been thinking of calling him Jonah." She had been listening to a Joyce Meyer talk and discovered the story of Jonah, impressed by the name.

"Then we should pray and think about it," I said in agreement. "We have always been in a 100% agreement about our children's names so if you aren't certain then we need to think some more." I was a little taken aback at how quickly I had agreed but I had just come back from a weekday Mass during which I had heard one of the episodes in the story of the biblical Jonah for the first time. There was that name again. The second time on the same day. And as it happened, the reading at

Mass was the second of a series that only occurred in that cycle of the liturgical year, which only came around every three years. I just happened to be at the right Mass!

As the sun was setting on our day and I called the family to prayer, I took hold of the children's song and storybook we had been using each night. I opened up to the relevant page I had routinely bookmarked after the previous night's prayer session. And there it was. "Jonah's song" was the title that stared back at me. I almost did a double take but realised just as quickly that the Lord had done it again.

"Therese, "I called out, "I think we have to call him Jonah!"

God had done more for me that night than just indicate our child's name. He had given his final word on the other doubts that had also plagued me – doubts about whether we should be bringing any more children into this cruel and sometimes savage world. But now I knew, once again, needing to be hit over the head with it just one more time, that God knew my son and he had a plan for him. He had revealed to us his name, which meant that God *knew* him. And perhaps, just like the biblical Jonah, so too my son might one day be God's chosen instrument for something great, an instrument for the salvation of many.

Despite being buoyed by this memory, I remained a little anxious just a few days before Jonah's birth, once again putting the Lord to the test, as I sat on my exercise bike and killed two birds with one stone, rosary beads in one hand and the palm of both hands on the pulse monitor checking my heart rate. The intention was the same. *Lord, through the intercession of Blessed John Paul II, prophet Jonah, St. Bruno and St. Gaetan, thank you for the safe delivery of our little boy.* At least this time I was thanking God in advance – this was progress!

Having completed two decades of the rosary, I spotted my missal on the bookshelf as my legs rode up that metaphorical hill (and the readings on the digital panel told me I was close). I decided to read the first reading of the Mass for Monday in the Sixth Week in Ordinary Time. It was a reading from the Letter of St. James.

"If there is any one of you who needs wisdom, he must ask God, who gives to all freely and ungrudgingly; it will be given to him. But he must ask with faith, and no trace of doubt, because a person who has doubts is like the waves thrown up in the sea when the wind drives. That sort of person, in two minds, wavering between going different ways, must not expect that the Lord will give him anything."

I let the sound of those final words hang in the air. *Thank you, Lord,* I muttered silently. I so needed to hear those words. Wasn't I being precisely *like the waves thrown up in the sea when the wind drives?* I was not surprised that the scriptures had been used once again to confirm the rational meaning of everything else that had surrounded the existence of Jonah.

A few days later, as we made our way to the hospital, I knew everything would be okay. During the ten-minute drive, I glanced across at Therese as she felt another strong contraction. They were still thirty minutes apart and experience told us that we should expect at least another twelve hours or so before delivery. I drove to the drop off point at the hospital entrance and was glad Therese accepted a wheelchair when offered one by the receptionist who came out to meet us. "I'll go and park and meet you up there!" I said, reassured that she was now in good hands.

As I arrived in the ward about five minutes later, I saw the obstetrician walking briskly towards me and waving happily. "Glad you are here," she told me. Rushing into the delivery room, I noticed the staff hadn't even had time to allow Therese to change into hospital clothes. She was also quite happy on gas, her best friend during labour. She was in the magical narcotic zone, enjoyed legally.

Barely forty minutes after our arrival at the hospital, little Jonah came into the world, our largest baby and Therese's least painful delivery. He was so beautiful. So vulnerable and helpless, but comforted when he lay on his mother's chest, close to the pounding of the heart that had been his drum beat for nine months. When I got to hold him, I held him all the more tightly, pleased that I could comfort him more.

Even as I write I wonder how many years it will be before I will learn to trust without any signs, confirmations and God-incidences?

My journey to a childlike faith is far from complete. Still, the Lord continues to give me further proof of his love and patience; his covenant promises renewed.

A short five months after Jonah's birth I found my soul once again plunged into the darkness of fear, as the reality of terror and despair made headlines across the globe. The persecution of Christians in Egypt, Syria and Iraq, the war between Israel and Hamas, and a plane shot down in Ukrainian airspace, the fruit of more war. I could not seem to get rid of images of human bodies falling from the sky.

My prayers for protection were desperate, filled with dread and no trust. But then, Josiah, just turned two years of age, opened his mouth barely a minute after I finally entrusted my children to the Lord with a spirit of hope. Turning to Josiah to give him his next spoonful of dinner, I was interrupted when he opened his mouth to speak.

Slowly, but very clearly, as if from an ancient oracle, he uttered three words he had never put together before and which amazed me, tears beginning to well up in me. Looking straight into my eyes, a serious expression on his beautiful little face, and with a confidence beyond his years, Josiah proclaimed, "Jesus ... lub...you."

This could not be just my son speaking. He blew me away with the breath of God!

I have been given children whose faith utterances were balm to me. And Josiah, at the tender age of 2, was beginning to follow in the footsteps of his older brother Joshua.

My children, 2014: Back row – Jacob, Joshua and Marie Grace. Front row – Josiah and Jonah.

THE MUSTARD SEED FAITH

⌘

Amen I say to you, certainly, if you will have faith like a grain of mustard seed, you will say to this mountain, 'Move from here to there,' and it shall move.
- Matthew 17:19

⌘

58

Dodo Bird on the Roof

"Daddy, Daddy, guess what?" Marie Grace shouted excitedly one afternoon when I entered the hallway after work. "Joshua's dodo-bird fell off the roof!"

"What?" I snapped incredulously. The conversation with Joshua the night before suddenly came to mind as I walked through our house to the children's playroom that looked out onto the back-yard lawn. And there, sure enough, was my son's dodo bird. *I can't believe it,* I thought to myself. *He has done it again.* I met Therese in what we called the "chill out room" where my children were momentarily playing. "I can't believe it!" I repeated. I recalled with her the dialogue I had with our son the previous day when he threw his toy dodo up on the terracotta coloured tiled roof - again - and expected me to take it down for him - again.

"Dad, can you help me get the bird down?"

"No, Joshua. This time your toy can stay up there. Next time make a better choice and stop throwing your toys on the roof!" I replied with self-righteous indignation, fed up with my son's new weird little habit.

But Joshua would go on to have the last word. During night prayer, my son prayed out loud when it came time for the intercessions. "Lord, could you send a strong wind to push the dodo bird off the roof, please?" *No, I don't want that prayer answered,* I thought to myself immediately, slightly insecure at the prospect of me pitting my own prayer against my small child's, given what I knew about the Lord's bias towards children!

The following day I approached Joshua, a defeated man. "Joshua, the Lord answered your prayer again, didn't he?" Joshua knew it was true. The confident look on his face said everything I needed to know. He had prayed for a strong wind to push his beloved toy off the roof, even though I had prayed against him, and he reversed the effects of his dance with fate. Nonchalant, as if the affirmative response to his prayer had been a fait accompli as soon as he had uttered his prayer the night before, he strutted off with a smirk.

This was not the first time his mother and I had marvelled at our eldest son's faith. He had been set up for it from a young age.

He was only two and a half when we saw him, hands clasped, sitting in mummy's lap, praying out loud. "Lord Jesus, bless my heart. Lord Jesus, touch my heart." As if touched by his own eloquence he added, "That's beautiful." Talk about the grace of Baptism and the presence of the Holy Spirit!

By five years of age it seemed that trust in the power of prayer was second nature to him and he was already synthesizing the implications of the story of Jesus' first public miracle at Cana.

"Dad, I want more lemonade," he said in a commanding tone after enjoying his first glass.

"No, Joshua, you have already had enough lemonade."

"Dad I *really* want lemonade."

"No, Joshua! I have already told you. *No more lemonade.*"

"Well, I am just going to ask Jesus to turn water into lemonade then," he huffed. His reference to the wedding at Cana in the Gospel of John, and the recording of Jesus' first public miracle, was almost as amazing as Joshua's faithful tenacity.

Joshua has more overtly prayed against me. I once heard him mumbling something to God about changing my mind, audible enough, (perhaps intentionally so) for me to hear. But generally, it has been when Joshua and I were in agreement that I have seen God manifest his grace after Joshua's prayer.

59

Moving Mountains

Joshua was about seven when I dropped him off at school one day. By the time we arrived it had started pelting down with rain, with no end in sight, and the mini deluge struck the car mercilessly. I knew we would find it difficult to make a dash for his classroom without getting drenched. In one of those extremely rare moments of childlike trust, which I truly believe was a grace in itself, I said to Joshua, "Let's pray that the rain stops so that we can get to your classroom."

I knew I was taking a risk. What if the prayer was not answered? What if Joshua's emerging faith would remain just that, or take a step backwards? But somehow, I knew that it was worth taking the risk, only if I asked Joshua to pray with me. Somehow, I sensed that his contribution would make all the difference.

I began to pray, with Joshua following suit, "Dear Jesus, please let the rain stop so we can get to the classroom." The prayer ended.

And, so did the rain! As soon as the last word was uttered! And as if turned off at the celestial faucet!

I looked at Joshua aware that mixed emotions were finding their way onto my face. Joy. Surprise. Awe. I almost gasped and hoped he only saw the awe.

"Joshua, what happened?" I seized this rare opportunity.

"It stopped!" The wonder on his face shone out as he answered.

"Who *did* that Joshua?" I continued not able to hide my astonishment.

"Jesus," he said without hesitation.

It was one of those moments where God's presence covers you like a sweet mist. I marvelled at how the heart of a child can change the natural course of even the weather. I knew that Joshua's part in the prayer was the clincher.

My son and I shared something deeply spiritual that day that was the continuation of a beautiful faith journey for him and a continuing one for me.

I wonder what the Lord has in store for Joshua, and indeed all my children. Their lives are still an open book on which can be written whatever their faith, free will and God will allow. But I have already seen some lines in Joshua's book that convinces me of the grace that comes with infant baptism, regardless of the polemic existing between Christians of different denominations about its efficacy. I have no doubt that when scripture testifies to whole households being baptised that infants and little children were included. God's mercy is just too generous.

One night the family gathered together for night prayer in the boys' room. When our prayer finished, I decided impulsively to lay hands over my children's heads and pray for them. It was a bold move – slightly charismatic I suppose and not our customary way of blessing our children.

I removed my hands from Joshua's head thinking that prayer time had come to an end. Joshua looked up, smiled and extended his own hands over my head, bowing his head in silent prayer. Taken aback a little, but not wishing to stifle the Spirit, I waited for him to finish and then watched him move across to his mother seated on the other side of my son's bed.

As he prayed, I gazed upon his small extended hands, with his head still bowed meditatively, and waited for him to finish. He kept going. Therese's head was bowed too, her eyes closed. As her eyebrows lifted and her head started moving back and forth as if caressed by a gentle wind, I heard her gasp, "Whoa Nelly!"

She went on to explain the warmth that she began to feel emanating from Joshua's hands, all the way down through her head, making her quiver.

Joshua completed his prayer and asked, "Mum, why are my hands so warm?"

"Joshua, that is a sign that the Holy Spirit is with you," I said, knowing he would understand. The Lord was once again working through my son.

None of us in the family are charismatic. None of us have the gift of healing. But I was struck by a beautiful thought; we shared one thing that night that is necessary as a conduit for any grace of the Spirit.

Love. That word, again! Especially, the love between mother and child. Joshua had begun to learn that faith and love go together long before that day at school when our collective prayer was answered the first time. I remember his prayer so early on - "Lord Jesus, touch my heart"- which he had prayed so tenderly.

Another incident, when Joshua was four, also helped build that bridge of understanding that love, this time between father and son, more than any other power, is a powerful magnet that draws God's healing power to the earth.

By the time I got home from work on May 25, 2009 I had begun feeling a mix of anger and sadness arise in me. Joshua was still sick and now his cough was a good deal worse. Never one for coping perfectly when my children are sick, I was quite disheartened by the time we lay him down to sleep. He had vomited from coughing too much and was beginning to wheeze. I was beginning to think the worst. Would we have to take him to emergency again like that other time when he was only nine months old and his listless body lay in my arms?

Tucking him in, the thought came to me to kneel by his bed and pray for his healing but loud enough for him to hear. I began the Divine Mercy chaplet that Our Lord entrusted to the Polish mystic St. Faustina in the 1930s, and which he asked her to promote throughout the world in order to draw upon his mercy. The main prayer that is repeated a number of times while meditating on the sufferings of Jesus, addresses the Father, reminding him of the saving death of his Son on the cross. "For the sake of his sorrowful passion, have mercy on us and on the whole world," I repeated earnestly, making my way through each decade.

Joshua listened as I prayed my heartfelt prayer, with tears beginning to blur my vision slightly.

It didn't take long before Joshua calmed down. Strangely, he coughed only once during the chaplet. Soon, he sneezed so effectively that a blessed blob of nasal contents fired out from his nostrils as if from a canon, clearing his sinuses and throat completely. A smile erupted on his face, his eyes still fixed on mine and he nodded in agreement when I announced with gratitude, "Daddy's prayer made you feel better, didn't it Joshua?"

"Can you pray more, Daddy?" he asked me, obviously touched. He continued to be well throughout the night.

I soon discovered that Joshua was not content to enjoy the gift of faith for himself. He became my little evangelist son. At age seven he wanted to make sure others knew about Jesus too. I didn't see it coming, I must admit. But come it did, and it seemed that nobody would escape it. Good news has to be shared, right? And what better time to start than at Christmas?

60

The Christmas Interrogation

The week before Christmas, Joshua had come to realise that not everyone believes in Christmas the way we do. The first time I noticed Joshua trying to change all that was when I lost him briefly, after our final kids' gym class for the school year. I was buckling my two other children in their car seats when I realised Joshua was absent. I glanced out the window and saw him behind the car, finishing his conversation with a grandmother of one of the other students.

"Do you know what this sign is?" he asked the unsuspecting old lady while pointing to the fish symbol on the back of our car.

"Yes, I do," she responded. By the time they finished the conversation, the old lady, a Christian herself, had passed his test and had guaranteed him that she would be praying for him when she gets to Heaven. She left with a smile on her face and perhaps wonderment at my son's faith and resolve.

The following day he managed to branch out to two other ladies who served us as we patronised their business at the major shopping centre near our home. We had barely entered the busy jewellery store when Joshua went for the jugular, while I cringed and wondered what would come next.

"Do you know what Christmas is all about?" he called out without any hesitation. I looked at the lady behind the desk, her face holding a note of discomfort, and I wondered how all this would pan out. After brief hesitation she said, almost under her breath, "It is about the birth of Jesus."

I breathed a sigh of relief. Joshua had asked two people, and both had answered correctly. The two of them then proceeded to have a discussion about the meaning of Christmas during which Joshua held his ground.

Thinking that Joshua's thirst for promoting the faith would have been quenched by the time we had lunch, I accompanied him to pick up the framed photo I had organised for my father's Christmas gift. He had asked for a photo of my wedding to match the ones of my siblings that he proudly hangs in his hallway. Once again, in fine fashion, pretty much as soon as the lady returned with the completed frame,

Joshua did not disappoint. He managed to insert himself into the adult conversation.

"Do you know what day it is soon?" he asked boldly. The lady replied, "Yes, it is Christmas." I breathed another sigh of relief. As we discovered, this lady was also Christian. By the time Joshua had finished she agreed that the most important thing about Christmas festivities was the birth of Jesus. "We will be going to church too," she said to Joshua's delight.

Given that there has been a pattern of decline in Australia's Christian demographic, (from 64% to 52% between 2011 and 2016 alone), I thought it quite providential that all the people Joshua had interrogated had at least some degree of Christian sensitivity.

And then came his fourth attempt at our local library's "Meet with Santa" session. The target this time? His own species – the children!!

Therese knew something was up when the librarian asked her, "So which church do you attend?" She was naturally curious as to why the librarian would ask such a direct question until I recounted what I had heard Joshua ask her. For the third time that week I found myself explaining that my son was apparently on a mission to find other believing Christians outside his home and friendship group and that he just can't understand why not everyone is Christian.

Earlier he had made his sentiments clear when he yelled out that Christmas was a celebration of "the Lord" in front of all the kids listening to the lady reading the Christmas story. He was also the one who blurted out that Santa was not real, potentially undoing myth that had been sustained by eager parents for years!! Fortunately, it probably did very little to spoil things for all who were in awe of the Santa look-alike handing out presents!

It is the child, Christ tells us, to whom the Kingdom of Heaven belongs and the stuff with which this Kingdom is constructed.

In that hour, the disciples drew near to Jesus saying, "Whom do you consider to be greater in the kingdom of heaven?" And Jesus, calling to himself a little child, placed him in their midst. And he said, "Amen I say to you, unless you change and become like little children, you shall not enter into the kingdom of heaven" (Matthew 18:1–3).

The simple faith of a child provides each discerning adult an opportunity to gaze into the face of Christ; even though, at times, this couldn't seem further away from the truth.

ALL IN THE HANDS OF GOD

⌘

In that hour, the disciples drew near to Jesus, saying, "Whom do you consider to be greater in the kingdom of heaven?" And Jesus, calling to himself a little child, placed him in their midst. And he said: "Amen I say to you, unless you change and become like little children, you shall not enter into the kingdom of heaven.
- Matthew 18:1–3

⌘

61

Lost Innocence

I knew something was wrong when I opened the freezer door and saw her. She was almost frozen, along with her young companion. It was pitiful. A smile that in other circumstances would have seemed purely evil, lit across my face. My two older boys were at it again.

This time their Machiavellian brilliance was shining through. When they placed Marie Grace's *Dora and Boots* figurine in a plastic cup filled with water and attempted to freeze them in their icy tomb, Joshua and Jacob, then eight and six, had decided that enough was enough. The allure of sweet revenge, as powerful as the scent of fresh blood to a hungry shark, was an elixir that promised relief to their suffering: No more frustrating rhetorical questions inflicted upon them or their sister by the bi-lingual Dora. No more verbal abuse by the annoying characters on the screen, offering redundant lessons in basic numeracy in Spanish, lessons that had been inflicted upon impressionable children against a background of childish plot devices. It was time to give the victim and her friend the break they needed and to send their younger sister a clear message: the age of the juvenile *Dora the Explorer* and her sidekick *Boots* had come to an end!

I must admit that my admiration for their ingenuity far surpassed my instinctive desire to reprimand them. And I laughed. As the eldest, and as instigator of the fiendish plot, Joshua giggled mischievously as he revealed how he had hatched the plan. But I couldn't help thinking that this event was more than just childish prankishness.

And it was: together my boys were expressing to me that they had come of age. Their prank was a sign that they were leaving a little of their childhood innocence behind, which I understood even more clearly when, a month or so later, I overheard a conversation as we were getting ready for their swimming lessons.

"Jacob, I'll leave the water bottle in the car. You tell Dad that you left it there so he can go and get it!" Joshua whispered.

Overhearing their discussion, I thought I had the victory when I told them I had no such intention of getting the bottle out of the car and leaving them alone inside the Aquatic Centre so they could do what they were planning to do, *whatever* that was. But Jacob, being quite astute, issued an intuitively prepared comeback, along with a smile meant to appeal to my vanity and self-importance: "It's a surprise for you, Dad."

I thought his remark was merely an attempt at a comeback for its own sake, but as I watched the boys walk toward the pool holding an orange coloured item between them, I realised that his words had a double meaning. Jacob's cautious eyes looking back at me revealed more than he would have liked: they had done it. They were attempting to conceal the toy that their mother had told them they could not bring to the pool. Their attempt at subterfuge had almost succeeded.

Antics such as these bring a smile to our faces. Such tomfooleries are, after all, still relatively innocent and only a drop in the ocean of the rebellion of which a child is capable. Still, with my eldest, Joshua, now in his fifteenth year, I no longer have to wonder how long it will be before all my children will lose every vestige of childhood. Will their ability to trust unconditionally disappear as cynicism sets in and my protection is no longer a guarantee 24/7? I know that there is as much chance of controlling my children's destiny as there is of travelling to the moon on horseback. We can coax and cajole, inspire virtue, and encourage goodness, but at the end of the day the dialogue between the free soul and the Maker of the universe occurs in the journey they embark on together. This journey began before I conceived of them and it will continue beyond my death.

I take comfort in the discovery that increasing age need not deny a soul access to a childlike faith. Such a faith can be discovered even in the frail and tired body of an elderly lady—in particular, one whom my children called *Great Grandma*.

62

A No-So Blind Faith

Still tall and slender and with a good mop of shoulder-length white hair, Doreen was eighty-four years of age when she boldly told me that she was "ready to go." It was the day of Joshua's First Holy Communion. Because winter viruses had taken up residence in our home in the lead-up to Joshua's big day, we thought it would be wise and courteous to apprise all invited guests of the situation in case they would choose to stay away. We particularly told Doreen, knowing how besieged she was by a litany of ailments such as high blood pressure, neuropathy in her feet, chronic airways disease, arthritis, and a host of other ailments. The last thing we wanted was for a visit to our home to lead to further complications. But in true Doreen style she decided to attend, nonetheless. Dressed as elegantly as she usually was in grey pants and cardigan, she quipped, "Well, I've gotta die of something. I'm ready to go." And she meant it. Her first great grandson's Holy Communion could not be missed.

When I first listened to her story, it was hard to believe that this mother of eight, and a great-grandma, was still attending gym twice a week, still held a driver's license, vacationed to exotic places and spent as much time going out as her frailty would permit. With her almost snow-white complexion not distracting from the gentleness of her face, she recounted the day in 2006 when she prepared for her cataract operation. "I had been sitting nervously in my granny flat kitchen waiting for my son Paul to take me to the hospital," she recalled. Cataract removal, regardless of how "minor" it was, was still surgery and she was nervous. "The words of my physician kept ringing in my ears: 'We don't use general anaesthetic for cataract removal anymore.' Anxious, I prayed, 'Please, Lord, don't let me worry about it.'"

Even though Doreen remained concerned on the way to the hospital, her fears disappeared completely upon arrival. "For the first time in my life I knew straight away that God had answered my prayer and had carried me," she told me.

I sat there perplexed and blurted out my question without thinking. "Do you mean that was the very *first* time you had a prayer answered?" I was in disbelief. The first time? At age 76? Doreen answered indirectly, maintaining the flow of her sentence. "And ever since then I have not worried about things. I just say, *'Dear Lord, I know you are going to be with me today; even if I get cancer, it won't matter; all I want to do is your will.'* It is so lovely that I don't need to worry. I came from him and I am going back to him. Trust is the biggest lesson."

Having gone there that day expecting tales of great faith experiences, I came out confused. Doreen's faith was not a result of what I had hoped would be quasi "mystical" experiences at all. Instead, Doreen was teaching me something more important.

Christians use the word *faith* a good deal. When questioned about the reason for their belief some Christians respond, "Well, I just do; it's my faith," without giving the matter much thought at all, as with a blind faith, accepted without question, irrational. Put another way, this faith could be merely used as a crutch to lean on when things can't be explained, and one has to make some sense of the world.

Yet, a blind faith can also be the strongest type—a sign of complete abandonment to the will of God, formed through great hardship.

To a person versed in the Judeo-Christian tradition, this understanding should not come as a surprise. If ever a story could knock any romantic notion of faith out of a person, it would be the story of Abraham and his son Isaac. A father is asked to kill his own child as a sign of his faith in God whom he cannot see—a hard task for sure, if ever there was one. But such a faith is born from the pangs of circumstance, fuelled by an unearthly trust that Doreen has made her motto for life. "It's all in the hands of God," she proclaims with the certainty of a disciple of Christ.

63

Beyond the River Nile

From her birth in 1929, Doreen was initiated into a life of change and adaptability. She was born in the ancient city of Cairo even though both of her parents were English. Her father, Albert Beatty, whose family came from Worthing, worked in the Army Service Corps and had already spent six years in India before his three-year stint in Egypt. Not long after Doreen's first birthday, the Beatty family moved back to England. "I believe we spent some time in Southampton, where my mother's family lived. I have a photo when I was only fifteen months old which was taken at the studio there," Doreen recalled. Southampton was only a short stop, however. The family soon made their home in the army barracks (Block D and then Block A) in Feltham, a town just two kilometres from Heathrow Airport and twenty-two kilometres outside London.

Located in the London Borough of Hounslow in Greater London, Feltham is known more for the Young Offenders institution and as a major centre of employment and leisure than for Army Barracks. The demographics of Feltham began to change in the 1930s, however, as the population increased, and industry developed. When Doreen's family arrived, it was a large village in the county of Middlesex and blessed with open green fields that delighted the children of the area. Feltham's garden suburb-style terrace homes contrasted greatly with the small Victorian terraced houses and blocks of flats found in London.

Listening to Doreen's account of her years in Feltham was like being invited to the premiere of a period piece on the big screen. War. Hospitals. Sickness. And of course, the bombs that exploded around her, both actual and of the emotional brand. Death, or at least the threat of it, seemed to be lurking around the corner.

In 1935, Doreen was diagnosed with scarlet fever and as the military hospital would not accept her, Doreen was admitted to an isolation hospital instead. She would see the concerned look on her father's face as he peered through the window that allowed Doreen and the other patients a view of the outside world. For Doreen, the time spent in that hospital seemed like ages.

The day of her "release" came and after Doreen was given what she could only describe as a "decontamination bath," she discovered that someone other than her parents was there to pick her up. She was not left waiting long for an answer. The maternal grandmother died, hence her parents' absence. At least she had met her once or twice in what seemed like a big house to curious juvenile eyes.

As for her paternal grandparents, well, Doreen had never met them. While growing up she had wondered why they were never spoken of, and she'd never asked. It wasn't until many years later, on a visit back to England in 1985, that Doreen found out the sad truth. Doreen's paternal grandmother had died in childbirth. Her father, Albert, was the child, and only four years later, he lost his father too. Albert and his siblings were farmed out to different relatives after their father's premature death. This was an era, it would seem, when keeping families together at all costs was not a priority. As if to symbolise the fracture that had occurred in Doreen's paternal family, her Uncle Jim's surname now had only one *t*—Beaty—rather than two.

As time passed, Doreen noticed that something was not right with her mother Elsie. "She never had any maternal instincts," recalls Doreen. Doreen was chosen to do many of the domestic duties that her mother found distasteful. The situation for the Beattys only worsened as the dark clouds of war began their descent over England and all of Europe.

64

The London Blitz and Doodlebugs

When Doreen reached her eleventh birthday, Feltham became a prime target of German air raids. Commencing in 1940, the year of the heaviest raids, they continued sporadically, whether by day or by night, until 1944. Despite its still mainly rural appearance, Feltham housed Britain's second largest railway marshalling yard, as well as the army barracks. Civilian fatalities were the collateral damage of Britain's decision to declare war on Germany, whose vengeance only grew as the war continued. At least Albert who was now retired from the army was able to remain with his family, including Doreen's younger sister Pamela, six years her junior, and Anne, born shortly before the start of the raids and two months after the start of the war.

The war changed village life permanently. Gas masks, flying glass, trenches, food rations, queues, people running maniacally towards shelters, "doodlebugs" (also called "buzz bombs"), and the drone of enemy engines, all became fixed in the local vocabulary and communal memory. The gas masks had to be carried throughout the war. I could understand why Doreen hated them. When I Googled *gas masks*, the pictures I found made me wonder if George Lucas, creator of the original Star Wars Trilogy, had in fact been inspired by them to create some of his alien creatures with the aardvark snouts!

At the start of the war, the mask came in a strong cardboard box and was held in place with a thick string. By the end, its packaging resembled a handbag and was much more user friendly, albeit still shaped a little "funny," as Doreen remembered. Each weekday morning, Doreen and Pamela made their way to school through their back fence. They threw their "stylish" gas mask "handbags" over their shoulders and obediently carried them along. They knew that if an air raid occurred before they were more than halfway to school, they could return home. If they were more than halfway there, as they had learnt via frequent practice in air raid drills at school, a series of actions needed to occur.

As the siren sounded, the teacher called the class to attention and reminded the students to put on their gas masks. "You know, every time I have been given anaesthetic in hospital I am reminded of the masks—the same smell of rubber," Doreen shared, screwing up her face to represent that all-too-memorable sensation. She would listen carefully as her teacher then ordered the students to line up in an orderly fashion. They proceeded to walk behind the teacher who led those in her charge to the shelters outside.

This type of shelter, known as the Anderson shelter, (named after Sir John Anderson who had prepared Britain for the air raids), would be hard for children of the war to forget. Many homes also had such a shelter. Doreen recalls the Anderson shelter outside her house. It resembled a mound of earth, except the walls were made of concrete and corrugated iron sheeting camouflaged by a layer of earth on the surface. The fleeing refugees would enter through the flat corrugated steel panel door and take a couple of steps down into a space that was not larger than a queen-size bed and about a metre deep. The school shelters were much larger and made of concrete cylinders that were adorned on both sides by seats.

Some homes were lucky enough to have an internal shelter that looked like a table in the corner of the living room known as the Morrison shelter, (named after the then Minister of Home Security). It had welded wire mesh sides that transformed the table into a cage housing a mattress. Should the ceiling cave in, the table-top would protect those sleeping under it. Doreen's neighbours, the Houghtons had this type and it spared them a time-consuming nocturnal trek outside. The Beattys were not that fortunate, their shelter being an older model of the outdoor type. "When the air raids began, we would be woken and make our way outside. At first, I thought it was all a bit of an adventure," she said smiling.

With all five of the Beattys in that small shelter the shelter was cramped. The smell of the little bit of food they brought with them wafted through the enclosed space. On nights when it was obvious that multiple raids were on the menu, the Beattys found lodging in the shelter for the entire night. There was little room to move, little privacy or comfort, but being there meant safety.

For a while after the raids began, Doreen managed to cloak their brutality with a veil of childhood ignorance. She marvelled at the fighter jets as she stared at them flying in formation like dancers in a troupe. She wondered how they could stay up there. "I was young and didn't know exactly what the war meant then." But the war lasted a long time. Doreen grew up. Without a faith.

By 1944, as the raids continued, Doreen passed into her teen years and the bright colours of childhood were replaced with the dull grey shades of adolescence. Every sound and colour of war suddenly told a different story. "You know, when I read a book about the war recently, it cast my mind back to these raids. It wasn't just England that suffered the bombing. Innocent people in Germany experienced the same thing. Innocent women and children all suffering because of the plans of mad men."

Doreen knew when disaster was about to strike. She was familiar with the sounds of the air raid siren. The one signalling the commencement of a raid was different from the one signalling its end. "That one was a monotone and we knew it was over," she said. But the relief did not mitigate the panic and seriousness of the danger just passed, because more danger was almost guaranteed. The shelters were no longer a novelty; going into one was like getting into a sleeping bag at a campsite. For the now fifteen-year-old Doreen, they meant life or death. And when the "buzz bombs" came, even the shelters would do little to protect them if one dropped nearby.

Buzz bombs! It would be hard even for a child to be complacent about these particular instruments of war. Known also as doodlebugs or "reprisal weaponry," these non-piloted V-1 flying bombs were launched by the Germans from Belgium and Northern France beginning in 1942. They cut out in eerie silence just moments—five seconds, to be exact—before exploding on their target. That silence was deafening. Would it land on us? That thought was ever present for Doreen. Those buzz bombs that were not intercepted by fighter planes, anti-aircraft guns, or "barrage balloons" did great damage. One of these bombs alone could kill ten Feltham citizens in one night. Feltham may have been spared the even more dangerous supersonic V2 rockets, but enough damage was done by the buzz bombs. "Even if they landed a block away," Doreen explained, "there would be huge debris—glass, massive masonry!"

Raleigh Way came to Doreen's mind as she attempted to recall the exact location of homes in her estate that had been bombed. The damage there was nothing like the destruction she saw in London, however. There she saw large craters in the streets, half-buildings still standing, chunks of flesh torn from its torso. The Beatty home was fortunately spared—except for one bomb that struck at its very heart in 1942, when Doreen still did not understand what faith meant. That was the day Mrs. Elsie Beatty abandoned her family.

65

Abandoned

It had come out of the blue. No note. No explanation. No goodbye. Doreen was thirteen at the time and her sisters were nine and two. Elsie managed to leave before the buzz bombs came. Doreen never saw her mother again.

"I was so angry," Doreen told me, shaking a little while describing her seventy-year-old wounds as if they were fresh. The pain of her mother's sudden departure in the middle of the war was as real now, all these decades later, as when it happened. "I had no idea why. I came home from school one day and she was gone." I was surprised by the raw emotion that the memory elicited in Doreen. She had learned many years later that Elsie had suffered from depression. Perhaps this explained the emotional absence of her mother long before her departure.

Doreen's pain lifted greatly during our discussion when my toddler, Josiah, walked into the room and started muttering something at me in his endearing gibberish, his large puppy dog eyes fixed on mine. Doreen's face lit up, her natural affinity for motherhood obvious. It was ironic that a woman who had been denied the love of a mother could understand so well what being a mother meant. When I tried to apologise for the distraction, Doreen wouldn't hear of it. "That's what little boys are meant to do."

Doreen's maternal instincts had kicked into gear the day her mother left. Because there was no child care or pension, Doreen's father decided that while he worked during the day as a store man in the army barracks to make a life for his three daughters, Doreen had to sacrifice her schooling and remain at home to look after her sisters.

"You could have ended up being taken away, couldn't you?" I asked Doreen. Having read about the terrible episode in Britain's history known as the Child Migrants Scheme, in which thousands of children had been sent as far away as Australia without their parents' permission, it struck me just how vulnerable Doreen's situation had been. Certainly, sending his children to an orphanage would have been an option for her father. But Doreen was one of the lucky ones, because her father could still provide for the family and did not ask for support.

"I paid the bills and the housework was easy for me. The gas and electricity were *pay as you go*. I remember putting pennies in the meter to make sure we had enough power to keep things running."

Our conversation was interrupted again when Therese deposited our month-old son, Jonah, into my arms. Josiah soon came in to dote on his "baby." Doreen's face lit up again. She asked Josiah to look at Jonah's little toes, which she held in awe, then addressed Jonah again. "You are so beautiful. You are a most precious gift of God," she said with that smile again widening her joyful gaze. I now knew from whom Therese had learnt that phrase, which she had often used in reference to our children. "That's your Daddy, yes, your Daddy," Doreen continued, imagining what Jonah might be thinking and feeling as his eyes fixed on mine, just as his brother's had earlier.

Doreen's words reminded me of what she had told me another time: how she marvels at the work of the Creator's hand, from the gorgeous tree to the tiny fingers of a child in the womb. "When I wake up, I marvel at the beauty around me and thank God," she had told me. "I now worry when I get behind the wheel, not because I am old but because I get too distracted by the beauty around me," she said.

This sense of awe has served Doreen well. When faced with the claims of those scientific naturalists who see in evolutionary "truths" evidence for God's non-existence, she is not fazed. "Evolution no longer worries me. Years ago, I remember looking at my hand and thought how absolutely fantastic all our body parts are—they couldn't have just happened by chance. Even the Earth has to have had some power behind it to do what it does." At the time, Doreen had been reading a book called *Unintelligent Design,* and it strengthened her faith rather than made her question it.

If it weren't for the suffering that Doreen endured both before and after her departure from England, one might be forgiven for thinking that she was nothing more than a modern-day Pollyanna, smiling all day and playing her *glad game* come what may. But her sense of gratitude had more than a fictional characterisation device behind it. "I talk to God all day long," she told me. "We come from God and will go back to him. And as for my suffering, well there is no point wasting it. I offer it up." I wondered where this strong faith had come from. It certainly hadn't come from her parents, or from her education.

As a child she had heard of Jesus, but she explained that she had thought of him as just a mythical figure. "I felt sad that he was killed, but it all seemed just a story to me. I didn't know he was real," she recalled while reflecting on her childhood education in an English state school.

Enter stage left one Catholic mother, a baker, and the allure of tea and currant buns!

66

Currant Buns

The war was not yet over when Doreen's appetite resolutely sealed her fate. "Doreen, the baker's been. I've got currant buns!" Mrs. Mona Houghton called out from the house next door. The hungry teenager approached the back fence and, using the post as a catapult, jumped over it and entered the Houghton home.

Visits with Mrs. Houghton were some of Doreen's most cherished memories. After Elsie's departure, Mrs. Houghton had to some extent taken her place. Invitations to tea can be dangerous liaisons. In the Houghton house, they were a precursor to a more, let's say, calculated invitation.

"Doreen, would you like to come to my son's baptism?" Mona asked Doreen one day. Doreen attended, and she did so with her father's permission, although he couldn't understand why his daughter had suddenly taken an interest in church. "How can you believe in God with all this suffering in the world?" he would ask, echoing a sentiment that has plagued countless others through the centuries. Doreen didn't know how to respond then. Her faith then was only a seed.

And then came another invitation. "Doreen, Father said you can attend the youth group in my parish, but he said that because you are not Catholic you really should attend Mass sometimes." Doreen, now seventeen, decided on her own steam that she would go. She met her husband, John, through this youth group, and became acquainted with Fr. Bishop, a convert priest in his early thirties who took Doreen and twenty-three other youth on a camping trip in Surrey. Sitting at Mass amidst faithful Catholic youth, watching them all go up to receive Communion, Doreen wanted more. Her longing to belong was a pull too great for her to resist. For the first time she was experiencing a family that was not dysfunctional. Her full reception into the Catholic Church in 1946 almost caught her by surprise.

"I have always said I feel I came into the Church through the back door—like I cheated a little," Doreen recounts. Doreen's conversion story is not the typical Damascus Road experience of the St. Paul type with which many are familiar. God has used many ways to communicate with a soul in need of conversion, whether through sudden illumination, a miraculous intervention, or a general inner knowledge. Conversions are often spectacular, witnessing to the fact that God's ways are not our own. Christians grow up feeding on a smorgasbord of stories like that of Paul falling to the ground, blinded by a heavenly vision on his way to persecute more Christians in Damascus. Unlike these more dramatic accounts, Doreen's conversion was not the fruit of a tangible experience of God's love, but rather the outcome of a longing for love in general.

In many ways, Doreen's longing reminded me of another longing that God used to draw another more famous soul to himself—one of Doreen's contemporaries, who was then still at his Oxford University post. The love for which Doreen longed through the tumultuous war years was much like the elusive joy desired by famous author and teacher C. S. Lewis. Lewis never took the boat across the Tiber to Rome, but his books have enticed generations of children and adults alike with their Christian imagery and teachings. Lewis's account of his conversion experience in *Surprised by Joy*, remains a vivid testimony of just how quickly God can creep up on a person in the silence of the heart, using whatever circumstances are available. I thought of his story as Doreen told me hers. A *deep longing* paved both of their paths to God.

Lewis's conversion occurred in 1931 while he was riding in the sidecar of his brother's motorbike on a trip to the zoo. He describes this conversion as quite sudden. At the start of the trip Lewis did not believe in Christ's Divinity. Yet, by the end of their destination, as if he had just woken up from a different reality, he had accepted that Jesus was indeed the Son of God.

Despite its suddenness, Lewis's conversion was the end-product, an epiphany moment, a joy that Lewis had realised he had been pining for all his life, even though he had tasted it as a child. Only later did Lewis realise that he had been neglecting the *source* of that joy.

For Doreen, God used a lady who knew that what Doreen needed was something more than a mere human could provide. The sense of belonging that Doreen felt in the Houghton's church was only the precursor to experiencing, as Lewis had, the source of that longing, though not always in ways one would choose.

67

The Getting of Wisdom

The following images now blur together in Doreen's mind: the war's end, her baptism, her blossoming friendship with John, their farewell at Kings Cross Station in London, her following him to Australia after praying for guidance. She still remembers visiting the nearest church to ask for guidance about going to Australia. She had resisted saying yes to John at Kings Cross, but only because she admittedly could dig in her heels when she felt she was being pushed into something. But it was inevitable. Their relationship of three and a half years before John's migration had to mean something. No doubt the glowing reports about Australia that John's mother had provided were a further confirmation that Doreen should follow John to the Promised Land!

Like a slideshow sweeping through her memory, she could see, with the wisdom that comes from hindsight and a developing faith, that life was not meant to be easy. Life in Australia was not as glowing as her mother-in-law had made out. The sense of belonging that Doreen had sought to nurture was only a stepping-stone to something more sacred in God's plan: the transformation of a soul, as demanding as that can be.

With a faith that had germinated a little more, Doreen now had plenty to offer to God in suffering. Not long after their marriage, John had begun working out in the country. Difficulties caused by the migrant experience, personality differences, and the challenges of a large family of eight children all took their toll over time. There were miscarriages too, and the struggle of varicose veins in pregnancy. And they were not well off. "At times we didn't know where to put our kids," Doreen recounted. "They just had to share. All those children!" The part of the marriage vows that spoke of *for better or for worse* certainly resounded deep in Doreen's mind.

Doreen underwent many more struggles as she discovered the plan of God for her life. "My faith was a grain of sand back then compared to what it is now," Doreen told me. "At times I would cry my eyes out and tell God I wished I was dead. But he pulled me through it. I didn't have trust then." I knew that to ask her for more information about her difficult marriage would be to trespass on territory that was sacred. Their story was their story, their journey of the cross. That Doreen could still see so much good in it, and maintain a friendship with her separated husband, spoke volumes to me. Doreen took her marriage vows seriously and she never divorced or remarried.

The sand-grain of faith she'd had as a young Christian had been nurtured in great part by John when he introduced Doreen to the Charismatic Movement. "Now I don't worry. I have learnt that Jesus is within me," she told me. She was always grateful that John had been the catalyst for her deepening faith. What Mona Houghton had started John had continued. The song that her children had learnt for their First Holy Communion, a song that is familiar to Catholics in Perth, came back to her: "God is dwelling in my heart," she would hear them sing. Only later did she come to understand: the image of God as judge just didn't cut it anymore. He dwelt in her heart every day and every minute. "The letter of the law got replaced with the letter of love," she recalled. "God was now personal to me."

I was particularly impressed by Doreen's answer to my question regarding her thoughts on grace. She averted her gaze for a moment, and I could see she was deep in thought. Then, after a few moments of silence, she said, "To me it means God's blessings, moments of peace and calm." Suffering had not taken her faith away; it had only strengthened it. She knew that God had carried her through each moment. "I feel so calm now, as if someone is saying, *'It is okay, I am with you.'*"

With a courage that reminds me of Australia's first canonised saint, Mary MacKillop, Doreen is a sign that the greatest crosses can actually be the greatest blessings. Just two years before her death, Mary MacKillop said the following about the love of the Sacred Heart of Jesus:

And in Its cause, since It deigned to raise me to It, I have never known aught but true peace and contentment of heart. Its love makes suffering sweet, Its love makes the world a desert. When storms rage, when persecutions or dangers threaten, I quietly creep into Its deep abyss; and securely sheltered there, my soul is in peace, though my body is tossed upon the stormy waves of a cold and selfish world (21 May 1907).

"Bit by bit I am coming to pieces. I think it's just part of my brain falling off," Doreen joked when commenting on what all the medication she takes is doing to her. Certainly, Doreen's experience of ageing has added to her trials. Her life has indeed been akin to a boat besieged by waves on a stormy sea. But her faith has not fallen to pieces. She has had recourse to that communion with God. What she has discovered there is a faith furnished not by mystical experiences but by simple, childlike trust. Her life has shown me that faith is indeed at its purest—most like that of a child—when, as Pope Francis wrote in his first encyclical, *Lumen Fidei*, one can see with the eyes of Jesus, understand the Father's plan for our lives, and entrust that life back to him.

Postscript

Doreen Freakley passed away on March 30, 2017 after a relatively brief battle with cancer. Joshua, her first great grandson, was able to visit with her a few days before her death and sang a favourite hymn to her as she listened. Family members present at her death, witnessed Doreen, in her final moments, lifting her hands as if reaching out to someone, while she smiled.

DARING TO BE A JOSEPH

⌘

"And whatever he did, the Lord made it succeed."
Genesis: 39:23

⌘

68

Fatherhood

The nearly 15 years that have flashed before me since I began writing the first edition of this book, have provided me with many opportunities to reflect on what it means to be a follower of Christ. In December 2014, a family crisis would bring this reflection into sharp focus. It sent all of us, especially our children, into a spin. The suffering that ensued was unexpected, and while life has returned to some semblance of normality, it will never be the same.

This book is not the place to discuss this crisis, but suffice it to say, while I always valued my role as a father, I have valued it even more since then. It is also a role I cannot fulfil properly on my own, relying on my own resources. I need, more and more, to rely on the grace and wisdom that comes from God's Word and his presence in my life, especially now that I have teens, facing new struggles and trying to help them navigate their own path.

I have heard myself say to my children so often, as if as an echo of the Father's own words to me all my life, *"Why don't you just listen to me? Actions have consequences. Think before you act. You think I am being cruel, but oh if you only knew how much I love you. You think I am asking you too much, but you can't see that I know what you need in order to cope in life and be the best version of yourself.... And no, if I treat your brother or sister differently, it doesn't mean I love you less!!"* It is as if God is saying to me, now that I have reached middle age - *"Now do you understand? Do you understand that even though I would love for you to listen to me, that I can't force you to? I would love for you to trust me in those things in which I simply know better than you. Can you see why I sometimes discipline you or why I let you go your own way? Can you see the potential of your children, their capacity for greatness, just like I see yours? And can you see that sometimes, being obedient, is just as nonsensical to those I love as it is to your own children, especially when you can't see the way out?"*

I needed to dare myself again to be like a person I had admired in my study of scripture. I had to *dare to be a Joseph* in my covenant walk with God.

69

Joseph's Legacy

Many readers may be familiar with the story of Joseph in the Old Testament; the guy that has been brought to life in Andrew Lloyd Webber's theatrical production *Joseph and the Amazing Technicolour Dreamcoat*. If you have small children, you may have seen the NEST production of it on DVD or on a Christian TV Channel such as EWTN or TBN. Either way you would know the story of Joseph is powerful.

Though Joseph is not in Christ's direct bloodline, (his brother Judah gets that privilege), he is much more like Christ than his older brother; a portrait of purity, steadfastness, integrity, trustworthiness and honour. The Catholic Men's faith sharing group which I hosted some years ago once spent a whole session reflecting on Joseph's story, based on Genesis 39: 7-28.

As we gathered in my old loungeroom, having eaten our snacks and bantered for a while, the men and I prepared our meditation. We slowly read of the sexual advances made on Joseph by his master Potiphar's wife, all of which Joseph refuses.

> *"Behold, because of me my master has no concern about anything in the house, and he has put everything that he has in my charge... How then can I do this great wickedness and sin against God?" (vv. 8-9).*

The wife's lies lead Joseph to being thrown in prison, and it is in this darkness, that his light shines all the brighter.

"But the Lord was with Joseph and showed him steadfast love and gave him favour in the sight of the keeper of the prison. And the keeper of the prison put Joseph in charge of all the prisoners who were in prison [paying] no attention to anything that was in Joseph's charge, because the Lord was with him. And whatever he did, the Lord made it succeed" (vv. 21-23).

What struck me the most in this sequence was not just Joseph's trust (and imitation of Christ, led like a lamb to the slaughter, never opening his mouth when condemned, refusing to give in to temptation) but God's pride and trust in Joseph. Even though it is Potiphar and the prison keeper who are depicted as trusting Joseph implicitly, it would seem that they point to the real "master" who places trust in Joseph, namely the "Lord [who] was with him."

God is depicted as the navigator of Joseph's perilous journey. It is God who grants Joseph an exalted place regardless of circumstances – his gift of dreams, his privileges in Potiphar's house and in the prison, and then his role in leading all of Egypt as second only to the Pharaoh. His exalted state is developed in crisis – while he is being rejected, sold into slavery, accused of rape and thrown into prison. God is a master who trusts that his servant will do precisely what he has been called to do, despite the difficulties; in fact, it would seem, actually *because of* the difficulties. Joseph would certainly be one of those about whom Jesus would subsequently say, "Everyone to whom much was given, of him much will be required, and from him to whom they entrusted much, they will demand the more" (Luke 12:48). It is exactly like me, when I depend on one child in particular, to help me with certain "jobs" because I know he can do them!

The story of Joseph greatly encourages me. Joseph reminds me that we are so important in the plan of God. He has entrusted great things to us which can only be discovered if we allow God's plan to bear fruit, by being faithful to his will and by having a transcendent vision that gives us the ability to see beyond the horrible circumstances of the present to a greater glory in a distant future.

More importantly, it is a vision that manifests as the ability to see in these same horrible present circumstances, the footprint of God who is walking by your side and perhaps even carrying you.

God had taught me this lesson in 2003 when my mother had died. Now, nearly two decades after her death, I am still needing reminding, that our Heavenly Father does indeed "know the plans I have for you …. Not for evil [but] to give a future and a hope" (Jeremiah 29:11), because for "those who love God all things work together for good … according to his purpose" (Romans 8:28).

Yes, I need, more and more, to have the courage to dare to be a Joseph, especially in the darkest moments of my life. It was in the darkness of Joseph's plight that God sowed the seeds for the salvation of all of Egypt (and the surrounding lands and their peoples, including the Hebrew people) from famine. Had Joseph not taken up the challenge of trusting in God, the result would have been extremely different. I wonder how different things might be if I face each challenge as an opportunity which is under God's loving control instead of as an indication that God has abandoned me?

Will you allow God to entrust even greater things to you so that his plans for the welfare of the human race can come to fruition? It is humbling isn't it, to know that God allows fallible human beings to participate in his work of salvation? It is more humbling still for me to trust that the seeds of this desire for our salvation, and the plan of our salvation itself, are planted in every individual in ways God alone knows they will understand. Some are called to greatness on the world stage – while others are called in more humble ways.

THE HOUND OF HEAVEN

⌘

I have loved you in perpetual charity.
Therefore, showing pity, I have drawn you.
- Jeremiah 31:3

⌘

70

The Pope and the Pilgrim

When I began the Roman leg of our European trip in 1998, I couldn't believe I had finally made it. Checking into our hotel on Via Nazionale late afternoon on January 5 my thoughts quickly turned to the Vatican. Seizing my chance to use the Italian I had learnt at high school and university, I enquired at the front desk, pretty chuffed with myself, and discovered that there would be a 9 a.m. Mass the following morning. All set; a Mass in St. Peter's Square would be our first outing in the Eternal City.

With parents in tow, and a quick bus ride down the street, I entered the piazza flanked by Bernini's colonnade that symbolically wraps pilgrims like a mother does a child. The Egyptian obelisk at the centre of the piazza grew as we passed it on our approach to the queue forming just beneath the steps leading to the portico of the Basilica. From a distance, pilgrims looked like ants before the great sentry-like statues of St. Peter and St. Paul.

Unfortunately, the distasteful scaffolding that groped the façade of the Renaissance basilica dampened my awe temporarily. Years of pollution had blackened the stone, a problem given the Great Jubilee barely two years away.

I was a little anxious going through security. Dressed in a thick trench coat, beret and strapped to a large old-fashioned video camera, I figured I would be stopped for sure. Instead, I was let through without a second thought.

The majesty inside the Basilica mesmerised my senses. Even before I reached my seat on makeshift pews behind the barricades that flanked the processional aisle, I began filming the mosaics bathed in gold, Bernini's bronzed pavilion-like structure rising thirty metres above the main altar, as well as the many statues, and the Basilica's opulent nave.

I couldn't wipe the smile off my face. Even my father seemed in awe. Both he and my mother had never been to Rome. I knew the Mass was about to begin when the choir began their Latin hymn. It was only minutes before the procession of bishops (and priests, soon to be ordained bishops), when I realised that this was not an ordinary Mass. It hadn't even crossed my mind that it was the Feast of the Epiphany.

Suddenly, I hear the crowd behind me cheering and clapping at an invisible figure at the end of the procession of white and gold-coloured vestments. I got the surprise of my life when I saw Pope John Paul II begin his long walk to the main altar above the tomb of St. Peter, the first pope.

The fact that I was almost hanging over the barricade by the time John Paul II had reached my location down the aisle had more to do with the excitement of pilgrims on my left who were all trying to get a better glimpse of their pontiff, rather than me attempting to defy gravity. But it didn't matter.

He shuffled his way up the aisle and the signs of suffering from the ongoing effects of his shooting in 1981, as well as Parkinson's disease, were obvious. Nonetheless, I had a smile on my face that I couldn't shake. His fragility was just another witness to his greatness.

Before me was a man of history - a man who was a major catalyst for the collapse of the Soviet Union, a saint who had defended human rights and dignity, (who travelled more than all the other popes put together spreading the love and mercy of God), and a Bishop who tried to bring to full realisation the true vision of Vatican II. Even his weakness witnessed to the dignity of human life at all stages of life. He could have retired by 1998, perhaps even earlier, but he fought the good fight for another seven years.

As he approached me, I saw that the muscles in his face were taut and he couldn't smile. But he looked directly at me and raised his hand in blessing. For the next three hours this same man remained but a speck to my naked eye as he celebrated Mass.

The words of St. Paul still come to mind when I think of my brief "private audience" with the Great John Paul II, made all the more poignant because of his frailty.

Because of this, I am pleased in my infirmity: in difficulties, in reproaches, in difficulties, in persecutions, in distresses, for the sake of Christ. For when I am weak, then I am powerful (2 Corinthians 12:10).

It was precisely in his weakness wherein lay his greatness; precisely in his ability to let go of the inevitability of decay for anything in us that is not of God, not eternal. And unlike John Paul II, and despite all I have already been made to understand in my walk with the Lord, the superficial still has a hold on me. Concern for appearance, for reputation, and for my floundering youth, still preoccupy me. I am far from entering that spiritual place that I know I am being called to.

If I am one day to approach the dusk of my life with true dignity, even as my body may fail me, I still have that one perennial lesson to learn to which John Paul II attested in his weakness. Indeed, we will all die, and there is nothing we can take with us except that which is eternal - faith, hope and love and their power and promise.

Those I have interviewed for this book have shown me that God has a way of helping us learn this lesson in a myriad of ways. Since my mother's passing, I have often wondered about the day my father will be called from this life. I don't feel either of us is ready for that. But not long ago, not long after my father entered his 74th year, he shared something with me that both surprised me, and encouraged me to remember, that God's Covenant plan for us never changes.

My photo of John Paul II, January 6, 1998, St. Peter's Basilica.

71

My Father and I

As soon as my parents and I arrived in Sicily in late 1997, three weeks or so before our sojourn in Rome, my father visited his Aunt Pippina who was very ill. Having lived with Pippina's mother - his grandmother, from the age of 4 until his migration to Australia, it was not surprising that Dad wanted to see his aunt. He had hoped it could be under better circumstances. Pippina was in a coma – in fact it had already lasted three months.

But when Dad visited her, the strangest thing happened. Pippina just sat up and spoke with him as if she were absolutely fine. They talked about family and whether Dad had gone to visit his parents' grave. It was surreal. The next day, his cousin Rosina notified us of her mother's death. "Bruno, she was waiting for you," Rosina told him. Somehow, she knew my father was coming and she held on just long enough.

What would become a trip of a lifetime, that not only included John Paul II but also Lourdes, Paris and meeting most of my father's family for the first time ever, had begun with the most amazing grace – a mercy for my father that, I hope, he understands comes from the hand of our Heavenly Father.

Dad and I have not always seen eye to eye. We are different in a number of ways. Growing up I didn't know him as well as I should. He worked so hard for the family and we didn't spend much time together. He spoke English with an Aussie accent that mirrored that of his fellow labourers more than my own. He was a bit of a larrikin while I was melancholic, and what he achieved through the work of his hands, I could only do so through my pen.

Certainly, he has a good heart – I only have to see how he cherishes my children to appreciate that.

The older I become the more I realise that one cannot judge the souls of others with any degree of certainty. It was my father who named me – after St. Renato. It was also he who specifically wanted a third child; namely, me. His stories, such as him being partly brought up by German soldiers in wartime Sicily, being named after Mussolini's son and playing in the tunnels that the soldiers had dug during their time in his land of birth, are ones I now treasure.

But we continue to disagree on matters of faith and the mysteries of the universe.

So, I was quite surprised when, after the birth of my fourth child Josiah in 2012, Dad dropped a bombshell. He told me of a dream that he had never forgotten and had kept with him for over fifty years. By the time he had finished telling me, I knew more than ever before, that my father and I had more in common than I thought. I knew then, and accept in faith and hope now, that what God did for my mother as she passed through to eternal life, he will also do for my father one day. Just as God kept his promise to me, he will keep the one he made my father.

**My father,
with his mother and Aunt.**

His beloved grandmother.

**Shortly before
migrating to Australia**

72

Apocalyptic

"Dad, let me record it okay? Say it in Sicilian," I asked, or rather strongly suggested to him when he told me of the dream that he says is as vivid today as it was when he first received it. I wasn't going to let him leave without it on file! I had thought that only my mother's side of the family was entrusted with the gift of dreams!

Dad looked a little embarrassed, but he consented.

"Here, hold the recorder," I directed. And after a slight chuckle, he began to recount his dream.

"I was walking along the countryside in the hills of Naso looking for bird nests which I always did. Soon, `I spotted a very large olive tree, with a huge stump, three branches and small leaves. In the middle, there was a nest.

"As I climbed the tree, I reached out to touch the nest, and a serpent slithered out, frightening me. Instinctively, I jumped down and ran away, down some steps nearby as I heard what sounded like a bouncing ball coming after me.

"The tree left my field of vision and I saw a gate. I ran through it, turned around the corner and watched as the ball bounced by. When it was safe, I proceeded back up the steps, through the gate and reached a relatively small flat open area. I looked up to see a gentleman, dressed in a striped grey suit, in an open field. 'Do you know who I am?' he asked me.

'Don Salvatore', I responded. I knew it was the Lord. He said, 'Let me show you something' and so I looked 300 metres down the hill and saw a large carriage being led by a fire-breathing dragon. About six soldiers flanked the carriage holding their spears, dressed in red.

"Don Salvatore then directed me to the dragon and said, 'That is the devil. He is in charge of the world. I will save you. Come with me.'

"We went down the other side of the hill to a road about ten metres away. In the cliff face adjacent to the road there was an earth coloured opening. When we entered, I saw about seven or eight marble steps, leading to a small landing followed by another three steps leading outside. I saw another landing leading to two further stone steps and a pergola about six square metres in size.

"Other people were there, seated, waiting for Jesus to speak. There were three containers full of fish. Jesus gave each person one fish each. To me he gave *three* fish on a plate. When we finished, I alone was transported with Jesus to a beach, with pristine emerald green waters buffeted by gentle waves.

"There were three large boulders on the beach, about ten metres apart. From each rock came out three beautiful women. Because I was cheeky, I pinched one in the leg, right in front of Jesus." *That's my Dad*, I thought. "Jesus then said to me, 'You will never change.' Then, I suddenly heard another man yelling. I could see him going down the hill in the direction opposite to us. I recognised him. He was cursing at the others. He wore a white shirt and was attempting to roll up his sleeves. I understood that the man was heading in the direction of the devil.

"Jesus said, 'Let me show you a new place.' There was another hill near the beach with another gate. We went through and I saw many people busily constructing a new building. He told me that when they finish this place, not many people will go there.

"I glanced at a wall against which rested a black steel step ladder. The last thing I noticed, as the dream ended, was that the second step was missing."

Dad never forgot this dream. He is still trying to work out the significance of the missing step and the symbolism of the number three. Until 2012 he had sort of worked that last one out. He had three children. His children, up until the birth of Josiah, all had three children. But when Josiah was born that blew that understanding out of the water as I broke the template. And Jonah's birth confirmed it further.

I will let Dad keep thinking about it. And while I may not be able to interpret the dream fully, I know one thing. It was a parable of God's Covenant promise to my father – "I will save you," he told him. And I will hold the Lord to it – and ask that he pass that same salvation down to each member of my family through subsequent generations.

God is truly the Hound of Heaven.

Into the Cloud of Knowing

EPILOGUE

One summer, sitting at the pool while watching Marie Grace during her swimming lessons, I saw her searching for me as our eyes met. A wide smile lit up her face. With her arm raised she waved at me. And with an equally proud smile I waved back.

There is something in all children that desires to scream out, *"Daddy, do you love me? Am I special? Watch what I can do!"* As I neared the final editing of this second edition, I realised more than ever the importance of needing to look at my children with awe, and of waiting patiently for the ways in which God would reveal his fidelity to the Covenant he has made with them, even if they do not understand it yet. I am slowly coming to terms with the fact that I cannot protect them from everything that may keep them from God. They do not just belong to me, as much as I wish they did. They are their own persons who will also need to wrestle with God and discover the plans He has for them. In faith, I will continue to trust that the plans God has for my children *will* come to fruition because He is faithful.

The heavy cross that began to affect my family in 2014 rattled the security of my children's life for a while, not to mention that of my own. For a time, I could not see a brighter tomorrow. But, as we all know, time can be a great healer, enabling us to cherish what is truly important in life. And through it all, I discovered anew the meaning of covenant and the nature of God's promises, as he repeated to me the words he breathed into my soul when my mother had died: *"I am with you always. I keep my promises. Trust in me!"*

This is the message I wish to pass on to my children, who remain precious to me, even as they are now beginning to seek and manage their growing independence.

I pray that the stories of the generous souls whose encounter with God I have recounted in this book, will not just be for my children, however, but for all who need to be reminded that God's covenant promises are eternal. In our suffering, our doubts, and fears, he is calling us deeper into the *Cloud of Knowing*, filled equally with mystery and God's certain presence, drawing us ever closer.

www.ingramcontent.com/pod-product-compliance
Lightning Source LLC
Chambersburg PA
CBHW071601080526
44588CB00010B/978